Drama

Drama

Drama

An Actor's Education

John Lithgow

An Imprint of HarperCollinsPublishers

A continuation of this copyright page appears on page 426.

DRAMA. Copyright © 2011 by John Lithgow. All rights reserved. Printed in the United States of America. No part of this book may be used or reproduced in any manner whatsoever without written permission except in the case of brief quotations embodied in critical articles and reviews. For information address HarperCollins Publishers, 10 East 53rd Street, New York, NY 10022.

HarperCollins books may be purchased for educational, business, or sales promotional use. For information please write: Special Markets Department, HarperCollins Publishers, 10 East 53rd Street, New York, NY 10022.

FIRST HARPERLUXE EDITION

HarperLuxe™ is a trademark of HarperCollins Publishers

Library of Congress Cataloging-in-Publication Data is available upon request.

ISBN: 978-0-06-208874-1

11 12 13 14 ID/OPM 10 9 8 7 6 5 4 3 2 1

To Mary

Preface

In the summer of 2002, my father was eighty-six years old. He'd been the picture of health all his life, but that summer he started to have some serious medical problems. There was an operation that could address these problems, but his doctors wanted to avoid it if at all possible. The operation involved major abdominal surgery, and they were afraid that it might be too much for an old man's system. But finally there was no choice. His health was plummeting and his doctors decided that, to save him, they would have to operate. So a date was set, and on the morning he went into surgery, the family was told that he had only a fifty-percent chance of surviving it. These were scary words, of course. But in fact he *did* survive it, and we all breathed a huge, collective sigh of relief.

But by the time he was discharged from the hospital, we had started to worry all over again. The operation had taken its toll. It had weakened him terribly and had drastically slowed him down. Worst of all, it had taken away his spirit. This genial man, with his impish humor and his boisterous laugh, fell silent and plunged into a deep depression. It didn't help that he and my eighty-four-year-old mother lived alone, with nobody looking after them. For years my brother, my two sisters, and I had repeatedly offered to set them up in a retirement community, but they had refused to even consider it. Instead they had ended up in a condo of their own choosing, outside of Amherst, Massachusetts, living like a little old couple in a cabin in the woods in a Grimm's fairy tale. And when my mother drove my father home from the hospital, that's where she took him.

There they were: my father struggling to convalesce, my mother struggling to take care of him—and *she* wasn't in such great shape, either. It was a catastrophe. Something had to be done.

Of us four siblings, I was the only one out of work. I had time on my hands. So with my wife's encouragement, I dropped everything, flew across the country, and moved in with my parents. My task was simple. I would tend to my father, help out my mother, organize

Dad's postoperative therapies, and figure out some system of ongoing care for both of them. The plan was for me to stay with them for exactly one month and have everything nicely in order by the time I left. I can do this, I thought. It'll be easy.

It wasn't. The first few days I was there, I practically fell apart. The situation was far worse than I had expected. I saw immediately that I was going to have to take care of my father, a frail old man, as if he were a little baby. He was too weak to sit up in bed. He was tormented by bedsores and a baby's burning diaper rash. He couldn't stand or walk without help. He couldn't get to the dining room table, let alone manage a bathtub, a shower, or a toilet. Worst of all, he had been sent home from the hospital with terse instructions to painstakingly change his own catheter, reinserting it every day, and to keep careful, written records of the workings of his own internal plumbing—at eighty-six years old! It was my job to help him through all of this, and I didn't know what I was doing. I was in way over my head, it was exhausting work, and it was unbearably sad. Every night I would get on the phone to my wife, back home in Los Angeles, and just sob.

The days passed and things improved. But they didn't improve much. My mother, my father, and I gradually fell into a predictable routine. I fixed their meals. I took Dad on short, halting constitutional walks. I bathed him, powdered him, and got rid of that awful rash. He'd gotten shabby and unkempt, so I trimmed his nails, shaved his stubbly beard, and cut his stringy hair. I prodded him to tell sunny stories of his early days and his young years with my mom. I coaxed him into word games and crosswords. I stumped him with scraps of Shakespearean trivia—anything, *anything* to cheer him up. But nothing worked. He made listless, halfhearted attempts to indulge me and my strenuous diversions, but nothing dispelled his feelings of gloom and doom. He felt tired and forgotten. He felt his life wasted and misspent. He'd lost his will to live. Without it, he was clearly not going to last much longer. I felt as if my mother and I were helplessly monitoring the slow decline of an old man who had just given up.

Then one day, halfway through my time with them, I had an idea. It was an idea that bubbled up through the soft-focus haze of my childhood, fifty years before. It was one of the best ideas I ever had.

In my grade-school years, my family moved a lot. There was an old burnt-orange sofa that traveled with us everywhere we went. That humble piece of furniture figures in some of the fondest memories of my youth. It was where I first heard stories. My siblings and I would cuddle up to my father on that sofa at bedtime and he

would read to us. He read the comics in the newspaper with near religious regularity. He read Kipling's *The Jungle Book*, a chapter a night. He read Dickens' *A Christmas Carol* every year on Christmas Eve. He read doggerel poems by Edward Lear, Lewis Carroll, and Ogden Nash from a set of bright-orange volumes called *Childcraft*. For all four of us, our most intimate memories of our father—his crinkly smile, his plummy voice, his husky smell, and his short-sleeved seersucker shirts—are connected to those lazy, luxurious evening hours on that scratchy wool sofa, all of us on the verge of sleep.

Most memorably, he read to us from a fat book called *Tellers of Tales*. This was a fifteen-hundred-page tome, edited by W. Somerset Maugham, that contained a hundred classic short stories. The book had been printed in 1939. By the fifties our copy was already faded and worn, its pages yellowing. Its spine was sprung, too, but my father had craftily repaired it with crimson-colored duct tape. He had even taken pains to neatly write its title in white ink on the taped spine. Characteristically, he had written it upside down by mistake.

When we were growing up, that homely old book was a kind of family Bible in the Lithgow household (wherever that household happened to be at the time), and story hour had all the gravity of a sacred rite. We would pick a story and my father would read it—savoring the wit, ramping up the suspense, and performing all the characters full-out. He worked a kind of hypnotic magic on us. We would hold our breath at the hair-raising suspense of "The Monkey's Paw." We would sniffle and sob when Krambambuli, the loyal Alsatian mountain dog, died of a broken heart. For the first time we heard the words of Ernest Hemingway, F. Scott Fitzgerald, Arthur Conan Doyle, Edgar Allan Poe, Jack London, Dorothy Parker, and on and on and on.

Did we have an all-time favorite? Oh yes. It was the funny one. It was called "Uncle Fred Flits By," by P. G. Wodehouse. This one was something special. Over the years I forgot most of the details of this story. Its plot and its settings all became a blur. But I remembered

"Pongo." I remembered "the pink chap." I remembered something about a parrot. And I remembered the outrageous Uncle Fred and his crackpot schemes, especially as portrayed by my father, a man with an abundant history of crackpot schemes of his own. Mainly I remembered how flat-out hilarious the story was. When we were growing up, any mention of "the pink chap" was enough to send everyone into fits of laughter, long after I'd forgotten who the hell the pink chap even was.

Cut forward to a half century later in Amherst, Massachusetts. There I was, a middle-aged man spending a month with my ailing parents in a cramped condo, immersed in memories of my early youth. It was probably just a matter of time before I hit on the idea of reading bedtime stories to them. I remembered *Tellers of Tales*, and I searched their dusty bookshelves for it. And there it was, only a little worse for wear, as if it had been waiting all those years for just such a moment. That very night, when they were all tucked in, my mother in their big sixty-year-old bed and my father in his little rented hospital bed drawn up next to her, I sprung my surprise. I showed them the old book and I told them to pick a story. And what do you suppose they picked?

"Uncle Fred Flits By," by P. G. Wodehouse.

So I read it to them. I launched into the first paragraph with only the dimmest memory of what I was reading. As the story unfolded, more and more of it came back to me. I was astonished. It was hysterical. I had never read anything like it. It practically caught fire in my hands. The characters revealed themselves, the complications kicked in, and one by one I recognized all those moments that we had thought were so damned funny all those years ago.

And then it happened. My father started to laugh. It was a helpless, gurgly laugh, almost in spite of himself. It was like the engine of an old car, starting up after years of disuse. I kept reading and he kept laughing, harder and harder, until he was almost out of breath. It was the most wonderful sound I'd ever heard. And I'm convinced that it was sometime during the telling of that story that my father came back to life.

I've thought long and hard about that moment. Starting the next day, Dad rallied. His health and his good spirits began to return. He lived another year and a half. Eighteen precious months. That may not sound like a long time, but it was much longer than any of us had dared to hope for. Better still, it was a happy time. The cloud of doom that had darkened his thoughts for so long finally dispersed. Those eighteen months provided a graceful coda to his life. They were months filled with visits from family, visits from friends, reminiscences, taking stock, fond farewells, more stories, more laughter. And I can't help thinking that it was Uncle Fred that got him going again. It was as if my father had fed off the irascible spirit of a long-dead author's fictional creation: that fabulous flimflam artist, Uncle Fred himself.

Acting is nothing more than storytelling. An actor usually performs for a crowd, whether for a hundred people in an off-Broadway theater or for millions of moviegoers all over the globe. Reading to my parents on that autumn evening in Amherst was something else again. It was acting in its simplest, purest, most rarefied form. My father was listening to "Uncle Fred Flits By" as if his life depended on it. And indeed it did. The story was not just diverting him. It was easing his pain, dissolving his fear, and leading him back from the brink of death. It was rejuvenating his atrophied soul. Lying next to him, my mother could sense that, by some mysterious force, her husband was returning to her.

Before he went to sleep, Dad thanked me for the story as if I had given him a treasured gift. But he'd given me a gift, too. It was the gift of a father's love.

I was fifty-six years old and had known him all my life. In all those years, our relationship had changed kaleidoscopically. We had been up and down, happy and sad, close and distant. Our fortunes had risen and fallen, ebbed and flowed, rarely at the same time. But in all those years I had never felt as close to him, nor ever felt as much love for him, as I did that night.

He had given me another gift, too, although he never lived to see it bear fruit. The period I spent with my parents was one of the most significant in my life. In that memorable month, that Wodehouse story was the most memorable hour. I had spent my entire adult life acting in plays, movies, and television shows. I had told stories. I'd had a gratifying, fun, and prosperous career. Only infrequently had I paused to plumb the mysteries of my peculiar occupation. That night, however, everything came into focus. Sitting at my parents' bedside and reading them a story, trying to help two old people feel better, came to seem like a distillation of everything my profession is about. In the years to come, my thoughts kept returning to that evening, even after my father was long gone. Finally, spurred on by the events of that night, I decided to write this book.

Drama

Drama

1.

A Curious Life

The first time I acted was before I even remember. At age two, I was a street urchin in a mythical Asian kingdom in a stage version of "The Emperor's New Clothes." It was 1947, and the show was performed in a Victorian Gothic opera house, long since demolished, in Yellow Springs, Ohio. A black-and-white photograph from that production shows me at the edge of a crowd of brightly costumed grown-up actors. Standing nearby is my sister Robin. She is four, two years older than I, and also a street urchin. We are both dressed in little kimonos with pointy straw hats, and someone has drawn dark diagonal eyebrows above our eyes, rendering us vaguely Japanese. I am clearly oblivious, a faun in the headlights. I stand knee-high next to a large man in a white shift and a pillbox hat who appears to have a role

At age two, I was a street urchin in a mythical Asian

not much bigger than mine. He reaches down to hold my hand. He is clearly in charge of me, lest I wander off into the wings. There is very little in the photograph to suggest that, at age two, I have a future in the theater.

But I do. Later that season, in the same old opera house, I was already back onstage. I played one of Nora's children in *A Doll's House* by Henrik Ibsen. I don't remember this performance either (and there's no photographic record of it), but Robin was there once again, playing another of Nora's children and steering me around the stage as if I were an obedient pet. In that production, the role of Torvald, Nora's tyrannical husband and the father of those two children, was played by that same fellow in the white shift from *The Emperor's New Clothes*. In a case of art imitating life, my onstage father was my actual father. His name was Arthur Lithgow.

Thus it was that my curious life in entertainment was launched, before I was even conscious of it, on the same stage as my father. So it is with my father that I will begin.

Arthur Lithgow had curious beginnings, too. He was born in the Dominican Republic, where, generations before, a clan of Scottish Lithgows had emigrated to seek their fortunes as sugar-growing landowners. I'm not sure whether these early Lithgows prospered, but they enthusiastically intermarried with the Dominican population. One recent day, as I was walking down a Manhattan sidewalk, a chocolate-brown Dominican cabdriver screeched to a stop, leaped out, and greeted me as his distant cousin.

Young Arthur got off to a bumpy start. Evidently, his father (my grandfather) was a bad businessman. He was naïve, overly trusting, and cursed with catastrophic bad luck. He and a partner teamed up on a far-fetched scheme to patent and peddle synthetic molasses. The partner absconded with their entire investment. My grandfather sued his erstwhile friend, lost the suit, and moved his family north to Boston, to start all over. At this point, his bad luck asserted itself. He fell victim to the Great Flu Epidemic of 1918, died within weeks, and left my grandmother a widow—penniless, a mother of four, and pregnant. Arthur was the third-oldest of her children. He was four years old. Growing up, he barely remembered even having a father.

But the situation for this forlorn family was far from hopeless. My grandmother, Ina B. Lithgow, was a trained nurse. She was smart, resourceful, and just as hard-nosed as my grandfather had been softheaded. He had left her with a large clapboard house in Melrose, Massachusetts, and she immediately set about putting it to good use. She flung open its doors and turned it into an old folks' home. All four of her children were recruited to slave away as a grudging staff of peewee caregivers, in the hours before and after school. The oldest of these children was ten, the youngest was three. Child labor laws clearly did not apply when the survival of the family was at stake.

At some point in all this, Ina came to term. She gave birth to a baby daughter who only lived a matter of days. Swallowing her grief, and regaining her strength, she went right back to work.

To my father, Ina must have been downright scary as she fought to keep her household afloat. But fifty years later, when I was a child, little of the fierce, formidable pragmatist was left. She had mellowed into my gentle and adorable "Grammy." Comfortable in that role, she was witty and mischievous, and entertained her grandchildren with long bedtime recitations of epic poems she had learned as a girl—"The Wreck of the Hesperus," "The Skeleton in Armor," "The Midnight Ride of Paul Revere." Only recently did it occur to me that, fifty years before, in the midst of all that hardship, she must have bestowed the same storytelling riches on her own fatherless children.

I picture my father eight years old, bleary-eyed and dressed for bed in hand-me-down pajamas. It is an evening in 1922. He is with his two older sisters and his younger brother, huddling around their mother on a worn sofa in the darkened living room of their Melrose home. He is a pale, thin boy with reddish-brown hair. He is quiet, bookish, and a little melancholy, miscast in the role of "man of the house," which fell to him when his father died. Tonight's poem is "The Wonderful One-Hoss Shay," by Oliver Wendell Holmes. I picture young Arthur listening with a kind of eager hunger, marking the meter, savoring the suspense, and devouring all those exotic new words. He is only a child, but I suspect he already knows, he can feel in his bones, that storytelling will define his later life.

And so it did. Growing into adolescence, Arthur commandeered a little room on the top floor of the Melrose house and immersed himself in books. Ghostly storytellers had found their most attentive listener: Rudyard Kipling, Washington Irving, Robert Louis Stevenson, Sir Walter Scott. And as he worked his way through all these timeworn treasures, he made a life-changing discovery. As an older man, my father described the moment when he "caught a fever": he came across the plays of William Shakespeare. Reading from a single hefty volume of the Complete Works, the teenage boy proceeded to methodically plow through the entire vast canon.

A few years later, such literary passions sent Arthur westward to Ohio, to Antioch College, in Yellow Springs. There his love of storytelling evolved into a love of theater. At Antioch, he poured his energies into student productions. Cast as Hamlet in his senior year, he caught the eye of an infatuated freshman, a Baptist minister's daughter from Rochester, New York, named Sarah Price. When Arthur graduated, he headed straight to New York City, where he joined the legions of aspiring young actors scrabbling for work in the depths of the Depression. Within months of his arrival, he was astonished to find Sarah Price on his doorstep, having dropped out of Antioch to follow him east. With no reasonable notion of what else to do, he married her. It was a marriage that was to last sixty-four years, until his death in 2004.

By the time my conscious memory kicks in, it was the late 1940s and the couple were back in Yellow Springs. In the intervening years, Arthur had turned his back on New York theater; he had taught at Vermont's Putney School; he had worked in wartime industry in Rochester; and he had completed basic training in the U.S. Army. Just as he was about to be shipped out to the South Pacific, I was born. Arthur was now the father of three children. According to army policy, this made him eligible for immediate discharge. He seized the opportunity and rushed home to Rochester.

The next stop for the burgeoning young family was Ithaca, New York, where the G.I. Bill paid for Arthur's master's degree in playwriting at Cornell. A year later, he was working as a junior faculty member in English and drama at his alma mater, Antioch College. He was also producing plays for the Antioch Area Theatre in the old Yellow Springs Opera House. Among those plays were *A Doll's House* and *The Emperor's New Clothes*. A year after that, when I was approaching four years old, I start to remember.

The Lithgow family lived in Yellow Springs for ten years. When we moved away, I had just finished sixth

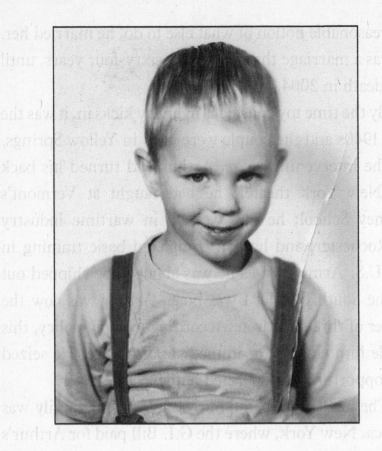

grade. Those ten years would prove to be the longest stretch in one place of my entire childhood. I've only been back to Yellow Springs twice for fleeting visits, and the last visit was almost thirty years ago. Even so, it is the closest thing I have to a hometown.

In the first show of mine that I actually remember, I had a lousy part. I was the Chief Cook of the Castle in a third-grade school production of *The Sleeping*

Beauty. It took place in broad daylight on a terrace outside The Antioch School. This was the lab school of Antioch College, where I was receiving a progressive, fun, and not very good education.

As the Chief Cook, my entire role consisted of chasing my assistant onto the stage with a rolling pin, then dropping to the ground and falling asleep for a hundred years at the moment Sleeping Beauty pricks her finger. I must have known what a bad part it was, but perhaps because of that I took particular care with my costume. I persuaded my father to make me a chef's hat befitting the Chief Cook of the Castle. With surprising ingenuity, he folded a large piece of posterboard into a tall cylinder, then fashioned a puffy crown at the top with white crepe paper. The hat was almost as tall as I was. I was delighted.

"Now we'll just cut it down to half this height and it'll be perfect," my father said.

"Oh, no, Dad!" I said. "Leave it!"

"But you'll run onstage and it'll fall off your head," he reasoned.

"No, it won't!" I insisted. "This is the hat of the Chief Cook of the Castle! It's got to be very tall! Leave it!"

The next day, I carried the lordly hat into my classroom. My schoolmates were awestruck.

"It's beautiful!" said Mrs. Parker. "But shouldn't we cut it down to half this height? You'll run onstage and it will fall off your head."

"No, it won't!" I exclaimed. "This is the hat of the Chief Cook of the Castle! The most important cook in the entire kingdom! It's got to be very, very tall!"

My vehement arguments prevailed. The performance was that afternoon. When my cue came, I ran onstage and my hat immediately fell off my head. After the show, I chose not to answer the eight or ten people who asked, "Why did they give you such a tall hat?"

This was perhaps the first instance of the extravagant excess for which I would one day become so well known. But considering what my father was up to at the time, such grandiosity is hardly surprising.

My father was producing Shakespeare on an epic scale. In the summer of 1951, in league with two of his faculty colleagues, he launched "Shakespeare Under the Stars," otherwise known as the Antioch Shakespeare Festival. It was to last until 1957. The plays that had sparked the imagination of that lonely boy in an attic room in Melrose, Massachusetts, came to life on a platform stage beneath the twin spires of the stately Main Hall of Antioch College. In every

one of those summers, my father's company of avid
young actors, many of them freshly minted graduates
of Pittsburgh's Carnegie Tech, would achieve the impossible. Each season they would open seven Shakespeare plays in the course of nine weeks, rehearsing in
the day and performing at night. Once all seven had
opened, the company would perform them in rotating
repertory, a different play every night of the week, for
the final month of the summer. In 1951, the company
began with a season of Shakespeare's history plays.
By 1957, they had performed all of the others as well,
thirty-eight in all, many of them twice over. My father
directed several of them and acted in several more,

with an exuberant flamboyance that banished forever his boyhood shyness.

Were the shows any good? In those days I thought they were magnificent. To my young eyes these were the greatest stage actors in the country, my father was the finest director, and Shakespeare couldn't possibly be performed any better. As the years passed, I began to doubt my childhood impressions. How good could the productions have been with such hasty rehearsals, such threadbare costumes, and such an untested troupe? A twenty-six-year-old King Lear? A professor's wife as Olivia? Grad students sprinkled among all the minor parts? Though I never lost my sense of awe at the magnitude of my father's achievement, a certain skepticism crept in when I grew to be a theater professional myself.

But then one day, only a few years ago, I received a package in the mail at my Los Angeles home. It contained an audio cassette. The cassette had been sent to me by a man whose late father, an actor named Kelton Garwood, had been a longtime fixture of the Antioch Festival, fifty years before. In going through Kelton's effects, his son had found an old reel-to-reel recording. It contained fragments of a live performance of *The Merry Wives of Windsor* from an Antioch production in 1954. Kelton was featured on the recording in the role of Simple. His son had made a copy of the recording and sent it to me. The day it arrived, I popped the cassette into my car's tape deck as I drove to work. Out came the scratchy sound of a scene involving a dizzy barmaid named Mistress Quickly, a sullen servant named Jack Rugby, and a manic Frenchman named Dr. Caius. Dr. Caius was played by my father. The scene was spirited, fast-paced, and riotously funny. The tape captured the sound of the audience, roaring with laughter and showering the actors with exit applause. The actors' unamplified voices were ringing and clear, their timing was expert, and their command of the material was unerring. They were hilarious. As for my

dad himself, he was even better than my oldest, fondest recollection of him. I pulled my car over to the side of the road. For a half hour, I sat by myself in a Proustian reverie, listening to the sound of marvelous actors, performing for me from the grave, fifty years after the fact.

For me, the lazy days of summer in Yellow Springs were a heady blend of Ring Lardner's Midwest and Shakespeare's Cheapside. I had my share of Little League baseball, Boy Scout camp, the town pool, even a couple of family car trips to the woods of Kentucky. But these episodes were brief and unmemorable compared to the fantastical pleasures of the summer Shakespeare Festival. Toothy, skinny, barefoot, and nut brown, my buzz cut bleached to near-white by the sun, I would hang out at the theater for hours on end, watching rehearsals, chatting precociously with the actors, and striking up unlikely friendships with them. On reflection, I realize that they must have been a pretty callow bunch, since none of them could have been over thirty. But as a child I considered them to be sophisticated, worldly, seasoned *artistes*. I was deeply flattered that they seemed to treat me as a peer. It never occurred to me that they were merely being nice to the boss's son.

Acting careers are ephemeral. Many of the young actors from those days flirted with stardom in the years to come, but few actually achieved it. Age, of course, has overtaken most of them and their moment has passed. But devotees of the American theater scene over the last fifty years would recognize the names of Ellis Rabb, Earle Hyman, Nancy Marchand, William Ball, Pauline Flanagan, Lester Rawlins, Laurence Luckinbill, and Donald Moffat. To my young eyes, they were the definitive King Lear, Othello, Katharina, Puck, Rosalind, Dogberry, Iago, and Justice Shallow, respectively. And I worshiped them all.

One of the big disappointments of my young life came during the first summer of the Shakespeare Festival. That was when my big brother David and my big sister Robin were cast as the two "princes in the tower" in *Richard III*. They wore tights, jerkins, capes, and floppy velvet hats. They even got to speak a few lines. Apparently I was too young for a speaking part. But I wasn't too young to be stricken with sibling envy.

The second summer was no better. Brother David got to play Lucius, the serving boy to Brutus, in *Julius Caesar*. Brutus was played by my father. One sweltering matinee day, David was queasy with stomach flu. A half hour before the performance, he asked to be

excused. In a near tirade, my father attempted to instill
in him the notion that "the show must go on." David
acceded. He played Lucius that day, waiting on his
father and struggling mightily to keep from vomiting
into the bushes in front of a packed house. But after
that, he never wanted to act again.

In time, my beloved brother Dave would craft his
own version of my father's vagabond lifestyle. It had
nothing to do with the theater. Boy and man, David's
exuberance and animation always verged on the hyper-
active. Hungrily inquisitive, a loquacious talker, and
a demon for speed and exercise, he figuratively and
literally took flight from the family business. He fell
in love with flying. All the passion, intelligence, and
energy that he might have poured into a career onstage
he channeled elsewhere. He chose a life of aviation—as
an Air Force pilot, an international airline captain, and
an official of the FAA. Lucius in *Julius Caesar* was his
swan song, at the tender age of twelve. And there was I,
sitting in the audience with my sister, dying, *dying*, to
go on in his place.

The next summer, I finally got my chance. The
season included *A Midsummer Night's Dream*, and I
was tapped to play Mustardseed, one of Titania's entourage of fairies (sister Robin was cast as Moth). I
searched the script and was thrilled to discover that

Mustardseed actually had lines. Lines! For the first time I would speak onstage! There were only seven lines in all, and none contained more than four words (the longest was "Where shall we go?" spoken in unison with the other three fairies), but this took nothing away from the exhilaration of that moment.

As with *Sleeping Beauty*, my costume was an issue. In its first incarnation, it consisted of a long-sleeved, bright-yellow leotard and a hat made of yellow fake fur. The hat was a miraculous creation. It had the shape of a tall seed pod, fastened under my chin and pointing straight up, rising two feet above my head. The dazzling yellow of the costume was set off by bronze-colored body makeup on my bare, spindly legs and several square inches of bold blue greasepaint

around my eyes. I absolutely loved the look. As I took the stage at the dress rehearsal, I was Mustardseed incarnate.

The next day, on the afternoon of our opening night, I walked into the company's big communal dressing room, eagerly searching for my costume. I was shattered by what I found. At the dress rehearsal, the leotard had been judged to be too bright under the stage lights, so it had been unceremoniously splattered with black paint to cut down the glare. This was bad enough. But the fate of my glorious hat was even worse. "Too showy," the director had decided. Just like the leotard, the hat had been splattered with black paint. And to my even greater horror, it had been cut down to half its size! "What is it," I must have wondered, "about me and *hats*?"

The woman who designed my androgynous Mustardseed getup also designed every other costume that summer. Of everyone who worked at the festival in all those years, she has emerged as perhaps the greatest star. She is the Oscar-winning costumer Ann Roth, who designed the clothes for *The English Patient*, *The Birdcage*, and over a hundred other plays and films. In 1981, we had occasion to work together again. She designed my entire wardrobe for the role of the transsexual Roberta Muldoon in *The World According to*

Garp. In one of my last appearances in the film, you may remember that I am wearing a stunning, broad-brimmed black hat.

Standing onstage at age seven in my first scene in *A Midsummer Night's Dream* is one of the most potent memories of my childhood. Oberon and Titania, the king and queen of the fairies, are quarreling over a mortal "changeling boy." In essence, it is a Shakespearean take on a hostile child-custody case. Poetry pours forth from both characters as Shakespeare seems to swoon at the chance to write dialogue for fairy royalty. And there I stood, half-forgetting that I was in a play, drinking it all in— the moonlit night, the pungent summer air, the cool breeze, the warm glow of stage lights, the distant shriek of cicadas, and the mysterious, half-lit faces of the audience, hanging on every word.

And such words! They washed over me in waves, unamplified and gorgeously spoken, especially in the honeyed baritone of Earle Hyman as Oberon. At age seven, I barely knew what any of those phrases meant, but their sheer beauty enthralled me. Years later, in my mid-teens, my father took me to a matinee of a touring production of *A Midsummer Night's Dream* at the Hanna Theatre in Cleveland. He had a couple of old friends in the cast, so for him it was an obligatory visit. But for me it was an afternoon of intense discovery.

I hadn't seen the play since that summer when I played Mustardseed. On this day in Cleveland, as I watched all of the fairy scenes, I was transported back to my childhood. I listened to every line as if it were half-remembered music. But this time, there was a kind of electric shock of recognition as I connected with Shakespeare's language. This time *I knew what they were saying!* I suddenly understood the chemical reaction between poetry and emotion, acted out onstage. My excitement was so keen that it almost matched the thrill of witnessing one of the greatest comic performances I had ever seen, or have seen since. In the role of Bottom the Weaver, I got to see Bert Lahr.

Oh yes, Shakespeare could make you laugh. Nobody knew that better than Bert Lahr. I once mentioned to his son, *New Yorker* critic John Lahr, that I'd seen his father play Bottom in *A Midsummer Night's Dream*. John told me that Bert had wanted to do the role for a very simple reason. Bottom draws a sword in the comic play-within-a-play toward the end of Act V. Bert had seen this as an opportunity to have his pants accidentally fall down around his ankles. This was comedy gold for an old vaudevillian. And I saw it happen! Bert Lahr drew his sword, his pants fell down, and the audience laughed for about five minutes. Eventually everyone onstage laughed, too. From the audience, I noticed Lahr mutter something to the other actors. They laughed even harder. After the show, I asked one of those actors what Lahr had said to them, in the midst of that torrent of laughter from the crowd. He'd said, "Let's wear them out."

It wasn't the first time I'd seen an antic character stop the show in a Shakespeare comedy. I can still picture so many moments of hilarity that I watched from my seat at the Antioch Festival. I see Petruchio waging a food fight, Sir Andrew Aguecheek waggling his sword, Dogberry cavorting with his night watchmen, like so many Keystone Kops. And I see my father, in my favorite of all his roles, staggering around as the drunken butler Stefano in The Tempest. These riotous performances represent my first lessons in the vulgar art of making people laugh.

One summer during those years, when I was twelve years old, I had the chance to put those lessons to work. The occasion was the big show on the last night of a week of Boy Scout camp, with hundreds of raucous boys in attendance. Our troop had been chosen to put on a skit. We had come up with a ten-minute version of the old melodrama involving a hero, a villain, and a damsel-in-distress tied to the railroad tracks. I must have been either the most accommodating or the most spineless Scout in camp, because I had ended up in the role of the damsel-in-distress.

That afternoon we haphazardly rehearsed for about fifteen minutes, then decided that in the evening we would just wing it. At showtime, I awaited my entrance in the darkness in my improvised costume. I wore a checkered tablecloth for a skirt and a Scout bandana for a headscarf. Combat boots completed the picture. The rustling sound of the crowd filled me with terror. I was a quivering bundle of nerves, anticipating the most mortifying humiliation imaginable. But alas, there was no turning back.

My cue arrived, I made my entrance, and I threw myself into the scene. I must have been emboldened by the memory of all those Shakespearean histrionics back at the festival. Whatever I drew on, it worked. The crowd of boys greeted my every fey line and my every mincing gesture with gales of laughter, hooting their approval. The hero, played by Eagle Scout Larry Fogg, untied me from the tracks, hoisted me into his arms, and fell backwards onto his butt with me on top of him. The laughter was earsplitting. It filled me with joy. Like Bert Lahr, we wore them out.

For a week, I had been a shy, despondent, home-sick camper. As of that night, I was a Scout Camp star.

If you hear enough applause and laughter at a young enough age, you are doomed to become an actor. After my performance as the damsel-in-distress, my fate was probably sealed.

The irony is that I had no intention of being an actor. Oh, I loved the energy and excitement of theater, I adored the Festival's plays and players, and nothing matched the giddy sensation of actually being onstage. But I never thought of any of this as anything more than a summertime diversion. I had another, altogether different, calling. I wanted to be an artist.

Early on, I felt myself in possession of an innate talent and facility for drawing and painting. In those early years, I would gravely announce to whoever asked (and to many who didn't) that I was going to be an artist when I grew up. I would lose myself for hours on end with colored pencils, pen and ink, and tempera paint. With my best friend, Eric Rohmann, I would write stories about warring tribes of good and evil elves, an ongoing saga to rival *The Lord of the Rings*. Then I would create elaborate illustrations for them. I even painted watercolors of scenes from the Shakespeare plays and presented them as gifts to my favorite actors.

All of this urgent artistic activity took place before I was ten. Years later, big sister Robin told me that she'd found it all insufferably pretentious. Looking back, I have to agree. But at the time, and for many years later, I was deadly serious.

Who knows where this preadolescent fervor came from? I had not yet had an art class or art teacher to inspire me, I hadn't had anything resembling an epiphany in an art museum, and, although my parents always made sure that I had the best art supplies in front of me, they did little else to point me in this direction. Perhaps the best clue to the source of these artistic urges can be found in my choice of a role model. At that time, American art was being revolutionized in New York City by the dark energies of Jackson Pollock, Mark Rothko, and Willem de Kooning. But growing up in quiet, peaceful, small-town Ohio, I chose to put on a pedestal their polar opposite. My great hero was that archetype of cheerful American normalcy, Norman Rockwell.

Imagine my excitement on the day I actually met the man! In my fifth-grade year, my father took a sabbatical from Antioch to dip his toe back into New York theater. The rest of the family was installed in Stockbridge, Massachusetts, three hours north of the city. Within days of our arrival in Stockbridge, I learned of a breathtaking coincidence. Norman Rockwell's painting studio was just above the candy store on Main Street, about a hundred yards from our rented house! One day after school I summoned up all my courage and set off to meet the great man. With a Brownie camera in my hand and a prized copy of *Norman Rockwell, Illustrator* under my arm, I marched up the back stairs of the candy store and knocked on Rockwell's door. The door swung open and there he was. He wore a homely brown sweater and corduroy trousers, and he held a pipe between his teeth. A huge half-finished painting for a *Saturday Evening Post* cover was propped on an easel behind him. A nervous, starstruck eleven-year-old introduced himself, asked for an inscription in his book, and requested a photo. The modest, silver-headed man obliged him.

And so it was that my first breathless brush with celebrity had nothing whatsoever to do with the entertainment business. I had met my idol. "My best wishes to John Lithgow," the man wrote. "Sincerely, Norman Rockwell." I was going to be an artist.

Such boyish certitude characterized everything in my life in those days. Back in Yellow Springs after that sabbatical year in Stockbridge, the family seemed to have nestled into a happy midwestern idyll. Our everyday life resembled a sunny novel written by Booth Tarkington. I was in a different school and a

different house, but everything else was comfortably the same. My old gang innocently prowled the leafy streets and backyards of Yellow Springs and the woods of nearby Glen Helen. Eric Rohmann was still my best friend, but now we competed for the attentions of the same girlfriend. My family had reached its quorum when my little sister Sarah Jane was born. She was ten years younger than I, and the focus of adoring attention from the other five Lithgows. We seemed to fit into the 1950s like the figures in a wholesome Norman Rockwell painting.

In school I was gregarious and popular. My schoolmates must have thought that my precocious aestheticism was pretty exotic, but it stirred admiration, never

derision. The two sides of my nature were nicely bal-
anced: a cross between Tom Sawyer and a preteen
Aubrey Beardsley. My days and nights at the Shakespeare Festival alternated with trips to Cincinnati
to root for the Redlegs. My afternoons of landscape
painting in the country were counterbalanced by long
innings of Little League baseball at dusk. I collected
a hundred different titles of "Classics Illustrated," but
I also spent endless evening hours in the summertime
playing marathon games of neighborhood hide-and-
seek.

Yellow Springs was a likely setting for this duality.
To all appearances it was a typical Ohio village, with
its whitewashed town hall, its battle monuments, and
its Lions Club lunches. But it was part of an Ohio ar-
chipelago of liberal-arts college towns, including Oberlin, Gambier, Granville, Kent, Bowling Green, and
Berea. And of all those towns, it had by far the most
radical, activist, and iconoclastic history. Antioch College was the wellspring of all this radicalism. In the
nineteenth century, Yellow Springs had been a major
way station on the Underground Railroad, and Antioch
warmly embraced the town's fervent abolitionist heri-
tage. The "Antioch Program for Interracial Education"
predated the Civil Rights Movement by several years,
and the progressive citizens of Yellow Springs shared

the college's pride in it. My parents were two of those proud citizens. They regularly hired student babysitters from the program for my siblings and me. Our favorite was a vibrant girl named Coretta. A few years after her babysitting days ended, Coretta would marry a young minister from Georgia named Martin Luther King, Jr.

Because of Antioch's presence, Yellow Springs teemed with pinko bohemians and tweedy anarchists. These were the early Eisenhower years, the era of Joe McCarthy and the House Un-American Activities Committee. The whole country was seized with anticommunist paranoia. But in Yellow Springs there was a gleeful defiance of the conservative tide sweeping the country. The Lithgow children absorbed the town's politics by osmosis. Adlai Stevenson was our messiah, Richard Nixon was our bogeyman. Our classmates whose professor fathers had been famously blacklisted walked among us with a special swagger. My parents bought their first television in 1954, just so they could watch the Army-McCarthy Hearings.

Mom and Dad hardly rated the blacklist. They were staunchly liberal, but far from revolutionary. For them, politics took a backseat to a shared passion for theater. Of the two of them, my father was not the only performer. Early in their marriage, my mother played big

roles in productions at the opera house. In later years, she loved to smugly invoke the memory of her Madwoman of Chaillot, her Madame Arcati, and her Green Maiden in *Peer Gynt*, but I have no memory of any of them. A photo from those days shows her as Cecily Cardew in *The Importance of Being Earnest*. With a distinctly Lithgovian pout, she is receiving the attentions of an ardent Algernon Moncrieff (played by an actor named Meredith Dallas, co-director with my father of several of Dad's Antioch enterprises).

But if Mom was wryly boastful of her brief career onstage, she was equally cocky about her decision to leave acting behind. With a household full of kids, a husband consumed with his theater exploits, and a gang of raucous actors constantly tramping in and out of her home, she took on the role of den mother. Her charges were her own children and the childlike adults that formed my father's company. If this was a grudging choice, she never showed it. Whatever histrionic urges she had left seemed to be satisfied by wistful evocations of dance recitals when she was a child in Rochester and periodic explosions of the Charleston performed in our living room and at boozy cast parties.

My father's nature mixed whimsy and furnace-like energy. His enthusiasms shot off in all directions, like an unattended fire hose. He shingled our entire house by himself, he constructed a ten-yard over-head wooden grape arbor in our backyard, he built beautiful maple bedsteads for each of us, he lined the master bedroom with knotty pine boards, he in-vented extravagant breakfast dishes with names like "bleeding heart omelets" and "eggs *spécialité*"—all of this with the same jaunty optimism with which he created a Shakespeare Festival. Late one night, at a supper party in our home, I remember lying in bed and hearing him downstairs declaiming to his adult guests. Someone had asserted that the first act of *The Tempest* was boring. Dad was passionately perform-ing the entire act, playing all the parts, just to prove the Philistine wrong.

Sometimes his whimsy tipped over into reckless-
ness. A typical example of this occurred a few years
later. When my sister Robin was in her late teens, she
went through a yoga stage. At the time, we were living
in a house with a single bathroom. Large and flooded
with light, the room was a beautiful space for practicing
yoga. One day, on a visit home from college, Robin was
languidly doing her yoga on that bathroom floor when
my father knocked on the door. She breezily told him
to come in, but he was mortified to think that he was
disturbing her privacy, so he apologized through the
closed door and went away. She heard nothing more
from him.

Later that same day Robin was doing some ironing.
The ironing board was set up in a room next to that
bathroom. She spread out a shirt, filled the iron with
water, steamed the shirt, and began to press it. She noticed a strange smell. She steamed the shirt again. The
smell was appalling. Caught between revulsion and
hilarity, she realized what had happened. Earlier that
day, Dad had peed into a half-filled pitcher of water
sitting on the ironing board and had forgotten to empty
it. Robin had filled up the iron with that pitcher. She
was steaming her shirt with her father's diluted urine.
The whole episode uncannily sums up my dad (somewhat at the expense of his dignity): his sweetness, his

courtesy, his ingenuity, his abstraction, and, above all, his soaring sense of humor. He roared with laughter every time he told the story on himself. And he told it often.

In the summer following my sixth-grade year I began to sense that something strange was going on. Whatever it was, it had taken me a long time to detect it. Looking back, I realize that my parents must have been living through a period of queasy anxiety, both in Stockbridge and in Yellow Springs. But they had a kind of genius for concealing this fact from their children. For my part, I must have been equally ingenious at ignoring their signs of stress.

The only evidence that anything was wrong was the fact that we kept relocating to different parts of town, house-sitting in other people's homes. For years we had lived in our own big, beloved ramble on Dayton Street, full of our own comfy, well-worn furniture. The house was the ideal small-town manse, with a broad front porch and a porch swing. It was shaded by a giant oak, and surrounded by fruit trees, peony bushes, and my father's splendid grape arbor. A weathered barn stood off by itself, but it was nothing more than a vast playhouse for us kids. An old jalopy was propped up on cinder blocks on the barn's dirt floor. My parents had bought it for my big brother David to indulge his passion for tinkering with engines. All of these childhood glories were suddenly relics of the past and the stuff of nostalgic memory. I don't remember ever asking why. Apparently, I was perfectly content to pack up and move on, three times in one year, to strange homes whose owners had temporarily left the premises, to do research, take a sabbatical, or get a divorce.

The last of these places was the most unlikely. We all crowded into a few rooms on the second floor of a farmhouse outside of town. It was August, weeks before the start of school. My family must have been floating in limbo, but, ever the cockeyed optimist, I was oblivious. I was having a wonderful time! With my equally adventurous big sister, I explored empty silos, cluttered toolsheds, groves of trees on the edge of vast cornfields, and a clear, swimmable creek.

For those weeks, Robin and I were billeted in the same bedroom. One night we were idly playing a board game, laughing and chatting with the radio on in the background. Paul Anka reached the end of "Diana," and the local news came on. Robin and I were barely listening until we heard our father's name. Our heads jerked up from the game, we caught each other's eyes, and heard the announcer's voice state that Arthur Lithgow had resigned from Antioch College and would leave his longtime position as managing director of the Antioch Shakespeare Festival.

My response to this news was inane: I was thrilled that my own father merited such attention on a radio broadcast. My older and wiser sister must have realized that the news was not good. In an instant, our lives had changed irrevocably, and not for the better. My childhood in the midwestern Eden of Yellow Springs, Ohio, was over. I was now destined to receive the best training any young actor could ever have. I had been cast as "the new kid in town," and I would play the role, over and over again, for the next decade of my life.

2.
A Kiss on the Neck

W hat in the world were we doing in Oak Bluffs, Massachusetts, on the island of Martha's Vineyard, a week after Labor Day, in September of 1957? Every year, at the moment the summer season ends, the Vineyard becomes almost ghostly. Its population plummets and almost all of the Cape Cod gingerbread homes are boarded up. In the towns, the streets are eerily empty. The carousel in Oak Bluffs is shuttered and silent. As the days pass, all signs of human life disappear from the windswept beaches, leaving them desolate and melancholy. Even the water in the ocean seems to turn gray. Why move to Oak Bluffs? And why at such a dispiriting time of the year?

There was a reason, but it was a strange one. Seven years before, my father had banded together with a troupe of young actors to present a festival of plays by George Bernard Shaw, in a shabby little summer stock playhouse in the piney woods of East Chop, on the outskirts of Oak Bluffs. Toward the end of that summer, a waspy summer resident from nearby approached Dad as he sat in front of his makeup mirror, preparing to go on in *The Devil's Disciple*. The man offered Dad the chance to buy a rambling five-bedroom vacation home near the playhouse. The price was astoundingly low. Dad jumped at the opportunity, thinking that such a house could serve as the perfect dormitory for his acting company the following summer. He never paused to ask himself why the house was so cheap. Only later did he learn that the residents of East Chop had conspired to lure lily-white neighbors into their midst. This was their ignoble attempt to fend off an incursion of middle-class African-American homebuyers. The attempt failed: in the last fifty years, Oak Bluffs has grown into one of the largest communities of vacationing black families in the United States.

As it turned out, Dad's impetuous purchase had been woefully misguided. "The following summer" never came. Instead of a Shaw festival on Martha's Vineyard, he started the Shakespeare Festival in Yellow Springs, which would consume his summers for the next several years. As a result, we were the proud owners of

a vacation home on Martha's Vineyard, for no good reason at all. In all those years, I can only recall one actual summer vacation there, which lasted about a week. I remember an untended front yard of knee-high, straw-colored grass, wicker furniture creaking from old age, the smell of disuse in all of the rooms, and the queasy feeling that we were poor relations visiting someone else's estate.

Our first and only extended stay in the house began in 1957, the year in question. When Dad precipitously quit Antioch, we had nowhere else to go. Bidding farewell to uncomprehending friends, we bolted from Yellow Springs and headed for Oak Bluffs, where the mournful, untenanted house sat waiting for us. Our sole purpose for moving there was to sell the place and plot our next move. With forced cheeriness, my sister and I picked out our bedrooms, settling into a drafty summer home for the cold months of a New England seacoast fall and winter. Dad sealed off half of the house with wallboard and mastered the workings of the big coal furnace in the basement, which roared to life after decades of idleness.

If I felt out of place in our huge saltbox manse, imagine my sense of dislocation in the Oak Bluffs public school. My classmates were the children of Martha's Vineyard year-rounders, a multiethnic mixed bag of fishermen and service-sector workers who catered to the recently departed population of vacationing rich folks. Half of my seventh-grade class had the last name of DeBetancourt, all of them descended from generations of Portuguese emigrants. The class was blessedly small. As an exotic newcomer, I was welcomed into their midst with a mixture of suspicion and offhand curiosity. Why had I arrived in Oak Bluffs at that time of year, when everyone like me had just left town on the last Labor Day ferry? I didn't even try to explain it. I barely understood it myself.

Our teacher was a tall, angular man in his forties named Mr. Troy. Looking back, I can't imagine what he was doing there. He was charismatic, intelligent, intense, and cynical, clearly overqualified to teach this roomful of ragamuffins. He would hammer their lessons into them and ruthlessly mock them when the information didn't stick. The class would respond to his mockery with squeals of delight—what did they care? One especially thick-headed student named Crosly sat next to me at the back of the room. Pasty and lubberly, he liked to twist his great bulk around in his seat and try to kill flies on the floor by smacking at them with a ruler: clack, clack, clack. One day Mr. Troy lost patience with this and, in an electrifying moment, interrupted our math lesson by hurling an eraser the entire length of the room, squarely nailing Crosly in the middle of his broad, fat back. The class cheered maniacally.

My mother and father dutifully showed up at school for Parents' Night, halfway through the fall semester. Afterwards, with hilarity shot through with guilt, Mom described their parent-teacher conference. Mr. Troy had kept the meeting short and to the point. Forgoing any introductory remarks, he had simply exclaimed, "Get him out of here!"

That December, I went to a school dance in the gymnasium. By this time, I had managed to work my way into the good graces of the seventh-grade Oak Bluffs "in" crowd (such as it was). I had accomplished this mainly by befriending the brawny, black-leather-jacketed class tough, Ashley DePriest, and by accepting his offer of my first cigarette. I got along fine, too, with the loud, raunchy girls who turned up the heat in all the flirty sexual interactions of our class. But although my hormones were approaching the boiling point, I was still the shy new kid in town and nowhere near secure enough to act on even the most chaste of my impulses.

So imagine my astonishment at the school dance when scrawny, bespectacled, and wildly sexy Ruthie Legg attacked me from behind, wrapped her arms around me, planted a moist, lipsticked kiss on my neck, and then ran back to a shrieking gaggle of girls, having made good on a dare. A glandular explosion erupted inside me. A breathtaking revelation almost caused me to faint: I was the object of a group crush! Impossible but true! I was attractive! Maybe life in Oak Bluffs was not the cold, barren tundra I had made it out to be.

Two weeks after this intoxicating episode, I was gone. The Lithgow family abruptly packed up and left Martha's Vineyard behind them. Unbeknownst to me, my parents had sold our house and engineered our next move. We were heading to a small town on the

Maumee River in northern Ohio, a move just as bewildering as the one before. I never saw any of my
Oak Bluffs classmates again. None of them, that is,
except one.

A crazy-quilt history like mine generates some
astonishing coincidences. Fifteen years after my
strange Martha's Vineyard adventure, I found myself
in New York City, a twenty-six-year-old unemployed
actor, married, with a six-month-old baby boy. A
friend invited me to direct two plays in a summer-
stock theater he had founded a year before. The theater
was situated in the gymnasium of the public school
in the town of Oak Bluffs, on the island of Martha's
Vineyard. Stunned by the coincidence, and grateful for
any work at all, I accepted. As I walked into that gym,
utterly unchanged in all those years, I headed straight
for the spot where Ruthie Legg had jumped me from
behind. I stood there for a long moment, savoring the
rich, exquisitely painful irony of life.

On the day I left Martha's Vineyard, having finished
my work on both of my shows, I sat with my wife and
baby in the Black Dog Tavern in Vineyard Haven,
waiting for the ferry to the mainland. During my
month on the island, I had searched the faces of everyone I passed, hoping to catch sight of one of those long-
lost classmates from Mr. Troy's seventh grade. I had

spotted no one. But on this morning, looking across the tables of the Black Dog, I recognized a large man in a mechanic's monkey suit leaning over a cup of coffee. He had greasy blond hair combed into a fifties-style ducktail. He smoked a cigarette. Except for a droopy mustache, he had not changed in fifteen years. I walked over to him.

"Excuse me," I said, "but aren't you Ashley?"

Silence.

"Ashley DePriest?"

"Yuh."

"This is incredible. I'm John. John Lithgow. You gave me my first cigarette."

More silence.

"From Mr. Troy's class. Seventh grade, remember? With Debbie DeBetancourt? Denny Gonsalves? Ruthie Legg?"

Ashley DePriest looked at me with bleary blue eyes, expressionless.

"I remember all of *them*. But I don't remember *you*."

Not remember!? How was that possible? Had all of these people, so vivid in my memory, retained no image of me at all? Had I simply slipped in and out of their lives, a forgettable minor player? Had Ruthie Legg forgotten, too? For the first four months of seventh grade,

I had desperately struggled to overcome my fear, to assert myself, to fit in. In my own mind, I had been a nervous, untested young actor, gradually winning over his toughest crowd. That morning, Ashley DePriest was my most dismissive critic. I had been completely unmemorable.

3.
Lachryphobia

As I recall it, the drive from downtown Toledo to the town of Waterville takes about a half hour. There were five of us in the car when I first took that short trip. My father, my mother, and my baby sister were escorting my big sister and me to our first day of school. It was halfway through the school year, and Robin and I were sick with anxiety. The January day was clear but brutally cold, with gusts of snow snapping across the flat, brown fields. By some innate wizardry, my mother had managed to secure yet another big house for us to live in, but we couldn't move into it just yet. For now we were billeted in a Toledo hotel, hence the January commute. On the radio, Buddy Holly was singing "Peggy Sue." I remember listening with intense concentration, mentally reassuring myself. "I know this song," I thought. "I'll have something in common with them."

So began the next chapter of the cockeyed story of my teenage years. My father was attempting to relaunch his summer Shakespeare Festival in a new setting. This time, the actors would perform in the outdoor Toledo Zoo Amphitheatre, where, in years past, the Antioch company had made frequent guest appearances, to the roars of lions and the shrieks of peacocks. He had five months to gear up for the summer season, and the sleepy town of Waterville was to be our bedroom community.

Joining a second seventh-grade class was bad enough. But joining it in the middle of the year was horrific. The small measure of confidence I had achieved in Oak Bluffs had vanished. My twelve-year-old's self-esteem had dropped to zero. I felt like I had been sent back to square one. In retrospect, my situation was hardly the stuff of a severe childhood trauma. There was nothing to fear from my cheerful, milk-fed new classmates, many of them sturdy farm kids with names like Weimer, Marcinek, Scheiderer, and Hiltabiddle. But I was terrified nonetheless. The causes were twofold: I was desperately afraid I would burst into tears (which occurred five or six times in the first week) and that someone would notice one of my inexplicable erections (which occurred every twenty minutes). I was a mess.

The fear of tears was a real problem. Call it lachryphobia. I simply couldn't get to the end of a day without crying, and every time it happened I was mortified with embarrassment. For example, I recall a halting conversation with a pleasant fellow named Denny Bucher across our lunch trays in the school cafeteria. In an act of almost corny kindliness, he asked me what Santa Claus had brought me for Christmas. His simple solicitude opened a floodgate of maudlin self-pity in me. I exploded with sobs in front of everyone, spilling tears and snot all over my chipped beef and biscuits.

By an uncanny maternal intuition, my mother sensed what was going on. Her response was swift and pragmatic. Behind the scenes, she arranged for me to simply walk home for lunch every day. Fortified by that daily half hour at our own kitchen table, I gradually got my sea legs and once again began to adapt. My first full day of school with no tears was a pathetically small victory, but a victory nonetheless. Within weeks I had collected a few friends, unveiled my nascent sense of humor, and put my days of lachryphobic geekiness behind me. As the winter weather gradually gave way to spring, my spirits continued to improve. Just as I had blended in with the deracinated young delinquents of Oak Bluffs, I now joined the wholesome ranks of Waterville's backyard boys and girls: riding bikes, flying kites, and playing intense rounds of kick-the-can until nightfall. I even spent weeks building a bright-red ersatz Soap Box Derby racer. My friends and I pushed each other around in it, up and down the leafy sidewalks of Waterville, hour after idle hour on end.

One evening that spring my father had something to show us. He had worked all day on a brochure to announce his upcoming summer season of plays. Using pen and ink, he had hand-lettered all the information in the brochure and created ink drawings to illustrate it. The drawings depicted scenes from each of five plays–*The Tempest, Charley's Aunt, The Devil's Disciple, Ah, Wilderness!,* and something called *Pictures in the Hallway,* billed as "a new play" adapted from the prose writings of Sean O'Casey. Dad was visibly proud of his own handiwork, and I recall being pretty impressed by it, too. I don't remember the slightest concern that the brochure looked cheap and amateurish. But in retrospect I can picture it vividly, and it did.

That evening, I didn't think to ask myself any of the questions that seem so obvious to me now. Why was my father making his own brochure? Why was he doing it on the kitchen table? Why did my mother have that anxious, skeptical look on her face? Why was there only one Shakespeare play included among the five offerings? And why were the plays going to be presented in the small indoor theater adjoining the Zoo Amphitheatre, and not in the huge Amphitheatre itself? And the biggest question of all didn't even occur to me: "Is anything wrong?"

There was plenty wrong. But, typically, my parents shared none of it with their kids. Years later, when my father was an old man, he told me the events of that year from his point of view. I finally learned what he and my mother had so expertly kept from me while it was actually going on.

Originally, the summer season was to be sponsored in large part by Toledo's major newspaper, *The Blade.* Assured of their backing, Dad had posted an "Equity bond" and had engaged a company of actors, signing their contracts himself. Almost all of these actors were friends and veterans of his former Shakespeare Festival. The new festival was to be precisely modeled on the old one, even using its distinctive unit stage design. Continuity was everything. He planned to capitalize on the reputation of the old festival and retain its huge following, both in Ohio and in neighboring states.

As it happened, my father relied too heavily on his own optimism and the good faith of his backers. To his shock and dismay, *The Blade* withdrew its funding, but too late for him to cancel the season. He was trapped, both by legal obligations and loyalty to his long-time troupe of actors. With a fraction of his projected budget and a stack of signed contracts on file, he had to come up with an alternative plan in a matter of days, and it had to be cheap. Hence the smaller theater, the shorter list of plays, and the tacky brochure on the kitchen table. The season went forward, and if memory serves, the shows were pretty good. But nobody came. By mid-August, my father's last-minute summer theater festival was a slowly unfolding catastrophe. But as the clouds gathered, I was blithely oblivious. My summer days were spent swimming at the quarry outside of town, and my evenings were devoted to playing third base for the Indians of the Waterville Little League.

Not once did I notice, even for a second, that both my parents had been seized by desperate panic. As Dad told the story in old age, the acute anxiety of those days still had the power to unsettle him. The fact was that by the end of that summer, he was in serious trouble. As a manager and businessman, he had always been vague and haphazard. But this time, with no one to look after the books, his negligence had caught up with him. In struggling to keep the company afloat, he had played fast and loose with payroll taxes. The season was drawing to a close. The festival was a washout. My parents were broke. Creditors were clamoring. Auditors were converging. In a nightmare scenario, Dad saw himself frogwalked to prison by the Feds, leaving his penniless family behind him.

At this juncture, a deus ex machina appeared in the form of a man named Hans Maeder. Maeder was the cheerfully despotic German headmaster of The Stockbridge School. This was a boarding school near Stockbridge, Massachusetts, the town where I had spent fifth grade. My brother David was just about to graduate from the school, having lived there for the previous three years (hence avoiding the mad vicissitudes of our recent moves). Out of the blue, Herr Maeder offered my father a job teaching English and drama. He even threw in a spousal appointment for my mom as a school librarian.

For my panicky parents, this dual offer was a lifesaver. They accepted it, but not before huddling with the Toledo festival's legal counsel. This man assured my father that he would find a way to clean up the financial mess that Dad had left behind. But at the same time, he urged Dad to get out of town as fast as he could. And so, as if grabbing the caboose railing on the last train out of the state, we loaded up our black Studebaker sedan and sped away.

For the second time in a year, I left behind a hard-won community of friends whom I would never see again. But this time, the change would be less of an adjustment, and far less wrenching. In Stockbridge, I would rejoin my old fifth-grade class from three years before. Familiar teachers, schoolmates, playmates, and crushes were all there, waiting for me, three years older. This would not be so bad.

Try as I may, I can't picture the moment when my parents announced this most recent disruption. I can't recall my reaction to the news, nor my emotional state of mind as we watched Waterville disappear in the rearview mirror. But I can guess. I imagine that

I was not so fearful this time, not so confused, not so resentful. I was heading back to Stockbridge, a world I knew and liked. And Waterville, like Oak Bluffs before it, represented a modest personal triumph, a hurdle I had cleared, a battlefield where, thirteen years old, I had emerged unscathed. I suspect that I felt pretty good. I was getting better at this.

4.
The Good Boy

After Oak Bluffs and Waterville, the world of The Stockbridge School was distinctly exotic. This was not your typical New England prep school, full of children of great wealth and patrician breeding. Oh no. With its renegade faculty and its raffish student body, The Stockbridge School was just the opposite. Its kids were roughly divided into two groups. Half were lefty New Yorkers, many of them Jewish and many of them children of divorce. The other half was a polyglot mix of foreign students, in keeping with Hans Maeder's internationalist mission (the United Nations flag flew alongside Old Glory at the school's entrance). An ultra-liberal, ultra-casual atmosphere prevailed. Dress codes were nonexistent. Every teacher was called by his or her first name. Folk ballads and union songs filled the air. The eighty-plus students were made to feel a part of a huge, mutually supportive family, in many cases replacing the fractured families they had left behind. The school shut down many years ago, unable to survive after the messianic Hans departed the scene. But while it lasted, it was an artsy, outdoorsy, gloriously anarchic mess of a place. In all of its years of existence, its most notable alumnus by far was Arlo Guthrie.

Although nestled in the Berkshire Hills in a splendid New England setting, the school was far from lavish. Serviceable cinderblock classroom buildings and dorms surrounded the large, white-shingled "Main House." The Lithgow family was housed in a tiny converted icehouse, painted gray with blue trim. This time, there were only four of us—my mother, father, three-year-old Sarah Jane, and me. David was at college now and Robin was enrolled, tuition-free, in the school's tenth grade, a boarding-school student a hundred yards from home. Hans wanted me to enroll, too. The school started in ninth grade, so he insisted that I skip a year and join the incoming ninth-graders. I demurred. I was worried about being a year younger than the rest of my class, and my parents shared my misgivings. Besides, I wanted to reconnect with my old gang at the public school in town, a half hour away by school bus. Hans was a hard man to refuse, but I managed somehow.

Though merely a faculty brat, I immersed myself in the quotidian life of the campus. The family ate most of our meals in the community dining hall in the Main House; I knew every student by name and befriended several of them; on Saturdays I tagged along on the students' "free days," traveling by bus to Pittsfield for burgers and movies; I rooted for the school soccer team, at matches played amidst the dazzling autumn foliage; I painted scenery for my father's wildly ambitious school production of *Peer Gynt*; and on Wednesday nights I attended an extracurricular crafts class run by a genius teacher named Bill Copperthwaite. From Bill I learned how to stitch leather bags, carve wooden bowls, and build furniture, skills which, though they lie dormant, I have retained ever since. All of this made me a de facto student of The Stockbridge School, even though most of its genuine students regarded me as little more than an eager, omnipresent mascot.

But all of this activity and bonhomie constituted only one-half of my schizophrenic Stockbridge existence. The other half was that of a Stockbridge townie. After the tearful transitions of the preceding year, starting eighth grade at my former school was a cakewalk. Everything was familiar. No real adjustment was necessary. And, as spotty as my education had been until then, I was a perfectly good student. Three years before, as a cowering fifth-grader, I had been terrified of the burly, glowering, red-faced eighth-grade teacher, Mr. Blair. But having become his student, I now found him colorful, crusty, and endearing. Despite his gruff demeanor, I won him over in no time and swiftly assumed the status of teacher's pet.

That first day, when I strode into class, my old friends were surprised and delighted, welcoming me back into the fold like the Prodigal Son. They were great guys—Vincent Flynn, Billy Sheridan, Peter Van Lund—and we picked up exactly where we had left off. In a replay of my fifth-grade year, the quaint town and its surroundings provided the setting for all kinds of adventures. In the autumn we climbed to the top of Laurel Mountain and explored the caves of the mysterious "Icy Glen"; when winter descended, we hiked in deep snow and skated on remote lakes and ponds; and in the spring, on the first day of fishing season, we rose before dawn and staked out a perfect spot on the banks of the Stockbridge Bowl, an impossibly picturesque lake in the heart of the Berkshires. The girls were pretty great, too. And although in matters of the heart I was still hopelessly shy, my fantasy life was vivid and feverish. A sweet girl named Carol Lowe, the object of an ardent fifth-grade infatuation, was still there, as dewy as ever.

A problem was emerging, but I didn't recognize it at the time. I had been forced to quickly adapt, three or four times, over the course of some crucially formative years. And here in Stockbridge I was leading a spirited social life with two separate and completely different crowds. I was developing Zelig-like skills to manage this odd dual identity. At first blush, this seems like an entirely good thing. After all, I had progressed far beyond the puling insecurity of my Waterville days. I was active, genial, and well liked in both of my social spheres. But in retrospect I have come to see a troubling side to this rapid-response adaptability. In my struggle to fit in, appearances had become everything. I was consumed by an eagerness to please, to cause no offense, to make no waves, to stir up no trouble for my stressed-out parents (however deftly they had hidden their stress from me). I was becoming a good boy, an utterly, unimpeachably *good boy*, and not necessarily in a good way. For when appearances are everything, the trade-offs can be poisonous. A good boy can be capable of appalling secret cruelties.

There was a girl in the freshman class at The Stockbridge School whom I shall call Esther Furman. Nobody liked her. From her first day at the school, she had been a social pariah. At supper one evening, as I sat with a group of older boys in the Main House dining room, one of them offhandedly mentioned someone named "Fau."

"Fau?" I said. "Who's Fau?"

"Esther Furman," he answered drily. "It stands for 'fat and ugly.'"

The boys cackled with laughter, and to my shame I laughed along with them. "Fau," it turned out, had become Esther's commonly used nickname around the school. In the next few weeks, I heard it dropped so often that I felt sure that Esther herself must have heard it too. And, most painfully, she must have heard what it stood for.

Starved for companionship, Esther turned to me. She had been ostracized by her fellow students, but since I was not one of her fellow students, she sought me out. In the dining hall, I would typically sit with the freshman boys, eager to be included. Esther would plop down next to me and chatter away happily. True to my carefully cultivated good-boy nature, I was pleasant and receptive (and, in fact, there was nothing about Esther to particularly dislike). But I was cringing inside. I feared that this hungry, hapless girl was ruining my bid for acceptance among the sophisticated young cynics of The Stockbridge School.

Everywhere I turned, there was Esther. She even took to waiting for me on spring afternoons, at the spot on the country road where the school bus discharged me. She began to fix on the idea of going fishing with me at the Stockbridge Bowl, off the school's private dock. I was mortified at the thought of being seen with her by any of my older friends, at being lumped with Esther as the object of their ridicule. To put her off, I made up all manner of bogus excuses. Weeks passed but Esther was cheerily persistent. At one point I claimed that I couldn't fish because my reel was jammed and I didn't have the proper tools to fix it. She said she would help. She would find some needle-nose pliers and meet me at my house at four. If we managed to repair the reel with the pliers, we could go fishing at last.

At the appointed hour, I was alone in the little ice-house, crouched in my bedroom. I heard Esther's footsteps along the wooden boards of the porch. She knocked at the door. I said nothing and sat perfectly still, hoping she would think I wasn't home. She knocked again.

"John?"

I stayed mum.

"Are you there?"

Still mum.

"I have the pliers."

A long pause. My heart was pounding.

"I know you're in there. I have the pliers. John?"

And I finally answered, with the three most hateful words I'd ever spoken.

"Forget it, Fau!"

After a moment, I heard footsteps again as Esther walked away. I never spoke to her again. I could barely even look in her direction. Everyone I knew continued to think of me as John, the good boy. But not Esther. Not anymore. And not I.

Someday I would be an actor. One of the most basic things an actor must learn is that human beings are capable of anything. Each and every one of us can be noble, courageous, and kind. But we can also be cowardly, cruel, and contemptible. And all of these qualities, good and bad, can often erupt from nowhere, when you least expect them, in the least likely people. Good people can do terrible things, bad people can astonish us with their goodness. This is one reason why life constantly surprises us. It is also, incidentally, at the heart of the best comedy and the best drama. We are capable of anything. A caustic three-word phrase barked out in an empty icehouse on the campus of The Stockbridge School was my first and most startling demonstration of that truth.

5.

Enter Messenger

For two years of my life, I lived on a fifteenth-century English estate. My backyard stretched out across a hundred acres. A vast greensward led up to a stately manor house graced with gables, parapets, Tudor beams, and hundreds of leaded-glass windows. The house had sixty rooms, including a great hall, a music room, a library, a billiard room, and a solarium. On the walls hung Old Master paintings, tapestries, armor, weaponry, and the stuffed heads of a dozen wild animals. A sycamore allée extended from the house in one direction, with seven-foot rhododendron bushes growing at the foot of the massive trees. In the other direction, a delicate birch allée led to twin gazebos overlooking meandering lagoons. There was a sunken English garden, a Japanese garden, a tennis court, and

a croquet lawn. Fountains splashed in the middle of a reflecting pool below a broad back terrace. An old Scottish couple named Sandy and Annie were the deferential retainers of the household. Rangy, red-cheeked Wilbur Turberville was the affable chief groundskeeper, tending to the lawns and flower beds. Flowers were everywhere.

Despite its grandeur, the estate had fallen prey to neglect and disrepair. Less than half of its formal gardens were maintained. Scrubby trees had long since sprouted through the crumbling asphalt of the tennis court. Overgrown reeds suffocated the abandoned lagoons where two feral swans fiercely guarded their swampy domain. A couple of bedraggled peacocks occasionally strutted out into the open and pierced the air with mournful screeches. Sandy, Annie, and Wilbur were themselves ghostly holdovers from a lost era, their prosperous employers long departed.

Besides the gabled manor house, there was a gatehouse, a gardener's cottage, and a carriage house. On the second floor of the carriage house, just above the empty stables and the porte cochère, lived the Lithgow family.

Where the hell were we now?

We were in Akron, Ohio. It was 1959. I was fourteen years old.

The estate was Stan Hywet Hall, the dream house of the early-twentieth-century rubber magnate F. A. Seiberling. Seiberling died in the mid-1950s, having long since lost the bulk of his fortune. As a tax dodge to benefit his offspring, he bequeathed his decaying Xanadu to the city of Akron, providing the town with a splendid site for a new civic cultural center. Noting his history of cultural midwifery, the board of directors of the fledgling center contacted my father. They invited him back to Ohio to become the center's first executive director. With dreams of a new incarnation of his beloved Shakespeare festival, performed on the back terrace of a Tudor manor house, he jumped at the offer. After a single year on the faculty of The

Stockbridge School, he was on the move again. Like a tennis ball thwacked back over the net, the family once again trekked out to Ohio, the old Studebaker groaning under the weight of our worldly possessions.

One evening, back at The Stockbridge School, my parents had sat me down in the living room of the icehouse and revealed to me their latest plans. This time I remember my response. I burst into tears, stormed out of the house, and ran off into the night. Alone in the middle of a field, surrounded by the Berkshire Hills and lit up by moonlight, I cried out at the top of my lungs, "WHY ME?! WHY AKRON?!" Looking back, I have to admit that this was all a bit theatrical. There was nobody watching, but I was acting my head off. Perhaps this was only fitting. In my next two years in Akron, events would begin to propel me, without my even knowing it, toward a career in the theater.

Over the course of those two years, I was a ninth-grader at Simon Perkins Junior High School and a tenth-grader at John R. Buchtel High (without ever learning who those two estimable Akronites actually were). These were my first big-city schools. With the onset of classes, I was confronted by throngs of students, multiple classrooms, thousands of lockers lining the halls, crowded assemblies, and clamorous pep rallies. I'd never seen anything like it. But this time the newness of the experience proved more exciting than overwhelming. And this time my skin was a little tougher. In an atmosphere of such energy and happy chaos, being a new student was far less of a trial than it had been in our preceding moves. Besides, I was welcomed into my new community in a surprising way. In those days, the curriculum of the Akron public schools was amazingly sophisticated. It accommodated and encouraged my most abiding, passionate interest. For two years, I was given the extraordinary luxury of starting every single school day with two elective periods of art.

And such wonderful classes! Every morning I would eagerly anticipate those early hours of school. Without fail, art class would launch me into the rest of my day with a heady creative rush. I did drawings in charcoal and ink, paintings with watercolors and acrylics, woodcuts, linoleum prints, silk screens, ceramics and mosaics. In those two years, my two teachers were twinkly older women, determined to unleash the creative juices of every one of their students. The second of them was named Fran Robinson. "Miss Robinson" was one of the best teachers I ever had. A distinguished craftswoman in her own right, she had invented her own highly individual medium. Using her Singer sewing machine, she embroidered fanciful tapestries in brightly colored thread. Occasionally her work would appear in the pages of *Art News*, and we would all feel the frisson of our teacher's fame. Pricked on by her encouragement and inspired by her ingenuity and flair, I grew more determined than ever to pursue the visual arts.

After only one year, my older sister Robin had left The Stockbridge School and had joined the family on our return trip to Ohio. So once again she and I were two grades apart in the same school system. I loved having her back in the household. She had absorbed the urbane tastes and left-wing politics of her Stockbridge schoolmates, and she now set out to find like-minded friends in her new Akron crowd. She found them all right. There were about five of them, all smart, vital young women. But the tone of Buchtel High School was fiercely conservative (its affluent students were known around town as "The Cake Eaters"), so Robin's new set of girlfriends was a tiny, heretical cabal. They reveled in their rebel status. They went to subtitled European films at Akron's lone art house; they attended concerts of Glenn Gould and Andrés Segovia at the cavernous Akron Armory; they collected the records of Pete Seeger, Joan Baez, and Theodore Bikel; they met early on Friday mornings before school to listen to entire Italian operas, following along in the scores. They even consorted with gaunt, long-haired college boys who drove them to nighttime meetings of the Young People's Socialist League.

I watched all of this hard-core beatnik activity with a mixture of curiosity, timidity, and longing. In the school classrooms, athletic fields, cafeteria, and gym, I had quickly formed my own circle of Akron mates, stolid crew-cut white boys with whom I shared the reliable common language of pro sports and dirty jokes. But my attentions were divided. Just as I had in Stockbridge, I found myself conducting a two-tiered social life. I liked my gang just fine, but I was crazy about my sister and her older, hipper friends. Outside of school, I cultivated their bohemian tastes, tagged along on their esoteric outings, and clung to them like a burr.

From day one in Akron, my artwork was my highest priority. My natural facility made me the top student artist in my class. My paintings, drawings, and prints hung in the school hallways and won "Gold Keys" in citywide scholastic art competitions. In the midst of such feverish artistic activity, I never imagined for a moment that I would end up an actor. But in a couple of instances, the catnip of theatrical performance began to assert itself for the first time since those early years in Yellow Springs.

In the middle of ninth grade, I initiated a school project as far-fetched as it was ambitious. I set out to produce and stage a fifteen-minute piece of theater, unconnected to schoolwork and unsupervised by any teacher. The piece was the "gulling scene" from Shakespeare's *Twelfth Night*. This is the scene in which the loathsome, puritanical Malvolio is tricked by four other gleefully vengeful characters in the play. I took the plum role of Malvolio and recruited schoolmates to play Sir Toby Belch, Sir Andrew Aguecheek, Fabian, and Maria. I gave everyone a little rudimentary direction and designed a simple set, consisting of a "boxtree," which I fashioned out of painted masonite and lime-green crepe paper. After a few weeks of after-school rehearsal, we presented the results at a school assembly. The audience of ninth-graders were attentive, if slightly bewildered. There were no gales of laughter, and at the end they applauded with a kind of grave, respectful admiration. But the tepid reception didn't bother me. For me, the show was fifteen minutes of undiluted triumph.

I remember almost none of the circumstances surrounding this bizarre event. Looking back, the whole thing completely astonishes me. How did it ever happen? When did I come up with such an idea? Shakespeare, performed by and for ninth-graders? Whatever possessed me? Was I crazy? Who did I think I was? Why, my father, of course. In hindsight, it seems quite clear that I was unconsciously aping him and his audacious schemes. Just like him, I was hurling Shakespeare at an unlikely, unpromising audience, and somehow making a success of it.

In tenth grade, the following year, I dusted off *Twelfth Night* once again. I reprised the entire gulling scene, this time playing all five parts. I performed it as a monologue in the category of "Humorous Declamation," for Buchtel High's National Forensic League team. On Saturdays, I would travel with a busload of brainy debaters to tournaments held in empty high schools all over north-central Ohio. The others would debate and I would perform, competing with teams from all over the region. I never did as well in my category as the debaters did in theirs. *Twelfth Night*, after all, was pretty heady stuff for a tenth-grader. In competition, I scored far fewer laughs than the students who recited the comic prose of Mark Twain and Robert Benchley, and I never won a thing. But watching my rivals in all those echoing auditoriums, I began to sense the beginnings of a smug certainty: I was the best actor in the house.

But it was during my Akron summers that theater began to truly take hold of me. This was when my father produced the Akron Shakespeare Festival. This festival was only to last two summers, but in both of those summers, I immersed myself in the pungent world of yet another of Arthur Lithgow's theatrical ventures.

For reasons that will shortly be revealed, the two seasons of the Akron Shakespeare Festival were presented in two completely different settings. The first was the terrace of Stan Hywet Hall, with the rear façade of the Tudor manor house providing a backdrop. For the festival's inaugural season, my father chose a repertory of four plays that echoed the start of his triumphant Antioch run. These were the first four history plays from Shakespeare's retelling of the War of the Roses—*Richard II*; *Henry IV*, parts 1 and 2; and *Henry V*. In keeping with his trademark style, the plays were staged simply, on a symmetrical arrangement of bare platforms, and performed by a small troupe of accomplished young actors imported from New York. But though the productions were straightforward and unadorned, the setting made them glorious. It is hard to imagine a more appropriate and more beautiful spot in America for this most English of historical pageants. The leaded-glass windows glinted behind Falstaff in his scenes inside the Boar's Head Tavern; Richard II cried out in defeat, "Down, down I come!" from a crenellated parapet high above the audience; and when Henry V declaimed "Once more unto the breach, dear friends, once more!" the looming, starlit manor house stood in for Harfleur Castle.

Initially, I just hung around rehearsals, much as I had done years before during those happy summers in Yellow Springs. But by now I was a gangly fourteen-year-old. I had arrived at the age when, to the forgiving eyes of an audience, I could pass for an adult. By the time the company began rehearsing the two parts of *Henry IV*, the play's big battle scenes forced the director, Edward Payson Call, to look for spear carriers anywhere he could find them. Inevitably, I was conscripted, and soon I was rehearsing five or six scenes in each of the last three plays. My first assignment was the only part I was remotely right for: I was one of Falstaff's wretched platoon of army recruits, old men and young boys whom Falstaff dismisses as "food for powder." I had a comic crossover with four other raggd peasants. For a weapon, I carried a rake.

But the summer wore on and I was quickly promoted through the ranks. The fight choreography grew more elaborate. I became more confident and histrionic. I dashed around with pennants and banners, swords and pikes. I yelled battle cries in English and French. I stoutly fought for the Yorks and the Lancasters, for the

English and the French, killing and being killed with near-operatic flourish.

And when *Henry V* rolled around, something wonderful happened. In a reprise of my "Mustardseed" moment from seven years before, I was given an actual role. I was cast as "A French Messenger." It was the smallest speaking role in the play, but a speaking role nonetheless. I had a single line. It was my job to walk into the French king's court and announce the arrival of Exeter, an envoy from England. For a week, I dutifully rehearsed with the full company. I ran my single line about a thousand times. On the night of the first performance, I waited nervously in the wings, dressed in black tights and a belted white tabard with blue fleurs-de-lys stenciled all over it. Nearby, pacing restlessly in the dark, was Exeter himself. He was played by the young David Carradine (yes, *that* David Carradine, from *Kung Fu*). As my cue arrived, I bolted up six stairs onto the stage-left platform and yelled as loud as I could in a piping, barely audible voice:

"Ambassadors from Harry, King of England, do crave admittance to your majesty!"

It was my first line spoken onstage as a grown-up actor.

Although I regarded this as another stunning success, I knew very well that I was on the lowliest rung of the company hierarchy. At the topmost rung was our acknowledged leading player. This was a splendid actor named Donald Moffat. His roles in the four plays included Richard II, the Chorus in *Henry V*, and a poignant and hilarious Justice Shallow in *Henry IV*, part 2. Donald was a thirty-year-old Englishman from the West Country, trained at RADA, and transplanted to New York with an actress wife, a gamine four-year-old daughter, and a baby boy. In the years following that summer, he grew to be a major actor in New York theater and a familiar face on screen (he played LBJ in the film of *The Right Stuff*). Nowadays he has slipped gracefully into retirement, embracing an old actor's obscurity with dignity and contentment.

In those days, Donald was a striking young man, a British edition of the young Max von Sydow. He had a rangy frame, a long face, penetrating eyes, and a soft voice. In a company of actors who relied on high energy and bluff athleticism, he was the quiet center of the storm, commanding the stage with poetic simplicity. He was quick-witted and intelligent, a man of uncompromising taste, with a warm smile and a stealthy sense of humor. Best of all, he was reflexively curious about all sorts of people and things outside the insular world of theater. From the moment we met, he took a bemused interest in me, especially in my precocious commitment to art. Such an interest was enormously flattering to a fourteen-year-old. I instantly put him on a pedestal and secretly made him my mentor. In the next few years, theater gradually seduced me away from art. I suspect this would never have happened if my father had never hired Donald Moffat.

For all its glories, the Shakespeare Festival's tenure at Stan Hywet was a flash in the pan. Following a familiar pattern, my father found himself on unsteady ground as the executive director of Stan Hywet Hall. After the close of the festival season, he soon learned that not everybody was pleased with its success. It became clear that half the members of the board of directors had vastly different priorities for Stan Hywet than my father did. These men and women were pillars of wealthy Akron society. They did not see Stan Hywet as a center for arts and culture. In their eyes it was a historic landmark, a museum, a garden center, a symbol of Akron's lost splendors, and a shrine to F. A. Seiberling. An outdoor Shakespeare festival, no matter how successful, had no place in their grand design. Massive lighting towers on the back terrace? Wooden risers and hundreds of folding chairs atop the reflecting pool? Sweaty, scrofulous young men in nothing but shorts and sandals, rehearsing noisy outdoor battle scenes or dashing through tapestried halls as they rushed to make an entrance? Cast parties on opening nights, with the campy squeals of happy, drunken New York actors, floating through the summer air? This would not do.

But my father pressed on. Either through defiance or denial, he began planning for a second summer of Shakespeare, giving only a nod to the everyday business of Stan Hywet Hall. Manned by its legions of volunteer ladies, Stan Hywet hummed along on autopilot. There were flower shows, salon concerts, a Christmas pageant, and a Festival of Tudor Sports. But Dad showed only a halfhearted interest. His passions lay elsewhere. He was intent on expanding the scope of his festival. Unbeknownst to him (or perhaps not), a quiet conspiracy was under way to prevent him from ever doing so.

And so it was that on a Sunday in April the following spring, Stan Hywet's board of directors met to decide whether to cancel the second season of the festival and, more ominously, whether to remove my father from his position. Once again, our fate hung in the balance. I was fifteen now, but apparently just as thick-headed as ever: like all those other times, my father's professional jeopardy took me completely by surprise. Adding to the drama of the moment was the fact that the fateful board meeting was held in a large common room in the carriage house, just beneath our living room floor. The whole family, including my father, sat around waiting while our future was being hotly debated down below. Dad had his ardent supporters, of course, so passions ran high on both sides. We could hear shouting under the floorboards. But a strange gallows humor prevailed, and all of us were manically upbeat. All of us, that is, except my five-year-old sister, Sarah Jane, who sat in a corner by herself, in uncharacteristic silence.

My folks had a peppy, exuberant friend on the board, a lawyer named Ralph Felver. Ralph was a forceful advocate of my father's cause. Several times during the meeting, he sprinted upstairs to give us reports from the front. Late in the afternoon he burst in and shouted, "They killed the festival! Now they're goin' after the kid!" He turned and ran back downstairs, in a last-ditch attempt to save my father's job. At that point, Sarah Jane stood, walked over to my father and asked in a quavering voice, "Daddy, what kid does he mean?"

Dad was fired that day. Our days at Stan Hywet Hall were numbered. And I was left with an abiding, life-long suspicion of small-bore civic boosters, genteel pseudo-aristocrats, conniving garden club mavens, and Ohio Republicans. For a few more months, Dad stayed on at Stan Hywet as a lame duck, but I can't imagine that he gave the place much attention. Apart from his understandable bitterness, he had something far more pressing on his mind. In an eerie echo of the Toledo episode, he had passed the point of no return in planning the upcoming summer festival. Once again, actors had been hired, contracts had been signed, and obligations had to be met. He had to put on another season of the Akron Shakespeare Festival. He was legally bound. And anyway, what the hell else was he going to do? The question was where.

6.
The Beefeater

A fleeting memory of my father has always stuck in my mind. It was a memory from when I was seven. On a hot afternoon in Yellow Springs in the days of his Antioch festival, Dad was directing a rehearsal for *The Taming of the Shrew.* This was a tall order, considering that he was also playing the leading male role of Petruchio. (Opposite him in that production was Nancy Marchand in the role of Katharina. Years later she would grab a lot more attention for playing Tony Soprano's diabolical mother Livia on HBO.) On the day of that long-ago rehearsal, my mother had packed a brown-bag lunch for my dad and had asked me to deliver it to him. Choosing my moment, I climbed up onto the stage and handed the bag to him. He took it from my hands without looking at me, removed a sandwich, unwrapped it, and bit into it, without taking his attention off of the rehearsal for even an instant. Looking up at him, I was filled with awe, admiration, and unease. There was something unsettling about his intensity. My father was not unloving, he was never harsh or cruel, he never punished me for anything (even when I most certainly deserved it). But he shared with every artist a forbidding fixity: when he focused on the work at hand, he was strangely absent.

I saw that same look on his face about a week after the Stan Hywet board of directors had fired him. He had been driving around Akron, scouting out a venue for his suddenly unmoored summer festival. I was along for the ride. Dad pulled the Studebaker into the parking lot of Perkins Park, a neglected, uninviting patch of city-owned ground. We got out of the car to explore the three or four acres of weedy parkland. Trash was everywhere. The air was full of the shouts of city kids and the barking of stray dogs. The place couldn't have been more different from the serene back terrace of Stan Hywet Hall.

Something caught Dad's attention. His whole nervous system seemed to quicken, like a dog catching a scent. Looking down a hillside at an open grove surrounded by dusty trees, he suddenly pictured a stage, with rows and rows of chairs set up in front of it. He pictured scaffolding with stage lights mounted on top. He pictured a lighting booth, a box office, and a concession stand. He swiveled around and calculated the number of parking spaces. In an animated stream of consciousness, he described out loud every detail of an imaginary outdoor playhouse. One week before, this man had suffered a terrible personal and professional setback, but now his mood was buoyant, almost giddy. His ardent expression was the same one I recognized from that *Shrew* rehearsal, all those years before. And just as I had back then, I felt oddly excluded from his flight of fancy. But this time, I was feeling something else, too. Looking down at the ugly expanse of Perkins Park, I knew that a Shakespeare festival would never be held there. I was asking myself, "Is my father completely out of his mind?"

Well, not quite. The second season of the Akron Shakespeare Festival did not take place in Perkins Park, but it did take place. My father found a venue only slightly less unlikely. This was the Ohio Theatre in Cuyahoga Falls, a derelict, run-down, four-hundred-seat theater perched on the edge of a gorge, across the Cuyahoga River from Akron proper. In its day, the Ohio had been a vaudeville house, a movie theater, and, most recently, a tabernacle for the Akron evangelist Rex Humbard. On the back wall, six feet above the stage, was a long-obsolete cement baptismal font. This dismal old building became the site of yet another of my father's quixotic exploits. He set to work fitting out the Ohio Theatre for Shakespeare, creating something from nothing on the scrubby banks of the Cuyahoga. Time was short and the task was enormous, but this only seemed to heighten his energy and sharpen his focus. He tackled the project with the missionary zeal of Rex Humbard himself. Shakespeare provided his text, and he would quote it with twinkling eyes and an impish smile: "Sweet are the uses of adversity."

Dad brought in an old friend, a man named Clyde Blakeley, to mastermind the rapid renovation of the Ohio. Wiry and bespectacled, Clyde might have stepped out of the pages of *Where's Waldo?* In a couple of my father's other ventures, he had proven himself a miracle worker in the area of theatrical barn-raising. Clyde was a theater professor at the nearby Lake Erie College for Women, and he brought with him four of his best students to form the core of his technical support staff. To this tiny platoon of youthful theater rats, my big sister and I were willing recruits. Robin even dragooned a couple of her Buchtel girlfriends. This gave us a backstage crew of eight. At fifteen, I was the youngest, two years younger than the next oldest, and the only boy.

As the days passed, ticking down to the opening of the summer season, I worked fifteen-hour days with this hardy band of young Amazons, performing every conceivable task. We painted the walls of the auditorium, perched on teetering scaffolds. We poured concrete for the stage floor. We stitched and stenciled a curtain to hang below the balcony of the unit set. We repaired dozens of battered, borrowed stage lights and outfitted them with colored gels. We hauled in and wired up two massive dimmer boards. We installed makeup tables, lights, and mirrors for the improvised dressing rooms. We mopped, we swept, we scrubbed. We even spent an entire day digging up a broken drainpipe and laying a new one for the one and only backstage sink. When water rattled down the drain and gushed through the new pipe, we cheered like a conquering army.

In the midst of all this feverish activity, the actors arrived from New York and started to rehearse the first play. My father was the director, and, of all things, the play was *The Taming of the Shrew*. I paid no attention. I was too busy to notice. I wasn't carrying a spear anymore, nor was I fetching my father's lunch. I was a working stiff. I had a Social Security number. I was paid by check. I got seventy dollars a week, less deductions.

I adored everyone around me. Among my sister's pals, I even had a crush. In secret, stolen moments, I was regularly reaching first base with her. I was in heaven.

Starting over from scratch, the festival was under extra pressure to bring in the crowds. Hence, Dad had chosen a slate of four Shakespearean warhorses. After *Shrew* came *Twelfth Night*, *A Midsummer Night's Dream*, and *Macbeth*. By August, all four were running in repertory. The productions were a little shoddy, but they were acted with the clarity and brio of my dad's best work. The quality of the acting company was very high. It was full of holdovers from the preceding summer, including my idol Donald Moffat in the roles of Gremio, Malvolio, and Macbeth. Amazingly, when the doors were flung open and performances commenced, audiences showed up. They kept coming all summer, though not exactly in droves. But if sellouts were a rarity, the very fact that the festival had happened at all was success enough for all of us.

I spent that whole summer backstage. I was in the cramped, sweltering lighting booth at every performance, operating the stage lights from one of the ancient dimmer boards. Mine held about twenty dimmers, each a disk of metal and cracked porcelain, a foot in diameter, operated independently of all the others by a ten-inch handle. On any given light cue, I would crank as many as eight of the dimmers at once, twisting myself into elaborate contortions and using three of my four limbs. The dimmers would sizzle and spark, spitting at me like so many angry cats, burning my forearms and zapping me with vicious bolts of electricity. And through all of this, I would hear familiar strains of Shakespearean verse, wafting toward me from the stage through the stultifying air.

One night in late summer, Arthur Lithgow pulled off an outrageous onstage stunt. Over the years, this stunt took on the shimmering aura of legend for everyone who knew him. It was the work of a mad theatrical alchemist. That night, for two dazzling hours, he summoned up the same cocksure wizardry that had produced the entire summer season. I can think of no better example of his creativity, his charm, and his lunatic optimism.

It happened like this. That summer the leading role of Petruchio in *The Taming of the Shrew* was played by a protean young actor named Kenneth Ruta. When my father had hired him for the season, Ken had specified a single night when he had to be away to attend a wedding. The night was in August, during the time when all four plays were to be performed in rep. Dad had played Petruchio several times before so he scheduled

The Taming of the Shrew for that night, intending to replace Ken for one performance only.

But once the season got under way, another problem arose. The actor playing the role of Baptista in *The Taming of the Shrew* left the company, so my father stepped into his role for the remainder of the season. The night was approaching when Ken Ruta would be absent, and, of course, Dad was scheduled to replace him as well. In the play, Baptista is the crotchety father of Kate the Shrew. Petruchio is her rambunctious suitor. Baptista and Petruchio share several scenes. Clearly another actor had to be found. Everyone wondered who that might be. My father stayed mum.

A couple of days before the crucial night, Dad instructed the prop woman to construct a freestanding coat rack to hold a single garment. Then he told the costume designer to whip up a full-length black cloak. When the two items were ready, he called an hour-long rehearsal. It was the morning of that problematic performance. At long last, he unveiled his plan for the evening. He announced to the incredulous company that he would play both Baptista and Petruchio *simultaneously*. In the scenes when both characters appeared together, he would act the role of Baptista in a little orange hat and the big black cloak. When Petruchio spoke, he would doff the cloak, reveal

Petruchio's bright, beribboned costume underneath, and drape hat and cloak onto the coat rack. Then he and every other character would relate to the coat rack as if it were Baptista, still onstage with them. When Petruchio made a bravura exit, he would don hat and cloak in one sweeping motion, without leaving the stage, and Baptista would reappear, as large as life. In the course of the play, he had plotted six times when he would execute this trick.

As they rehearsed the key scenes, the skeptical cast was gradually converted. That evening, he made a curtain speech to the audience, dressed in the black cloak and the orange hat. He explained to them what they were about to see. As he described the forthcoming Baptista/Petruchio switcheroo, he demonstrated it by whipping off his cloak and hat. I was watching from the wings as he thoroughly charmed the crowd. I remember his concluding words verbatim, all these years later:

"I beg you not to look for any Freudian significance in the fact that the same actor is playing both son and father-in-law. If you do find such a significance, that's *your* problem. Our problem is to put on a performance of *The Taming of the Shrew*. I hope you enjoy it."

They did, and wildly. My father was in his element, and the crowd ate it up. The show got the biggest laughs and loudest applause of the summer. Looking back, I realize that my father was an unwitting teacher that night. And, backstage, stooping over my dimmer board, I was an unwitting student. His succinct lesson has stayed with me ever since: make a pact with an audience and they'll follow you anywhere.

Within weeks of my dad's big night, the summer season was over. But before it ended, I got the chance to emerge from my lighting booth and do my first substantial piece of acting on a professional stage. In those last weeks, when day-long rehearsals were a thing of the past, a couple of gung-ho young company members came up with the idea of a workshop. Eager to try their hand at directing, they wanted to present a single extracurricular program of short dramatic pieces after an evening performance, inviting the paid audience to stick around and watch. To cast these pieces, they first tried to enlist the actors who were doing the heavy lifting in the festival repertory. Not surprisingly, they came up empty-handed. So, to my delight, they turned to the backstage crew. Being the one and only male in that group, I was perfectly positioned to land a part.

One of the pieces on the workshop program was a one-act play by George Bernard Shaw called *The Dark Lady of the Sonnets*. Written in 1914, the play is Shaw's argument for a British national theater, embedded in an amiable comedy of mistaken identity. It is set at the end of the sixteenth century, on the grounds outside of Windsor Castle, and the main character is William Shakespeare himself. As it opens, Shakespeare is loitering at the foot of the castle, awaiting a tryst with his "dark lady." Instead, Queen Elizabeth enters, sleepwalking outside the castle's battlements. Thinking her his lover, Shakespeare awakens her, then immediately recognizes her. In the droll dialogue that follows, Shakespeare becomes Shaw's mouthpiece as he passionately makes his case to the queen for a royal playhouse.

But before Queen Elizabeth arrives onstage, Shakespeare is confronted by a Beefeater, a royal guardsman patrolling the castle grounds. Although the Beefeater is a tiny part, it is a witty, colorful, and very noticeable one. With so few willing volunteers available, the part was mine. And then, to my near disbelief, Donald Moffat himself consented to play the central role of William Shakespeare. I had been given the chance to rehearse, to run lines, and to act in front of an audience with my revered mentor. It was incredible! And even more incredible, Donald seemed perfectly happy to be acting with me.

As it happened, my performance as the Beefeater was a modest triumph. But, curiously, my success in the role was a direct result of my own ineptitude and obliviousness. Let me explain.

In *The Dark Lady of the Sonnets*, the Beefeater is a rough-hewn, plainspoken, working-class man. But he has the uncanny habit of tossing off phrases from *Hamlet*, a work that hasn't even been written yet. In the course of his conversation with Shakespeare, he speaks several such phrases: "Angels and ministers of grace defend us," "Frailty, thy name is woman," "You cannot feed capons so," and many more. Every time this happens, Shakespeare avidly jots down the phrases in a little notebook and curses himself for not thinking of them first. It is a device Shaw uses about ten times, to greater and greater comic effect. At one point Shakespeare even cries out, "This man is a greater genius than *I* am!"

Oddly enough, of all the Shakespeare I had absorbed up to that point, *Hamlet* was a glaring omission. Just like the Beefeater, I was completely unaware that I was speaking famous lines, and no one had thought it necessary to inform me of the fact. As a result, every time I spoke one of these lines in front of our audience, it was greeted with inexplicable gales of laughter. During those booming three-second laughs, Donald's face would crinkle with pleasure and his eyes would signal congratulatory approval. I was thrilled, of course, but at the same time I was completely befuddled by all that laughter. And I suppose that befuddlement was precisely what was called for. That night, I was the definitive Shavian Beefeater, and I had no idea why. Afterwards, everyone praised me for my knowing performance and my crafty comic timing. I said nothing to disabuse them.

Somewhere in the hurly-burly of that crazy summer, my father got another job. Unbeknownst to me, he was invited to join the staff of the McCarter Theatre at Princeton University for the coming fall. At the Ohio Theatre, closing night came and went. The company disbanded with the usual combination of merriment and melancholy. The crew hung around to undo all of their own work from the preceding spring. Then the crew disbanded, too. The Akron Shakespeare Festival was no more. Since then, my memory has played its usual tricks. I have no recollection of moving out of the Stan Hywet carriage house, loading up the Studebaker, calling friends to say goodbye, kissing my almost-girlfriend for the last time, or driving off to central New Jersey. But all of it happened. My Akron episode came to an end. While it lasted, it was so jam-packed with vital new experiences that now, in my memory, it seems like a dream. Maybe it has become so dreamlike because, in all these years, I've never been back.

7.
Most Creative

There is a road in New Jersey that leads from Route 1 into Princeton. The road is less than a mile long. It runs through broad fields, is lined with tall trees, and crosses a stone bridge over a pretty, man-made lake before it takes you past the college and into the twee village. Traveling that road, you pass from the concrete commerce of Jersey to the groves of preppy academe. It is hard to imagine a greater change in so short a distance, or a more beautiful entrance to a town. As the Lithgow family motored down that road in September of 1961, I felt like I was passing through a gateway into a totally different life.

It was different all right, and mostly for the better. My father was now an employee on the outer fringes of Princeton University. The family was billeted in junior faculty housing down by Carnegie Lake, far from Princeton's faux-Gothic quadrangles. In that status-conscious college community, my father's professional standing barely registered. He had been hired by the university's estimable professional theater company, in residence at the McCarter Theatre, but he certainly wasn't in charge. His title there was "Education Coordinator." His task was to travel up and down the state, presenting school assemblies to thousands of high school kids, preparing them for student matinees at the McCarter. It was an admirable mission but lonely work, involving hours of solitary driving on wintry roads, endless crowds of unruly teens, and little contact with his artistic peers. And despite Princeton's prestige, the job was unquestionably a comedown for him. He was strenuously promoting McCarter's theatrical fare, but he had virtually nothing to do with the productions themselves.

But if this was an indignity to him, he didn't show it. Indeed, he was flattered by his association with an Ivy League school, and his reduced responsibilities seemed almost a relief to him after his recent years of prolonged cultural combat. He attacked his new job with good humor, renewed vigor, and zest. His high school assemblies evolved into lively dramatic monologues, firing the imagination of the students and priming them for their first experience in a theater. Back at McCarter, he was on hand to greet the raucous young crowds at every matinee. He even created a New Jersey Festival of High School Performing Arts, inviting the winners of drama competitions from all over the state to perform on the McCarter stage. He accomplished all of this with a seasoned producer's ingenuity and resourcefulness. For a pittance, he purchased a couple of jalopies to serve as company cars for his cross-country junkets. He nursed them along with loving care, tinkering with their wheezing engines and alternating them for each trip. He even gave them Shakespearean monikers. The bilious green Plymouth was "Glistering Phaeton" and the faded maroon Dodge was "Plumpy Bacchus with Pink Hind."

As for me, I was off to yet another new school. By extraordinary good fortune, I was destined to finish off my nomadic secondary school career at Princeton High School. Of the eight public schools I attended in all those years, this one was by far the best. For eleventh and twelfth grade, my last big push en route to college, I grabbed the brass ring. My teachers there included three or four of the best I ever had. There was Henry Drewry, a vibrant, fiercely intelligent African-American young man who made electrifying connections between nineteenth-century U.S. history and our early-1960s world. There was Elizabeth Stecchini, an English teacher who bubbled over with the love of language and fine literature (and who could have been the twin sister of Fran Robinson, back in Akron). And best of the lot, there was the brilliant and hilarious Carmine Prezioso, a wildly flamboyant polyglot with the manic energy of Roberto Benigni, who somehow managed to have me speaking French at the end of my very first year of study.

At Princeton High, I felt free to reinvent myself. My big sister, Robin, had moved on to Barnard College in New York City, heading straight from Akron to her Emerald City of Oz. I missed her, of course, but I no longer required her proximity, her moral support, or her community of bohemian girlfriends. I was on my own and I liked it. I had already reached my full height of six-foot-four, and I resembled a scrawny young Ichabod Crane, but I had finally begun to feel at home in my gangly body. Having weathered the last four or five moves, I had developed a kind of genius for fitting in, acquiring social skills worthy of a seasoned politician. I made friends instantly, with no terror and no tears. The student body at the school was a mixed bag of professors' children, blue-collar New Jerseyites, and farm kids, and I managed to connect with all of them.

One source of my newfound self-possession was harsh experience. By now I was an old hand at being the new kid in town. But there was another source, too, one that I was barely aware of at the time but which now strikes me as perfectly obvious. It was theater. In those difficult years prior to the Princeton move, theater had been my godsend. Time and again, it had delivered me from my shell. The *Twelfth Night* assembly and the Malvolio monologues, the nights in the lighting booth and the days of rehearsal, my precocious comradeship with adult actors and my flirtations with Lake Erie College girls, the spear-carrying and banner-waving, the French Messenger and the Beefeater—all of these moments of performance, onstage and off, had emboldened me. If all of the old insecurities still bubbled inside me, I could at least project the *appearance* of a near-Clintonesque confidence and social ease.

Armed with this theater-bred adaptability, I shot up the social hierarchy of Princeton High School with astonishing speed. And my rapid ascendancy had a clear connection to those same theatrical roots. On a Wednesday, three days after the start of school, everyone was required to enroll in one of dozens of extra-curricular clubs. For me, the choice was a no-brainer. I picked the drama club, archly dubbed "The Tower Thespians." That afternoon, I took a seat in the school auditorium as the other club members gathered. None of them sat near me. I watched as their numbers swelled to ten, twenty, thirty. I grew more and more alarmed as I looked around me. Every single Tower Thespian, everyone but me, was a girl. "What kind of a nerdy club is this?" I thought. "And how do I get out of it?" Five minutes later it was too late. They had elected me club president.

Two days later, I was sitting in the same auditorium at a meeting of the leaders of every student organization

at PHS. Two months after that, in stage whiskers and old-age makeup, I scored a personal triumph in the huge role of Noah, in the school play of the same name. Two months after that, after delivering a sly, self-mocking campaign speech to the entire student body and sweeping the two co-captains of the varsity football team in a school-wide election, I was the new president of the Princeton High School Student Council. The new kid in town had snowed everybody. By the time I graduated, my class had voted me "Most Creative," "Most Popular," "Most Likely to Succeed," and "Best Dancer." In secret, the student editor of the yearbook called to inform me of these four honorifics. She told me I had to pick just one. Still nursing my dreams of being an artist, I went for "Most Creative."

Yes, in spite of all my giddy success in student theater and school politics, art remained my primary calling. But at PHS, my dogged artistic ambitions fell prey to a cruel irony. For all of its pedagogical glories, the school had awful art classes, far inferior to the ones back in Akron. At the beginning of my first year, I dutifully signed up for the single art elective. My teacher, whom I shall call Alfred Stipek, was a dark, dour bantamweight with a strictly vocational approach to his subject. My fellow art students seemed to have had no aspirations beyond print advertising and industrial design. Mr. Stipek's dry, academic lessons seemed calculated to extinguish the slightest glimmer of artistic fire in any of us. A typical assignment was to spend three weeks doing a charcoal drawing of a plaster copy of an Egyptian sculpture of a cat. It was excruciatingly dull.

Halfway through that semester, we were finally allowed to set aside our charcoal. Mr. Stipek set up a still life and told us that, for the next few weeks, we were to render it in colored pastels. For days I toiled over my drawing, fending off boredom as best I could. But Mr. Stipek was not happy with my technique. Where I was working in the light, sketchy style of Degas and Lautrec, he wanted me to massage the colors with my thumb, smushing them together to simulate oil paint. Whenever he walked up to my desk and repeated his instructions, I would nod obediently, then proceed as I had before, completely ignoring him. The days passed and Mr. Stipek became more testy and impatient. Finally, after about two weeks of work, he crept up behind me with a paper towel, reached across my drawing board, and violently scrubbed the entire surface of my picture. Inwardly I was shocked and enraged. But passive-aggressiveness had become my strong suit: I calmly put down the board, gathered up my things, walked out of the class, and never went back.

This wrenching incident was a blessing in disguise. I reported it in detail to my mother, the most ardent supporter of all my creative activities. Once her maternal wrath was spent, she swung into action, researching the best art instruction outside of school. She came up with a three-hour Saturday-morning figure drawing class for teenage kids in New York City, at the venerable Art Students League of New York. Sifting through commuter schedules, she found a Trailways bus trip from Princeton to the Port Authority Bus Terminal, departing Saturdays at 7 a.m. Then she scoped out the right subway route from the Port Authority to West Fifty-seventh Street for the 9 a.m. class. The very next Saturday she fixed me a bagged lunch, drove me to the tobacco store, bought me my ticket, waited with me until the bus arrived, then dispatched me to Manhattan. By the end of that month, this solitary day-trip through central Jersey had become my regular Saturday routine, and the glamorous, clamorous, tawdry world of New York City had opened up to me like a van Gogh sunflower.

The Art Students League never changes. It is a grand Beaux Arts rock pile, within yelling distance of Carnegie Hall. Inside, the smell of linseed oil and turpentine hangs in the air, century-old dust gathers in the corner of every studio, and the halls echo with the ghosts of New York painters from decades past. The first time I timidly stepped through its doors, this atmosphere exhilarated and intimidated me in equal measure. I was directed upstairs to a large, skylit studio, cluttered with easels and stools. These were arrayed around a low wooden platform, with space for two models. The studio was already filling up with a class of teenage art students, most of them on a Saturday-morning busman's holiday from Manhattan's High School of Music and Art. This young crowd was intense, driven, focused, and very talented. They scared the hell out of me. In the first seconds, my Princeton High School savoir faire evaporated. I was a frightened clam once more. I spent my first late-morning break huddled in a stall in the men's room like a hunted animal, wolfing down my mother's packed lunch.

My new teacher was a far cry from the kindly, maternal Fran Robinson. She was Ethel Katz, a tough-minded Jewish woman in a drab, workmanlike smock. She was in her mid-sixties, half my height, and shaped like a cinderblock, with close-cropped gray hair and gigantic horn-rimmed glasses. Ethel was all business.

That morning, without a word of greeting, she brusquely assigned me an easel and sent me downstairs with a shopping list to the in-house art-supply store. I was back to charcoal again, but this time I would be working on heavy, textured sheets of paper, and on a huge scale. And this time I would be drawing nudes.

Nudes! I was sixteen years old, an age where anything with a curved surface was the source of runaway sexual fantasies. I had never seen a naked woman in my life and I was feverish with anticipation. I nervously adjusted my easel and pinned a sheet of paper to a drawing board, waiting for two radiant sirens to emerge from behind a screen, step onto the platform, and stand in front of me in all their seductive glory. Out they came. Clearly the wise minds at the Art Students League had had the sense to dampen the sensual enthusiasm of their teenage students. In two years of Saturday mornings, I saw a weekly parade of uniquely peculiar male and female bodies—old, fat, wizened, weathered, deformed. They were marvelous subjects for a figure drawing class but none could be called remotely attractive. All business.

Ethel was a gruff, unsentimental, altogether marvelous teacher. She challenged me as no art teacher had before. Simple truths poured out of her, in the coarse, nasal accent of a waitress at Katz's Delicatessen on Houston Street. Under her watchful eye, my crabbed little scrawlings became bold and dramatic, with sweeping lines filling up the frame. She taught me to visually organize the complex shapes of two naked bodies. She ordered me to keep my eyes on the models, noting my tendency to fix my gaze on my own drawing as it grew tighter and less fluid. She tore photos of athletes out of the New York Times and brought them to class as chance examples of elegant abstract composition. Like a sponge, I soaked in every word and every image, then put it all to work. At a certain point, Ethel decided I was ready to move over to the other half of the studio where she unleashed me on watercolor still lifes. My big paintings swam with brilliant, liquid color, like nothing I'd ever dared to do before.

In all of this, Ethel would encourage me but never compliment me. In her view, nothing was ever completely mastered. There was always something more to strive for. And this could sometimes make her downright merciless. Her most pointed critique has stayed with me ever since, resonating with every other aspect of my life. She told me one day that I had a distinct, facile talent but that I had to be watchful. My facility was my greatest asset, but it was also my greatest drawback. It allowed me to get by with glib, hasty, lazy work. Things came easy for me, so too often I was perfectly willing to skip over difficult tasks. Art is hard, she insisted. If you're going to be great at it, you can't fake it. Faking it, of course, is the very essence of acting. Ethel Katz may have been telling me more that day than either of us realized, and more than I wanted to hear.

My Saturday classes at the Art Students League ended at noon. At that hour, the second half of my weekly Manhattan adventures would begin. Between midday and midnight, when the last Princeton bus pulled out of the Port Authority, the city was my oyster. Most Saturdays I would jump on the subway at Columbus Circle and head uptown to meet Robin in her Barnard dorm room. Then off we would go, to museums, galleries, art house films, and Greenwich Village coffeehouses. We occasionally tracked down beloved actors from the recent Ohio theater seasons, meeting them on their home turf. Sometimes they actually had jobs and we'd go see them act in tiny off-Broadway houses. On big occasions, Robin and I would splurge for tickets to shows we knew only from record albums in faraway Akron—*The Fantasticks, The Play of Daniel, Beyond the Fringe*. At one point, Robin even directed a Barnard student production of a one-act Yeats play and hired me to create masks and paint an enormous show cloth for it. New York seemed to me then, as it does to this day, a world of limitless creative energy and possibility. And experiencing it for the first time in Robin's company sustained the brother-sister bond that we had forged in our itinerant grade-school years, worlds away from Manhattan Island.

Halfway through our first year in Princeton, a stroke of good luck befell my father. In a happy reversal of fortune, he was invited back to Ohio to create yet another summer theater festival. This one was to be called the Great Lakes Shakespeare Festival. It would take place in the town of Lakewood, just outside of Cleveland. The beauty of this invitation was that the new enterprise would not conflict with his Mc-Carter job. He would be employed year-round. And, blessedly, we would not have to move. All of us were thrilled with this news. The new festival would have all the earmarks of Dad's earlier ventures, and many of the same players. And once again he would be guiding the fortunes of his own theater company.

This time, however, I would be far away from the action. I was heading to Europe on my first trip outside the country. I had joined a group of East Coast prep school kids for a summer travel-camp tour of a dozen cities, towns, and villages in France. The trip was part of a program run by an old college friend of my parents who had offered a French tour to me gratis, in an effort to persuade my father to lead a corresponding tour to England. For weeks Dad strung along his old friend as plans for his new Shakespeare festival took shape. In the end, the festival was launched and Dad didn't go to England—but I got my trip anyway. And what a glorious trip it was. I traveled to Brittany, the Loire Valley, the Riviera, the Alps, and Paris. I saw museums, galleries, chateaux, plays, operas, and towering alpine peaks. I ate *foie gras, crêpes Suzette,* and *croques mes-sieurs.* On streets, beaches, and hillsides, I spent languorous hours sitting with a box of watercolors and a *bloc de feuillets,* painting landscapes and street scenes in my best imitation of Maurice Prendergast and Raoul Dufy. I was drunk with the experience of an exotic new culture and played the role of budding artist with romantic flair.

In the company of so many children of Yankee privilege, I was something of a poor relation. But in our seven weeks abroad, the fifteen of us grew into a happy, adventurous band. And by the midpoint of the trip, I had my first girlfriend. She was a feisty, worldly, guitar-strumming Jewish girl named Jane, born and bred on Manhattan's Upper West Side. Sexually, I still lived in a cave of benighted ignorance, but Jane led me toward the light. Although neither of us lost our virginity that summer, the swoony eroticism of perfumed summer nights in France kept us in a constant state of orgasmic groping. When I returned to Princeton for my last year of school, I crawled back into my cave, as sexually reclusive as ever. But my summer travels had vastly broadened my horizons, and I began my senior year of high school with a substantially broader sense of myself.

8.
Big and Little

Of the crowded cast of characters from my high school days, one person played perhaps the most important featured role. This was my little sister Sarah Jane. As with so many supporting players, Sarah Jane was ubiquitous, delightful, and sometimes slightly taken for granted. In hindsight, she completes the picture of my life during those Princeton years.

Back in Yellow Springs, when Sarah Jane was two years old, Harry Belafonte was a big deal. His album *Calypso* sold in the millions, and its first song, "Day-O," was part of the sound track of the American scene. The album became the most frequently played music in our household, having finally displaced the swing jazz of Benny Goodman and Glenn Miller. The most lively, danceable song on Belafonte's record was something called "Dolly Dawn"—

She gonna dance!
She gonna sing!
She gonna cause the rafters to ring!

For baby Sarah Jane, that song was her first ecstatic musical experience. She had only just started to walk, but every time she heard it, she would dance. For the whole family, Sarah Jane dancing to "Dolly Dawn" on the living room floor became our favorite entertainment. It was probably inevitable that she would become known to all of us as "Dolly." Until her arrival, I'd been the youngest of my parents' three kids. She was an afterthought child, ten years younger than

I, so in effect she grew up with two actual parents and three surrogate ones. She was a beautiful child with an ineffably sweet nature, and the five of us smothered her with doting affection.

By the time our gypsy family pitched our tent in Princeton, Dolly was five years old. I was fifteen. Sister Robin and brother David had long since departed the scene. Dolly and I were the only kids left in the household, and we were a constant presence in each other's lives. With her as my little sister, I happily embraced the role of big brother. I was her go-to babysitter and frequent schlepper, but I never begrudged either job. Mainly I was her primary source of fun, and she mine. I read her books, sang her songs, and littered the house with all kinds of crafts projects. Our big housing complex bordered a large woodsy tract of land on the edge of town. This became an exotic playground for us and the site of endless adventures. In the winter I taught her to skate on the vast expanse of ice covering Carnegie Lake. Together, we turned even mundane household chores into giddy drama. The layout of our building required a fifty-yard trek to its garbage bin. Dolly and I invented the characters of two undercover agents, named "Big" and "Little," and turned the garbage run into an hour-long espionage mission, packed with suspense and hilarity. In spite of our cover names, at such moments we were no longer a big brother and a little sister. We were playmates, pure and simple, uncannily attuned to each other's sense of adventure and fun.

Although the thought never occurred to me at the time, those idle hours with Dolly provided me with an unwitting primer on parenthood. Years later, when I became a father, I put all our projects, adventures, and games back to work. As a parent I was far from perfect (ask any of my children), but as a gonzo entertainer I was way ahead of the game.

As a matter of fact, gonzo entertainment was to become a major sideline to my professional career. Anticipating parenthood in my mid-twenties, I began to teach myself guitar, intending to sing and play songs for my first child. My playing never advanced beyond grinding mediocrity, but it was good enough for "She'll Be Comin' round the Mountain" and "Go Tell Aunt Rhodie." Within a few years I was singing in my son Ian's classrooms and school assemblies. I started making up my own daffy songs. I fashioned a fifty-minute concert for kids and perfected the demanding skill of unleashing and harnessing their wild enthusiasm without ever losing their attention. As the years passed, the concert venues got bigger. I performed with major orchestras. The concerts spawned CDs and bestselling books. I clowned around for two thousand children on the stage of Carnegie Hall. But if the scale of these escapades grew exponentially, their spirit remained the same. I never lost the sense of goofy fun that I discovered entertaining my little sister.

My own children outgrew my kids' concerts years ago, but I've never stopped doing them. The more I perform for children, the more I love it. They are a sensational audience for a stage performer and an exhilarating change of pace from adults. The goal of theater is a suspension of disbelief. With grown-ups, you never completely achieve it. Adults never entirely forget that they are watching actors pretend. You can certainly have an impact on them. You can surprise them, move them, shock them, and make them laugh. But you're not fooling them for a moment. Adults always sit in a theater with the unwavering knowledge that they are watching a calculated piece of fiction.

Not so children. They barely know what a theater is. For them, there is little difference between artifice and reality. Irony means nothing to them. Their disbelief is in a constant state of suspension. Over time I've invented all sorts of tricks to take advantage of their innocence. My concerts are full of them. For example, I always stride onstage for my first song wearing a jaunty bowler hat. I finish the song and begin to greet the kids. One of the musicians tugs at my sleeve, whispers to me, and points to my hat. I reach up, feel the hat, and shout out, with shock and dismay:

"Oh, no! I've done it again! I do it all the time! I put on my hat, I sing the song, *then I forget to take off my hat*! It's my worst habit! If I do it again, be sure to tell me, won't you?"

In the next hour I wear about six hats. Each one is more ridiculous than the last. There's a top hat, a pith helmet, a beanie with a little propeller, a pair of kangaroo ears, and so on. Every time, I forget to take off my hat for the next song. Try to imagine what the kids do when this happens. The sound reaches the decibel level of a Beatles concert at Shea Stadium.

Then there is "Guess the Animal." On the concert stage, I place a huge easel at stage left. Using the easel, I play a game with the children: I tell them I'm going to draw an animal on a big piece of poster board and they must guess what it is before the drawing is completed. In bold felt pen, I begin a large drawing of, say, a hippo. Soon it is a clearly recognizable hippo. The children have begun shouting "It's a hippo!" I turn to them and say, "It's a what? It's a *what?*" "It's a hippo!" they scream. I stare at them, puzzled, and say, "Funny. I thought you'd get this one." By this time they are shrieking at the top of their lungs, "IT'S A HIPPO!!!" After working them into a state of frenzy, I finally cry out, "RIGHT! IT'S A *HIPPO!*" I finish the drawing and launch into Flanders and Swann's blissfully silly "Hippopotamus Song." Hugely pleased with themselves, the children sit back and listen.

I repeat the game six or seven times in the course of the concert, but they never tire of it. They play the game passionately, over and over again, blithely unaware that I'm doing anything to manipulate them. They absolutely love to be tricked in this way. And in their response you can see the first stirrings of a grown-up's appetite for entertainment. Deep down, adults long to be tricked as well.

And when did I invent Guess the Animal? On a rainy Princeton afternoon with Dolly when there was nothing else to do. She taught me to connect with children, to understand them, and to entertain them. And somewhere along the line, she must have picked up some of these skills herself. For years she has been a superb teacher in Ithaca, New York. She has directed spectacular school musicals and student productions of Shakespeare. And she has raised four marvelously talented and creative sons. Whenever we see each other, we revert to an adult version of our long-ago childhood selves, giggling and teasing like Big and Little. But she is Sarah Jane now. Nowadays there are only a handful of us left who remember that she was ever known as Dolly.

9.
Curtains

I was a curtain puller for Marcel Marceau. For decades, the immortal French mime was a yearly one-night-only fixture at McCarter Theatre, presenting his delicate art in hypnotic silence for wildly appreciative full houses. On one of his visits, I was pressed into service. I was assigned the job of raising and lowering McCarter's massive red-velour curtain for Marceau's single performance. It was one of many backstage jobs that I undertook at the theater, for piddling wages but mostly for fun, during my two high school years in Princeton. At various times I had run lights, painted sets, fashioned lobby displays, and operated the fly lines that hoisted flats and set pieces up and down. But pulling the curtain for the great Marcel Marceau was the best gig of all. I was humbled by the honor.

In those days Marceau was a one-of-a-kind Gallic superstar, his slight frame and unique persona recognizable everywhere. In performance, his face was painted stark white, with his mouth, eyes, and eyebrows delicately outlined in red and black. He wore white pants cut to halfway down his calves, a striped shirt, a tight, short jacket, ballet slippers, and a little blue hat with a flower sprouting out of it. In this emblematic costume, he performed a show that was simplicity itself. He would present about a dozen short mime pieces, most of them in the character of Bip, his alter ego. Marceau would chase butterflies, struggle against the wind, grow drunk at a cocktail party or seasick on board a cruise ship, all in pantomime. The entire performance took place on an empty stage, without props, sets, or supporting players. Or rather, all of these things were there but invisible, created by the magic of Marceau's physical gifts, by the eloquent lighting, and by the imagination of the audience. Clearly, the rise and the fall of the curtain was also pretty damned important.

On the day of Marceau's performance, I watched worshipfully from backstage all through his afternoon technical rehearsal. Although he had been through the drill a thousand times over the years, his preparation was exhaustive and precise. When it came time to rehearse the curtain call, his stage manager instructed me in broken English to raise and lower the curtain in a steady rhythm as Marceau took several bows. This was known as "bouncing the curtain," and it required that I quickly master a complex new skill. In the wings, I stood in front of two thick ropes. I would pull on one of the ropes to ring down the curtain while the other rope shot up in the opposite direction. When the curtain was almost down, I would grab the second rope and allow it to lift me four feet off the ground. At this point, my counterbalancing weight would reverse the direction of the two ropes, I would drop back down to the floor, then pull on the second rope with all my might. The curtain would "bounce," barely touching the stage, then gracefully rise up again. For Marcel Marceau I was to repeat this maneuver ten times: five times up and five times down. It was a tricky business, demanding enormous effort and split-second timing, but by the end of the tech rehearsal, I had mastered it.

The evening performance was sensational. Each of the mimed mini-dramas was greeted with clamorous adulation. I and the entire McCarter crew performed our backstage tasks with self-assurance and a sure hand. Marceau had craftily saved his best material for last, and in the final moments of his performance the audience was completely transported. I'd never heard such an ovation.

Then came the curtain call.

I brought the curtain down on cue. After a poetic pause, I switched ropes and pulled it back up again. I switched again, ready to "bounce the curtain." The second rope hoisted me high off the ground. The curtain reversed course and came back down. I switched ropes and was hoisted up again, the curtain bounced nicely off the stage and went straight back up. Perfection! I switched again, gaining confidence, as the cheers rang out. Down, up, down, up, as Marceau smiled, clutched his heart, and grandly bowed. On the fourth bow, the curtain came down, I switched ropes, and once again I lurched back up in the air. But by this time, my strength was flagging. I lost my grip and fell in a heap onto the stage floor. I scrambled to my feet and stared at the two ropes as they gradually slowed to a stop. Terror engulfed me. I had no idea which one I should grab next. Hoping for the best I reached for the one on the right and pulled on it for all I was worth. I pulled. And pulled. And pulled. And pulled. Bit by bit, the rope offered less and less resistance. The roar of the crowd was oddly diminishing. A ghastly thought slowly dawned on me: Had I grabbed the wrong rope? I turned and looked out at the stage. What I saw filled me with horror.

Between Marcel Marceau and the audience was a massive pile of dark-red velour, about eight feet high. It was McCarter's grand show curtain, lying on the stage like an enormous felled giant. Instead of bringing the curtain back up, I'd brought it down, down, down, piling it up, up, up on the stage. This mountain of fabric was attached to a long metal pipe and a series of tangled wires. These hung down from McCarter's fly space in full view of the audience, swaying slowly from side to side. The crowd had fallen into a deathly silence. As for Marcel Marceau he was standing erect, with his hands on his hips, his weight on one leg, and a foot turned out. He was staring at me with stony fixity. His immobile face, with its bone-white makeup, its knit brow, and its gashlike red sneer, could only be described as a mask of rage. Predictably, the famous mime said nothing.

The moment was indelible. I cannot say that it had anything to do with my eventually becoming an actor, but it most certainly persuaded me that I had no business being a stagehand.

My evening with Marcel Marceau was one of many memorable nights at McCarter Theatre in those two years. Blessedly, it was the only catastrophe. In most cases, I was an engrossed spectator. In my memory

McCarter was a kind of conservatory of the performing arts, with me alone making up its entire student body. And the faculty of my private conservatory included some of the greatest figures of that era, in theater, music, and dance.

Where else could you find such a roster of brilliant teachers? Then as now, a parade of world-class artists and ensembles shared McCarter's stage with its resident theater company, presenting to the university and to the greater Princeton community a vast smorgasbord of performances. And under the protective guise of a staffer's brat, I became an expert at sneaking in to see them. I would casually stride through the stage door at the back of the theater, pass through the scene shop, costume shop, and rehearsal room, slip into the inner lobby, and mingle with the gathering crowd. Having bypassed the ticket-takers, I would walk into the auditorium with the paying audience, climb up four flights, and perch myself on the top stair at the very back of the balcony.

During the first half of any given performance, I would spot an empty seat far below in the first few rows. I would note down its exact location. During the intermission, I'd seek out the seat and confidently plant myself in it. And for the second half of the evening there I would be, a dozen feet away from Dame

Joan Sutherland, Pete Seeger, Rudolph Serkin, Odetta, Isaac Stern, Dave Brubeck, Julian Bream, every major symphony orchestra, and the dance companies of Alvin Ailey, Merce Cunningham, and the American Ballet Theatre. I would bask in the glow of their brilliance and drink it all in. There was even a visit from the Cambridge Circus, a young comedy troupe from England, featuring a tall, thin fellow with an especially anarchic streak. I worked with him forty years later and we deduced that, yes indeed, he'd been there and I'd seen him. His name was John Cleese.

On those nights of cultural cat burglary, I was given the gift of extraordinary artistic riches. But in retrospect I see a strangely forlorn side to it all. On my furtive McCarter capers I was a solitary teen, alone in a crowd of privileged adult sophisticates, creeping around like a spy behind enemy lines. Once again I was straddling two worlds, and in one of them I was a secretive loner.

In the other world, I continued to fly high. All through my senior year I seemed to leap from one shining moment to another. In my schoolwork I got nothing but A's. As Student Council president I presided over weekly all-school assemblies, crafting a droll, self-deprecating public persona. I initiated a series of after-school concerts featuring solo performances by student musicians. In the foyer of the school library I created a gallery for student art, and its initial offering was an exhibition of my own watercolors. I invited actors from the McCarter Company to speak before meetings of the Tower Thespians, giving myself the unique opportunity of introducing a spirited Shakespearean monologue, performed by my own father. I even created a cottage industry of woodcut Christmas cards and peddled them to the parents of my classmates. My eagerness to please verged on the pathological. At the awards assembly at the end of the year, I routed my competition. Oh, what a good boy was I!

But in the gleaming patina of such a triumphalist year, cracks occasionally appeared. In my year-long victory lap, I experienced a couple of queasy moments. And it's a good thing that I did: they taught me more than I could ever have learned in schoolbooks.

The first of these moments shows what a rarefied and repressed social circle I was traveling in at Princeton High. One of my classes that year was Advanced Placement Social Studies. Our teacher was a squat, round, wryly cynical man named Mr. Roufberg. One day, Mr. Roufberg surprised us with an unusual assignment. He asked us a simple question: "What is the issue in your life that most concerns you?" He gave us all ten minutes to write down anonymous answers and pass them in. A day later, he reported on the results of his pop survey, rattling off our deep concerns with deadpan bemusement. The answers were heavily weighted toward such ponderous topics as nuclear disarmament, world poverty, and civil rights. I myself had written down some garbage about creeping commercialism.

Then Mr. Roufberg sprung a surprise, hitting us with a kind of sociopolitical ambush. He proceeded to summarize the answers to the same question that had been written by students from his other classes, a few levels lower in the school's rigid social hierarchy. These answers were stunningly different from ours, far more personal and far more urgent.

Should I go steady?

Should I pet?

Should I have sex?

Should I tell my parents that I've had sex?

What'll I do if I'm pregnant?

Listening to this list, all of us in AP Social Studies felt curiously chastened. We flushed and lowered our eyes. Our skin prickled with embarrassment. We were accustomed to feeling an offhand superiority to the working-class majority of our classmates—smarter, more worldly and sophisticated. Yet here they were, these earnest, impassioned townies, anonymously expressing emotions that we barely allowed ourselves.

Creeping commercialism? Who the hell cared? Could it be that we were learning a lot more about social studies and they were learning a lot more about life?

And then there was my hard-earned lesson in political chicanery. My sweet-natured mother turned downright wrathful one day when I bragged about one of my Student Council initiatives. As president, I had proposed to my Executive Committee that we use Student Council funds to purchase several of my Christmas cards to send to members of the high school faculty. The committee had briskly passed the measure and I had handily pocketed thirty-five bucks on the deal. When I came home brandishing a check and crowing about my entrepreneurial coup, Mom's face turned crimson. In no uncertain terms, she ordered me to return the money and make the cards my personal gift to the school. Then she sat me down and explained to me, in words that seared into my brain, the concept of "conflict of interest." What I had done, she said, was enough to get me impeached from any elected office out there in the real world. I was seventeen years old by this time. At such an age, I certainly should have known better. What kind of amoral idiot needed such elementary ethical counseling? I learned about conflict of interest that day, but I also learned how blithely corruptible I was. Corruptible and, I might add, unregenerate: I recall, to my shame, that I never quite got around to returning that check.

Finally there was Patty Brown. Her story was my first real insight into the ugly realities of racism. In those days, the American Friends Service Committee ran a program that brought talented African-American high school students north from segregated schools in the Deep South. The idea was to give them a year-long experience of the fully integrated and presumably more enlightened world of public education in the North. This was 1962, remember, and the civil rights movement was only just beginning to take hold. As such, the program was well ahead of its time. If it was a little patronizing and naïve, it was also bold, idealistic, and worthy.

The program sent two students, a girl and a boy, to join the Junior Class of Princeton High School in my senior year. The girl's name was Patty Brown. Patty was short, compact, and bespectacled, a smart, vibrant kid with a dazzling smile, a daring sense of humor, and an explosive laugh. It was easy to see what had made her a star student in her Alabama school and a prime candidate for the AFS program. She arrived in Princeton ready to seize this new experience with both hands, and her classmates responded in kind. She and I hit it off instantly and maintained a fun, teasing relationship that entire year.

When spring came around, Patty asked me to take her to her Junior Class prom. She asked over the telephone. Her voice was halting and uncharacteristically shy. Clearly the request had taken all her courage. Near tears, she touchingly added that she would understand if I felt I had to say no. I said yes. And so, for what was surely the first time in the history of PHS, a white male Student Council president would escort a black girl to a school prom. And not only that. The *vice* president, an African-American junior named Art Brooks, invited a white girl and asked Patty and me to double date. I said yes to this, too. Long before its time, we were all set to enact a four-character version of *Hairspray*.

As our plans fell into place, my mother nearly burst with pride. She saw the event as a radical social statement on my part, and it warmed the cockles of her lefty heart. When the evening arrived, I did my best to ignore the political baggage she had attached to it. The four of us gathered at the home of Art's date and we ate supper together. The air was charged with nervous anxiety, but probably no more so than any of our classmates were feeling, in households all over town.

We ate together in near-silence. The anarchic humor that Patty and I usually shared had disappeared. We were a perfectly typical quartet of shy, tentative teenagers heading to the prom.

But at the prom itself, we cut loose. The awkwardness of the early evening gave way to Patty's usual high spirits. She revealed herself to be an electrifying dancer and I did my best to keep pace with her. At one point she kicked off her shoes and danced in her bare feet. A crowd gradually formed a circle around us and clapped in rhythm, urging us on. We were having a ball. As the two of us reached a fever pitch, I noticed Florence Burke elbowing her way into the circle. Miss Burke was the school's assistant principal, a large, florid, middle-aged woman, full of sunny rectitude. Ordinarily she enforced school rules with her own brand of edgy good humor. But tonight she glowered. She brought Patty and me to a halt, declaring that dancing in bare feet was strictly prohibited at school dances. Patty was unfazed. She cheerfully put her shoes back on and we continued to dance, with only slightly less abandon. I barely gave it a thought when, in the last hour of the prom, I noticed several white girls dancing in bare feet.

When I walked into my homeroom on the following Monday morning, a letter was waiting for me. The letter was written in blue ink on pink stationery. It was short, to the point, and unsigned.

> *John,*
> *You have desecrated the Junior Prom. We don't*
> *want any nigger lovers at our school.*

As I read the letter, my knees went weak. I was seized with a mix of shock, rage, and nausea. For the rest of that day, I stared balefully at the faces of my classmates in the halls and classrooms, suspecting every one of them of harboring secret poisonous prejudice. I was due to preside over an assembly that midday, and I spent the entire morning preparing to read the obscene letter out loud to the student population and declaim against hatred and racism. When the time came, my courage failed me and I conducted the assembly with sullen ill humor.

Instead of spewing my feelings in public, I unburdened myself to Henry Drewry, my revered African-American history teacher, in his office after school. I sat down at Mr. Drewry's desk, handed him the letter, and watched him as he read it. The written words did not appear to surprise or distress him. He merely sighed with a kind of world-weary resignation. In the conversation that followed, he gave me the profound gift of his own experience of racism and instantly took his place in my pantheon of personal heroes. He said that he could list hundreds of examples of this kind of hatred and cowardice from his own experience, even within the leafy confines of liberal Princeton. He said that I was lucky to be made aware of this subterranean evil but that I should not allow it to turn me bitter or vengeful. He reassured me that I had been wise to stay mum on the subject in front of the gathered student body, but that I should find ways of judiciously fighting prejudice in my own life. Leaving his office, I felt that Henry Drewry, that amiable, mild-mannered man, was the strongest person I had ever met. The next day, I clung to his words when a car sped by as I walked home from school and a red-faced young bigot screeched out at me from the passenger-side window: *"Lithgow's a nigger lover!"*

But the Patty Brown episode was a dark moment in the midst of sunny times. For my entire family, things were looking up. That spring, my father was asked to put aside his high school hucksterism and take over as artistic director of the McCarter Theatre. This was far and away the most prestigious assignment he had ever been given. For the moment, he arranged to also continue as head of his summer Shakespeare festival in Cleveland, thus providing his core company of actors with year-round employment. The family packed up for another move to Ohio, but this time just for a summer gig. Dad hired me to work in the company as an apprentice and bit-part actor, and I embraced his nepotism with undiluted enthusiasm. It would be three months of exhausting work, but I also planned another project for my spare time. Typing, of all things, had been one casualty of my scattershot high school education. And so, armed with a graduation-gift used Remington and a how-to manual, I intended to teach myself to type. This was more a necessity than a whim: I'd been accepted to Harvard College on a full scholarship for the following fall.

Over the course of a freakishly hot month of May, I rang down the curtain on my grade school years. I marked all the sentimental rituals that bring high school to a close—Senior Prom, Commencement, and a series of desultory end-of-the-year parties. All through those weeks, I recall feeling an enormous sense of relief, as if I had reached the end of a marathon that I never thought I could complete. But the days were also suffused with a curious sensation of unease, if not guilt. I had made a great success of Princeton High School, but that success felt oddly similar to sneaking into a front-row seat during an

intermission at McCarter Theatre. I couldn't escape
the sense that I had pulled the wool over everyone's
eyes, that I was leaving town just in time, before anyone found me out. All around me I saw classmates
with a shared history, young adults who had lived
their entire lives together, in the same small town. To
them, saying goodbye at the end of high school was an
agonizing rupture. Not to me. I had just been passing
through, shuffling identities like a riverboat gambler.
My genial self-assurance had been the performance
of a lifetime. Although it never occurred to me at the
time, the haphazard circumstances of my school years
had prepared me, to an uncanny degree, for a life of
acting.

10.
Pinch Me

For someone with no intention of becoming an actor, things were getting pretty serious. In late June of 1963, days after my high school graduation, I arrived in the leafy confines of suburban Lakewood, Ohio, to join the Great Lakes Shakespeare Festival for its second summer season. I was a bona fide member of a professional repertory company. My father had hired me as one of a team of five apprentices, with the usual long list of backstage duties, ranging from scene painting and prop making to mopping the stage. But along with all that drudgery, we five apprentices were expected to fill out the lower ranks of the acting company. All summer long I was going to *act*.

Like so many of my father's early ventures, the festival took place in a bizarrely unlikely setting. The plays were mounted in the large, echoing auditorium of the Lakewood High School, twenty minutes from downtown Cleveland. At show time, theatergoers filed into the school building beneath an enormous polychrome sculpture of a blond, Nordic-looking young farmer, on his knees planting a sapling. Apparently the figure was originally intended to be Johnny Appleseed until some unsavory historical facts about Appleseed's sex life had been uncovered by Lakewood's prudish citizenry. Now the sculpture was simply called *The Early Settler*. This was the source of great amusement to the waggish New York actors who arrived at the start of the season. They decided that the Early Settler was actually Lemuel Gulliver, jerking off into the soil.

These were the years of the festival's infancy, but it has survived to this day, nearly fifty years after my father launched it. Now known as the Great Lakes Theater Festival, it has long since expanded its repertory beyond the Shakespearean canon and has relocated to downtown Cleveland, where it is housed in the venerable Hanna Theatre (by coincidence, the site of Bert Lahr's long-ago performance as Bottom the Weaver). Nowadays, the festival's publicity materials tend to banner the names of two famous alumni. One is Tom Hanks, who played major roles in three seasons there early in his career. The other is John Lithgow, who was there for two seasons, several years earlier. No mention is ever made of how tiny his roles were.

But to me, size did not matter. I was giddy at the prospect of playing actual parts, no matter how small, in the summer's entire repertory. On a large casting grid, my father had put my name down for roles in each of six plays. I was to be little more than a minor player—the roles averaged only about a dozen lines apiece. But each part was a big step up from spear carrier, and each character had a name. And though most of those names had only one syllable (the best parts were Nym, Froth, Pinch, and Le Fer), at least I would have a line to myself in every playbill. The following summer I would return to the festival and would take on larger roles with more syllables in their names (Hortensio, Guildenstern, Lucilius, Artemidorus), but for the moment, little monosyllabic parts suited me just fine.

The Comedy of Errors was the first show that season. My father was set to direct it and I was to play the small but juicy role of Dr. Pinch. Although I didn't realize it at the time, Dr. Pinch was by far my biggest challenge to date. On my first day, I put my head down and started to rehearse, blithely unaware of how carefully I was being scrutinized by the rest of the cast. Acting is a highly competitive game at every level, and if the boss's son does not deliver the goods, the unspoken judgment of his onstage colleagues is instantaneous and withering. By the same token, a smashing Dr. Pinch would gain me acceptance from everyone for the rest of the summer. And as luck would have it, I was a smashing Dr. Pinch.

The play is Shakespeare's most frivolous, his reworking of an ancient Roman farce by Plautus. The plot involves two sets of identical twins. One set are both named Antipholus and the other are their servants, both named Dromio. Each master-servant pair believes that the other was lost at sea. The fun begins when one Antipholus arrives in the other one's city, accompanied by his rascally servant Dromio. Mistaken identities, cross-purposes, and romantic complications kick in and escalate. At the very height of the mayhem, Dr. Pinch has his one and only scene. He is a schoolmaster and mountebank conjuror, brought onstage to exorcize the demons that have supposedly possessed one of the mistaken Antipholi. It is a scene clearly calculated to be explosively over-the-top, and from day one of rehearsals, I set out to make a meal of it.

By that summer I was a few months shy of eighteen years old and thin as a rail. Although I towered over most of the company, I only weighed 175 pounds, *fifty pounds lighter* than I am today. As Dr. Pinch, I wore a form-fitting gray wool costume resembling the working clothes of a Victorian governess. Atop my head was a tall, sausage-shaped black hat with a flap covering my ears and the nape of my neck. For every performance I sculpted a pointy putty nose, I glued wispy strands of gray crepe hair to my eyebrows and chin, I sported round wire-rimmed glasses, and I painted my face with yellowish greasepaint and spidery wrinkles. I looked like a distant cousin of the Wicked Witch of the West, a pencil with jaundice. With my father's prodding, I devised all sorts of frenetic comic business involving an outsized book of spells, magic potions in little bottles, and a bag of confetti, which I tossed around like fairy dust. The tech crew even concealed a flash pot on the stage so that when I screeched out my final, climactic imprecations, they were accompanied by an explosion and a six-foot-high mushroom cloud. All of this nonsense was greeted with gales of crippling laughter, and every night, when I skittered off stage, I heard the glorious sound of exit applause at my back.

I couldn't see into the future, of course, so I had no way of knowing. But looking back, it is perfectly obvious: in that first show of the summer I had created the precursor to Dr. Emilio Lizardo in *The Adventures of Buckaroo Banzai*, far and away my most outrageous screen performance, and, secretly, one of my favorites.

In a larger sense, that summer I was creating a template for the wildly varied range of roles that would unfold over the next several decades in my checkerboard acting career. Every actor weaned on Shakespeare inevitably emerges as a character actor. Shakespeare's plays shift briskly from one genre to the next. In *Hamlet*, when Polonius speaks of the arrival of traveling players and of the plays they perform—"tragedy, comedy, history, pastoral . . .

tragical-comical-historical-pastoral"—he could be describing Shakespeare's own output. Hence an actor in
a Shakespearean troupe becomes accustomed to abrupt
mood swings, night by night, between romance, hero-
ism, horror, and lunatic farce. He develops a taste for
this constant change of pace, and the more radical the
changes the better. On any given night in my two seasons in Lakewood, I could be a crotchety uncle, a cowardly French soldier, a sadistic courtier, an Egyptian
eunuch, a cockney thief, a foolish aristocrat arrested in
a brothel, and, yes, a crackpot conjuror. I went through
ten pounds of greasepaint, wore out a dozen costumes,
and had the time of my life.

These two summer seasons put me into a heightened
new relationship with my father. The air was thick
with Oedipal complexity. I was his employee now,
one of a gang of working actors who were not always
happy campers. Most were veterans of several seasons with my father. They liked and respected him,
but they were far from reverential. Of the twelve plays
that I appeared in, Dad directed half. For the first
time, I watched him at work, up close and personal.
I witnessed his interactions within his own company,
I compared him with other directors, and I took his
measure. The festival's workaday routine and the

actors' occasional grumbling took their toll on my fil-
ial idolatry. My high estimation of him never flagged,
but, in my eyes, his untarnished image gradually gave
way to a much more realistic picture. I began to see
his undeniable strengths counterbalanced by weaknesses that I'd never quite noticed.

In general, my father's directorial modus operandi
was to find the best actors he could get, put them
together with a slate of Shakespeare's plays, and just
let 'er rip. Such an approach was daring but dodgy. By
any rational standard, he scheduled too many productions in too little time, requiring plays as complex and
demanding as *Hamlet* to be mounted in as few as eight
days. Besides, the quality of acting in the ensemble was
wildly inconsistent. As a consequence, it was almost
impossible to achieve a consistent company style. By
necessity, Dad's direction tended toward the "louder/
faster" school. A lot of attention was given to the break-
neck pace of the dialogue and the running time of the
entire play. He was even known to bring a kitchen timer
to rehearsals and require that scenes finish before the
timer went off. When he was directing, our workdays
were supercharged with his genial, positive energy, but
there was little time given to subtlety or detail. He was
impatient with close textual analysis, nuances of character, emotional truth, or historical context. Indeed,

his most frequent direction to his actors was to face the audience, fill up your lungs, and *"just speak the words!"* For him, Shakespeare carried a kind of biblical weight, an almost magical power. He fervently believed that if you just speak the words, everything else will fall into place.

If Dad's "faith-based" approach was sometimes haphazard and off-key, it often paid miraculous dividends. His passion for Shakespeare's work was infectious, and the youthful energy and raw talent of his actors often carried the day. And every once in a while, watching him at work like a bench player eyeing his coach from the sidelines, I would witness flashes of genuine brilliance.

In *Romeo and Juliet* I was cast in the trifling role of the Second Musician, so I had plenty of time to watch. A day before our first performance, the cast was plowing through a daytime dress rehearsal. Things were not going well, but my father, sitting in the dark at the back of the house, was letting the actors struggle through the play without stopping. I sat in the first row, watching the sodden production lurch from scene to scene. Chiefly responsible for the theatrical doldrums up onstage was the actor playing Romeo. He had a flowery name, six syllables long, but I'll call him Devereaux. Devereaux was a vain, baby-faced pretty boy, consumed with narcissistic self-regard. His favorite pastime was sitting languorously at his makeup table for an hour before every show, staring at himself in the mirror, his face framed by a whole gallery of photographs of Elizabeth Taylor in *Cleopatra*. As Romeo, Devereaux's coiffed blond hair, meticulous mascara, and fey, self-styled costume were far more important to him than his character's impetuous flesh-and-blood passions. Romeo's scalding love for Juliet was barely an afterthought.

As I sat and watched the dress rehearsal that day, Romeo and Juliet began their famous balcony scene. Five minutes into it, Dad broke his resolve to let the cast slog through to the end. He unfolded himself, stood up, and walked all the way down the aisle, bringing the two actors to a halt. He put aside his notes and began to speak, his demeanor exuding an eerie forced calm. With an almost canine sensitivity, I recognized that tone in his voice. I shifted in my seat, sensing a gathering storm. He directed all of his words toward Devereaux. They were carefully chosen and enunciated, as if he were composing an academic essay.

"The problem with the production as it now stands," he began, "is that it has no Romeo."

That quiet declaration hit Devereaux like a rifle shot. He lowered himself to the floor, carefully arranging his powder-blue cape with its dainty pink piping.

His eyes were glassy and his body slumped as my father's gentle critique slowly built in intensity. Peppering his speech with quotes from the text, he described Romeo's renegade sexuality, his hotheaded irrationality, his feverish fixation on Juliet. With every sentence he grew louder, more passionate, almost angry. Within minutes, his helpful prodding had bloomed into a full-blown tirade.

"If *this* Romeo tried to vault Juliet's fence," he bellowed, "he'd break his stick! If he climbed in bed with her, he wouldn't know what to *do*! That's not Romeo! Love for Romeo is not flowers and perfume. It's urgent, it's sweaty. He's an animal! He's carnivorous! So is Juliet! If he doesn't have fire in his loins, then neither does she! You're giving the other actors onstage nothing! Romeo is not there! And without Romeo, the whole play is as limp as a limp *dick*!"

I had never seen my father like this. Witnessing his tantrum, I was frozen in my seat, caught between anxiety and relief. I hated to see Devereaux treated so ruthlessly, but I was enormously relieved to see him finally getting the thrashing he needed. His passion spent, Dad instructed Romeo and Juliet to begin the scene again from the top and then strode back to his seat. Devereaux had been shaken to the core, but he climbed to his feet, shook his head and his hands, and began again. The second time through, the scene was transformed. Devereaux never grew into a great Romeo, and the entire play never quite caught fire. But my father's harsh medicine had been both necessary and effective. From that moment on, Devereaux, Romeo, and the production itself were all mightily improved.

That day I felt that I had seen my father at his very best. His love of Shakespeare and his passion for theater were abundantly on display. He filled me with admiration and pride. Questions hung in the air, of course. Why did he wait until dress rehearsal to tear apart an actor's performance? Why did he allow Romeo to wear that awful costume, makeup, and hairdo? Why was such a fatuous actor ever cast in the first place? Besides compromising the production, wasn't this a cruel disservice to the actor himself? Such questions went to the very heart of my father's strengths as a theater manager. But as I sat watching him in that darkened auditorium, either those questions didn't occur to me or I scrupulously ignored them. And why should I have cared, anyway? What emotional investment did I have? After all, this was not my career. I wasn't going to be an actor. This was a lark, a fun summer before I went off to college. It was years before I asked all those questions about my father. When I finally did, the answers would weigh heavily on me.

11.
Veritas

The dreams of an artist die hard. Despite all the fun of my first season with the Great Lakes Shakespeare Festival, I was still nursing ambitions of being a painter. And so it was that, halfway through my freshman year at college, I set my sights on Skowhegan, Maine, for the upcoming summer. As it is today, Skowhegan was the site of a summer-long art school and the seasonal retreat for a whole colony of high-powered New York painters. In my dorm room I filled out an application, typed out a brief essay, assembled slides of drawings and paintings from my Art Students League days, and sent off the whole package. I was bursting with high hopes and creative zeal. What with the hectic frenzy of the summer festival and the crushing workload of my freshman year, my

artistic output had slowed to a trickle. I was count-
ing on a meditative summer in Maine to get it going
again. In the weeks after I mailed my application, I
awaited word.

While I waited, I went home to my family in
Princeton for Spring Break. On my first day back,
my father had a bright idea. Since arriving at
McCarter Theatre, he had made the acquaintance of
Ben Shahn, an authentic American master of painting and printmaking whose home and studio were in
nearby Roosevelt, New Jersey. For years Shahn had
been a summertime fixture at Skowhegan and a dom-
inating presence at the art school there. To boost my
chances of admission, Dad called up Shahn himself
and asked if I could visit his studio to talk to him
about the summer program. Shahn said yes, and a
few days later Dad and I drove out to Roosevelt to
meet with him.

When we walked into his bright, airy studio, the
bespectacled Shahn was working on a series of small
watercolors. He was enthroned like a pasha, surrounded
by a happy clutter of drawings, paintings, photos, and
art supplies. Afternoon sun poured in the windows,
filtered through the spring leaves of birch trees out in
his yard. Mozart played softly on the radio. I took in
the scene with awe and envy. It was everything I had

dreamed of: a serene creative idyll, perfectly conducive to the unfettered flow of art.

But Ben Shahn himself was anything but serene. In his late sixties, he had the big head, broad shoulders, meaty hands, and expansive girth of a longshoreman. He spoke in a deep growl and his manner was brusque. His defiant, left-leaning politics, frequently expressed in his social realist paintings, seemed to color his every word and gesture. He needled and challenged me, rabbinically testing my fiber with irascible good humor. The questions came thick and fast. What have you done? Where have you studied? Whose work do you like? Why do you want this? What do you aspire to? Where do you stand? I burbled my earnest answers, feeling utterly intimidated and inadequate. Then came the biggest question of all:

"If you want to be an artist," he barked, "what the hell are you doing at *Harvard*?"

I went to Harvard because I got in. This is not the best reason to pick a college, but in retrospect, it's the best reason I can come up with. In those days, to an even greater extent than today, the very word "Harvard" represented the pinnacle of high school achievement, the ultimate flatterer of a seventeen-year-old's vanity. The heady aura of the place swept aside all other considerations. This was still the era of Jack Kennedy's pre-Dallas Camelot, and the place shimmered with his reflected glory. Admittance to Harvard was a gilded invitation to join the company of the best and the brightest, long before that phrase had taken on its dark, ironic overtones. If you got in, you went, simple as that. My letter of admission arrived, I accepted without hesitation, and the following September I arrived in Cambridge and moved into Wigglesworth Hall, my freshman dorm, in the shadow of Widener Library. I was a newly minted Harvard undergraduate, Class of 1967, without knowing a thing about the place and, in fact, without ever having laid eyes on it.

From the moment I arrived at Harvard, I sensed something in the air. It emanated from the moist red bricks of Sever Hall. You heard it in the Brahmin drawls of the all-male undergrads. You saw it in the lazy waggle of their cigarettes and the droopy forelocks of their unbarbered hair. You could practically smell it on their damp tweed sport coats and crimson wool scarves. It was a certain indefinable culture of languid male success, an unspoken awareness that having gained access, you were expected to effortlessly excel, both at Harvard and beyond. Everyone there bore these great expectations in one of two ways: they either regarded them as a mantle of privilege or as an onerous burden. This made the Harvard men of those days highly susceptible to virulent strains of self-importance, self-doubt, self-contempt, or some complex combination of all three. However you responded to the pressures of the place, one thing was clear: to thrive at Harvard, or even to survive there, you must stake out some domain where you can *succeed*, and move into it like an invading army.

It didn't take me long to find mine.

By centuries-old tradition, Harvard turned up its nose to formal training in the arts, an attitude that is only just giving way in this day and age. And yet its student body at any given moment has always been packed with students of exceptional talent, ready to pour their energies into extracurricular artistic activity. How else can you explain the long list of career artists that Harvard has produced over the years: Robert Frost, Leonard Bernstein, Alan Jay Lerner, Arthur Kopit, Jack Lemmon, Pete Seeger, and John Updike from earlier generations; and more recently Yo-Yo Ma, Terrence Malick, Christopher Durang, Bonnie Raitt, John Adams, Peter Sellars, pianist Ursula Oppens, sax player Josh Redman, and movie stars Natalie Portman and Matt Damon. All of these notables were feverishly active in the arts at Harvard.

Only one or two of them actually studied their discipline there.

Read over that list again. You will notice a glaring omission. Not one of these impressive artists worked in the visual arts. Ben Shahn was right. You didn't go to Harvard to paint pictures. The year before I'd arrived, Harvard had unveiled the Carpenter Center for the Visual Arts, a stunning piece of sweeping architecture designed by Le Corbusier. A seductive photo of the building had caught my eye the year before, when I was sifting through college literature and choosing schools. On one of my first days on campus I went inside it and snooped around its glass, steel, and concrete interior. The bright rooms were weirdly empty. The walls were covered with what looked like technical drawings, analytical design projects featuring black-ink outlines of geometrical shapes, seemingly intended to transmute fleshly art into bloodless science. By all evidence, art at the Carpenter Center had to meet some dry, academic, almost technological standard or it was disallowed. There were no paint-smeared rags, no turpentine smell, no racks of unfinished canvases, no plaster dust, no clutter, no mess. It had the feel of an art school where actual artists had been told that they need not apply. Clearly this was not the place for me. I walked out the gleaming glass doors and for the next four years I barely went back.

That same day, I sought out another building. This one lay blocks away from Harvard Yard, crouching on Brattle Street like a mutinous exile. This was the Loeb Drama Center, a state-of-the-art two-theater playhouse entirely devoted to extracurricular dramatics. The building was only two years old but already looked comfortably lived in. The walls were lined with photos of student productions. The bulletin boards were crammed with casting calls and handbills. Coats and book bags were flung in every corner. Laughter and fast talk echoed in the halls and spilled out of the open doors of rehearsal rooms. And lolling everywhere, with an air of cocky ownership, there were students. These students, the denizens of "the Loeb," were funky artistic types of both sexes, and included the first Harvard upperclassmen and graduate students I had ever laid eyes on. They were a breed apart from the timorous, tentative young men in jackets and ties who huddled together at meals in the Freshman Union. Taking it all in, my heart raced and creative juices pumped through my veins. I could hardly believe my good luck. In my very first week, I had found my place at Harvard.

In the meantime, I had also found a friend. He was hard to miss. He was my roommate. Weighing our histories, Harvard had housed me in Wigglesworth Hall with two other freshmen with an artistic bent. One of them was David Ansen. David and I could hardly have been more different. He hailed from Beverly Hills High School, a child of Hollywood whose father had written short films and trailers in the movie industry. In those days, David was an aspiring writer of fiction, poetry, and plays. His serious demeanor and bookishness were belied by a worldliness, sly humor, and vivid sexual history. We probably found each other equally exotic. When he walked into our dorm room for the first time, I was already there. I had staked out a corner desk and was laboring away at a woodcut, barely acknowledging his arrival. A woodcut! An hour after arriving at Harvard! Who *was* that strange boy? David later told me that, at first sight, he had thought I was a painfully shy hayseed from the South, invited to Harvard as part of an outreach program, there to practice and refine some kind of arcane hillbilly handicrafts. From such unpromising beginnings we soon became best friends, and we've been best friends ever since.

With his Hollywood pedigree, there was absolutely nothing that David did not know about film. Within days of that first meeting, we went to a movie. It was the first of scores of films that we saw together over the next four years. He became my de facto professor of the history of film, eager to drag me to both new movies and old ones that he'd seen several times before. And what a time for an intensive movie tutorial! This was the early sixties, and our generation was drunk on cinema. Boston was dotted with revival houses, presenting an unending repertory of classic films from every era and every genre. New international movie trends kept crashing on our shores like waves. In France there was the Nouvelle Vague, in Sweden there was Ingmar Bergman, in Italy there were Fellini, De Sica, Visconti, and Antonioni. As for American filmmakers, they were on the verge of their greatest period of innovation, with Stanley Kubrick in the vanguard. Ansen was there to mark every development, trace its roots, and tell me all about it.

But David was no cinema snob. His interests extended far beyond art films. He was just as eager to see *Goldfinger, Lawrence of Arabia, A Hard Day's Night*, or, for the umpteenth time, *Casablanca*. And whenever he got home from a movie, he would take out a little notebook and add the title to a master list he kept of every film he had ever seen. In the same book, he wrote down his personal picks every year for Oscar winners in every major category, along with his predictions for what the actual winners would probably be. It is amazing that, given David's obsession with movies, it never occurred to any of us (himself included) that he would end up a film critic. But of course that is exactly what he became. For over thirty years he was the lead critic for *Newsweek*. I never thought I'd be a movie actor, either, but in the course of those three decades, David Ansen, with studied neutrality, reviewed my performances on film ten different times.

12.
Utopia

Within weeks of my arrival in Cambridge, the floodgates had opened and I was swept into the world of Harvard undergraduate drama. Days after that first visit to the Loeb, I auditioned for the first big Main Stage show of the year and landed a major role in it. I was to be Reverend Anthony Anderson, one of the two rival leading men in Shaw's *The Devil's Disciple* (my father had played Dick Dudgeon, the other leading man, back in Oak Bluffs when I was five years old). I was the only freshman in the show, and as I rehearsed with the rest of the cast in the basement of the Loeb, I keenly felt my rookie status. I was an unlicked whelp among a lot of swaggering juniors and seniors, the youngest actor playing the oldest of the major roles. But my years of experience fortified me. In rehearsals I held my own, and in performance I was self-assured and commanding. The joke went around that in three more years I'd be running the place.

As it happened, my Harvard years were the most active and creative of my life. The fact that there was no academic program in theater meant that all of us operated in an atmosphere of reckless, unsupervised creative abandon. It was the last time I worked in the theater for the pure, unfettered joy of it. Some of the work was excellent, much of it was dreadful, but its quality was never really the point. Joy was the point. If someone wanted to try something, there was somewhere to do it, a starvation-level budget to pay for it, and an entire army of eager classmates ready to join in. These were smart young kids, brilliant students of science, math, economics, political science, you name it. Only a tiny fraction of them ever dreamed of actually pursuing a life in the creative arts. They were merely looking for an outlet, a social context, and a little fun outside the demands of a Harvard undergraduate education. And yet hundreds of them spent more than half their waking hours feverishly slaving away—as stagehands, set builders, costumers, lighting technicians, musicians, designers, producers, directors, and, yes, actors—on one of the fifty-odd shows which, at any given moment, were in various stages of production on that vast, sprawling campus.

To illustrate the variety and creative ferment of those Harvard years, here, in a rough chronology, is a sampling of my extracurricular entanglements there:

- I played the title roles in *Tartuffe*, *Macbeth*, Christopher Marlowe's *Edward II*, and Lord Byron's *Manfred* (I bet you've never seen *that* one onstage).

- I played the ancient, blinded Duke of Gloucester in *King Lear* (I was eighteen at the time and wore a wig once worn by Sir John Gielgud).

- I directed and acted in a one-act play by Molière called *The Forced Marriage* (I also designed the set and created masks for all the characters).

- As president of the Gilbert and Sullivan Society, I directed and played the Learned Judge and the Lord Chancellor in *Trial by Jury* and *Iolanthe*, respectively.

- I recruited dancers from the Boston Conservatory and staged a double-bill of one-act opera-ballets made up of Stravinsky's *Renard* and Menotti's *The Unicorn, the Gorgon, and the Manticore* (I made the masks for that one, too).

- I directed, designed, and played the role of the Devil in a fully staged version of Stravinsky's *L'Histoire du Soldat.*

- In a Radcliffe College common room, I recited Dylan Thomas's poetic reminiscence "A Child's Christmas in Wales." Beside me, a Radcliffe girl in a black leotard (future actress Lindsay Crouse) did a Jules Feifferesque dance interpretation of the entire piece.

- With a few ringers from the New England Conservatory of Music, I staged Mozart's *Le Nozze di Figaro* in a dorm dining hall (the conductor grew up to be the Pulitzer Prize–winning composer John Adams).

- I played the role of Sparky in *Sergeant Musgrave's Dance* by John Arden (the title role was played by a student from Texas, a year younger than I, named Tommy Lee Jones).

- I directed John Gay's *The Beggar's Opera* in yet another dining hall (the orchestra's harpsichord was played by future world-class conductor William Christie, and the cast included a talented, bawdy young actress named Stockard Channing).

- I designed the sets for Sean O'Casey's *The Plough and the Stars* (though in truth they were the ugliest, most ungainly sets ever seen on the Main Stage of the Loeb Drama Center).

- I designed and directed an elaborate production of Georg Büchner's *Woyzeck* at the Loeb. This is a dark, expressionistic German work, seething with hot-blooded sex, sulphurous jealousy, and murderous vengeance. Although I was a senior by this time and twenty-one years old, I didn't have a clue about even the most basic of these primal human emotions. But more on that particular blind spot later.

Of the many students swirling around me in those days, several were destined to intersect with my professional life in years to come. One of the actors in that Molière one-act was a fellow named Tim Hunter. He wasn't much of an actor, but he later became a notable filmmaker and directed me in an episode of the TV drama *Dexter*. The stage manager of every show I directed was a peppy, tart New Yorker named Victoria Traube. Still one of my best friends, she is a longtime executive of the Rodgers and Hammerstein Organization and an indispensable fixture of the New York theater scene. In my senior year, an eager freshman named Tom Werner arrived on the scene. Although I never knew him at Harvard, years later he too became a good friend. He also became my boss. His company Carsey-Werner produced the six seasons of *3rd Rock from the Sun* for NBC-TV. Also showing up that year was a young would-be journalist who immediately started writing for *The Harvard Crimson*. Before long his gimlet eye would be sizing up my performances on Broadway in his role as drama critic for the *New York Times*. His name was Frank Rich.

But all of these estimable figures in the cultural landscape of the future were happy amateurs like me in those days, with unformed notions of what was to come. We were all fiercely ambitious without being entirely sure what the object of that ambition was. For the moment, we were grabbing at everything Harvard had to offer, unguided missiles trying on different versions of ourselves in an effort to figure out who the hell we really were. True, I was wide open to periodic spasms of insecurity and self-doubt all through those years. But those moments were rare and fleeting. Mostly I was having a wonderful time.

Years later I had a rare opportunity to vicariously recapture the excitement of all that extracurricular activity. In the twenty years after I graduated from Harvard, I had little to do with the place. I rarely even told people that I had gone there. When you are struggling to establish yourself as a working actor—trying out for a soap opera, for example, or for a laxative commercial—you tend to keep a Harvard degree to yourself. But in my forties, in the midst of a thriving acting career, I finally restored the Harvard connection. I was elected to a six-year tenure on Harvard's Board of Overseers, a thirty-person governing board chosen by the alumni. As the first candidate from the creative arts since Robert Frost in the 1930s, I was a shoo-in. I even outpolled Bishop Desmond Tutu. From 1989 to 1995, I attended seven Cambridge meetings a year, in the company of bankers, lawyers, corporate magnates, college presidents, and senators (among them Tommy Lee Jones's old roommate, Al Gore). For the first three years of my service I was an empty suit, wondering what in the world I was doing in the company of such movers and shakers.

But then I began to make my presence felt. I embraced my role as "the overseer from the arts." I launched an initiative on behalf of Harvard undergraduates that, since then, has evolved into an essential Harvard institution. It is called Arts First. It was the best example in my life of the power of a simple idea. Arts First is an annual festival of undergraduate arts, held on the first weekend of every May. It is an exhilarating celebration of springtime, of the completion of the school year, and of youthful creativity and talent. And it is arguably my proudest achievement.

First produced in 1993, halfway through my time as an overseer, Arts First has grown into Harvard's version of the Edinburgh Festival. By now it is impossible to imagine a year at Harvard without it. During its four-day span, hundreds of students act, dance, sing, play music, exhibit their art, and show their films. Thousands more watch. Every theater and concert hall on the campus is pressed into service. Twenty-odd college buildings are converted to performance spaces. Harvard Yard is flung open to the public and nearly everything is free. And every spring I show up, an eager vicarious participant. Each year, my hair is a little grayer and there's a little less of it, but my enthusiasm never flags. The students regenerate me. In them, I see my dimly remembered self of many years ago, with all the reckless, inexhaustible excess of youth.

And what about my actual Harvard education?

As a student, let's just say I was a very good actor. Concurrently with all of my frenzied extracurricular exploits, I managed to fake my way through my studies. I had chosen an extremely rigorous major, English History and Literature. This was an academic field packed with star professors and driven, high-powered students. Although I never completed the reading for a single class and sat mute through most classroom discussions, nobody seemed to notice what a plodding intellectual slowpoke I was.

Oh, but I was crafty. A prime example of my craftiness was an "independent study" I cobbled together for course credit. It focused on London in the eighteenth century, taking Daniel Defoe's *Journal of the Plague Year* as its central text. To my shame, I never even read the book. My one-on-one teacher was an amiable young assistant professor named David Sachs. The course consisted of three or four pleasant conversations in his office, spread over an entire semester. In years to come, Sachs would achieve a distinguished career in academia. I ran into him by chance a few years ago, and he gently reminded me that I still owed him a paper.

But despite my academic sleight of hand, my distracted brain managed to absorb great swatches of knowledge. Most of my professors were grizzled old superstars of the Harvard firmament who had long since learned how to put on a great show. Lecturing for as many as six hundred students at a time, they were masters at conveying and inspiring a genuine passion for their various subjects. The names of these venerable men barely register now, but in those days they were spoken of around Harvard with solemn reverence.

I learned the Homeric epics from John Finley, the history of drama from William Alfred, Romantic poetry from Walter Jackson Bate, art history from Seymour Slive, a smattering of psychology from Erik Erickson, and on and on. And if I did the least possible amount of studying to get by, get by I did. I never got less than a C (and I only got one of those), I wrote a sixty-page honors thesis (on satire in Restoration comedy), I graduated magna cum laude, and I was one of a handful of my classmates inducted into Phi Beta Kappa. On the day I graduated, I secretly felt as if I had gotten away with murder.

So in this whirlwind of grinding academics and amateur theatrics, when did I decide to embrace my destiny and become a professional actor? I can narrow it down to a minute-long span of time late one evening in December of 1964.

It happened like this.

From that long list of student productions from my four years at Harvard I've left one title out. It is *Utopia, Limited; or, The Flowers of Progress,* an 1893 operetta by Gilbert and Sullivan. An epic-sized and overdrawn satire of British colonialism on a South Sea island, *Utopia, Limited* is the least known and least performed of the entire G&S canon. It is a raucous, vaguely racist piece of work that probably deserves its obscurity, but in my own modest history it looms large. Although an unlikely candidate for a life-altering experience, *Utopia, Limited* was the show that distinctly altered my life.

Early in the autumn of my sophomore year, a production of the operetta was slated for the Main Stage of the Loeb Drama Center. Its director was an intense and brilliant young man named Timothy S. Mayer. As seductive as he was abrasive, Tim Mayer was one of the most extraordinary characters I've ever known, and he looked the part. He was stoop-shouldered and pocky, with a rope of dark brown hair always hanging in front of his piercing, bespectacled gray eyes. He sported expensive tweeds and penny loafers, but the clothes hung shabbily on him and he wore no socks. He spoke in a language all his own, rapid-fire and dazzlingly clever. A heavy drinker and nonstop smoker, he was a man whose prodigious talent was matched by an equally prodigious strain of self-destructiveness. During his Harvard career, he would churn out a long string of electrifying productions, but he never scaled the same heights in the hazardous world of professional theater. As if consumed by his own demons, he died tragically young, of cancer, in his early thirties. By a quirk of fate, this amazing young man was to have a catalytic effect on the next several years of my life.

Of the many shows Tim directed at Harvard, *Utopia, Limited* was his maiden effort. He was fiercely determined to make a splash with it and to disprove the old adage that Gilbert and Sullivan is more fun to perform than to actually watch. His take on it was startlingly original. In W. S. Gilbert's creaky, campy Victorian humor, he saw hidden strains of bitter, almost savage anti-imperialism. For all its high spirits, this was to be the thrust of his production. He pitched it on a grand scale, with an enormous cast, a thirty-piece orchestra, and lavish, pastel-colored costumes and sets. But as Tim conceived it, all of this extravagance was shot through with acid irony. He had joined forces with Gilbert to skewer Victorian smugness and arrogance, seventy years after the fact. With the bravura that would soon earn him the nickname "The Barnum of Brattle Street," Tim touted *Utopia, Limited* (accurately) as the biggest spectacle yet produced at the Loeb.

All fall the Loeb was abuzz with breathless rumors of this magnum opus. But perilously late in the rehearsal period, the production was dealt a crippling blow. The actor playing the central comic role of King Paramount, ruler of the island nation of Ulalica, abruptly walked off the show. Suddenly this colossal enterprise had no leading man, and Tim Mayer, a frazzled director at the best of times, was desperate for a replacement. By now, my performances in Shakespeare, Marlowe, and Shaw had accorded me an embryonic star status in the tiny world of Harvard theater. So Tim sought me out. The phone rang in my dorm room. I answered. Mincing no words, he got right to the point:

"Can you sing?"

I'd never sung onstage in my life, and I told him so. But I knew plenty of songs. And so a half hour later I was standing on the stage of the Loeb, belting out an a cappella version of an English music hall song titled "I Live in Trafalgar Square." I sung the last note and stared out into the house. With a shout, Tim cast me on the spot, and that evening I walked into my first rehearsal, leaping onto the speeding train known as *Utopia, Limited.*

In the run-up to our first performance, I was rushed through a kind of musical-theater boot camp. I was spoon-fed my recitatives and arias; I was drilled on the bass line of all the four-part singing; I was even sent downtown to the New England Conservatory for a few last-minute voice lessons. Ideally, the role of King Paramount should be sung in a big, resounding bass. For all my efforts, I never got beyond a thin, reedy baritone (and over the years, I haven't improved much on *that*). But my pitch was reliable, every word was crystal clear, and I strove to squeeze every drop of wit out of Gilbert's lyrics. And in all the book scenes, on much firmer ground, I was effortlessly funny. As rehearsals sped by in the countdown to our opening night, I methodically proceeded, scene by scene, to steal the show.

Act II of *Utopia, Limited* begins with a comic septet, taking its title from the first line, "Society Has Now Forsaken All Its Wicked Courses." This number is sung by all of the principal men in the cast. As the plot unfolds, the island nation is transformed into an absurd Polynesian parody of English society. The song's verses, sung by King Paramount, provide a long list of examples of that transformation. The verses are broken up by a snappy refrain sung at top speed by all seven men:

> *It really is surprising what a thorough Anglicizing*
> *We have brought about—Utopia's quite another*
> *   land;*
> *In our enterprising movements, we are England*
> *   with improvements*
> *Which we dutifully offer to our Mother-land!*

The format of the septet is that of an English music hall minstrel show, with the seven men in white tie and tails seated on seven chairs, King Paramount in the middle. Every time the refrain is repeated, the men leap to their feet, producing all manner of instruments. As the song builds, so does the loopy energy of the singers. The lyrics are funny enough, but the theatrics of the staging make the number over-the-top hilarious. By tradition, it is such a hit that the seven singers plan a couple of encores just in case they're needed, ready to perform ever more elaborate variations on that manic refrain.

Our production was no exception. All eight times we performed the song, we stopped the show with it. But for me, the first time was the life changer. That night, when the song proper came to an end, the applause was deafening. We all remained onstage, poised for our first encore. The conductor powered up the orchestra again, silencing the crowd. I repeated the last verse, and the seven of us bellowed the refrain. This time I did a frenzied mock tap dance with one of the men rapping on the stage floor at my feet with a pair of drumsticks. This brought an even bigger response from the crowd. Once again we stayed onstage, and once again we performed an encore. For this one I produced three Spaldeens, spray-painted gold, and juggled them inanely all through the refrain. An even *bigger* response. By now the crowd was delirious. We had only plotted the two encores, so the other six men picked up their instruments and chairs and walked into the wings. I remained onstage alone, ready to begin the next scene. *But the audience did not stop applauding.* The applause swelled into cheers. The cheers became a roar. I suppose the ovation must have lasted about twenty seconds, but to me it seemed five minutes at the very least. I stood there, grinning like an idiot, dizzy with the overdose of adulation pouring down on me.

That twenty seconds was all it took. There was no longer any question. I was going to be an actor.

13.
Hard Times on
the Great Road

I n 1966, the ground began to shake under our feet.
The Vietnam War had grown into a major confla-
gration. Every Harvard student was grappling with
the queasy reality of the draft. SDS antiwar rallies on
Mt. Auburn Street were drawing larger and larger
crowds. American rock and roll had risen to the challenge thrown down by the Beatles and the Stones. Bob
Dylan had gone electric. Late-night dorm-room dope-
smoking sessions had been a dark, paranoid ritual; now
they were an offhand folkway. Students from California were returning from breaks with lubricious tales of
LSD trips and orgies. The confluence of feminism and
the Pill was transforming sexual mores and reducing
Harvard's rigid "parietal rules," which barred women
from men's dormitories, to a travesty. Suddenly half the

male student population were sporting long hair and scuzzy beards, and finding ingenious ways to mock the school's fusty dress code. The social and political cataclysm of 1968 was still a couple of years away, but an atmosphere of liberation, radicalism, and incipient rebellion already hung in the air.

But the rushing waters of social change were flowing right past me. In September of 1966, before the start of my senior year at Harvard and a month shy of my twenty-first birthday, I got married.

I married Jean Taynton, the daughter of the librarian of the Philadelphia Orchestra. Jean was six years older than I and had been living and working in Cambridge, just blocks away from the Harvard campus. In those days she taught special education to public school kids with a wide range of emotional problems. We had met a year before, working together at the Highfield Theater, a summer light-opera company in Falmouth, Massachusetts, on Cape Cod. The theater was a summer adjunct of Oberlin College and its Music Conservatory, out in Ohio. Years before, as a student at Oberlin, Jean had spent several summers at Highfield, performing a long list of comic character roles. As a lark, she had returned there to appear in *Patience*, yet another Gilbert and Sullivan warhorse. She had come at the behest of the show's young director, a rich, precocious Harvard boy from nearby Cotuit who had been hanging around the Highfield summer playhouse for years. Those summers had been the source of the boy's early infatuation with musical theater. By sheer persistence he had landed a directing job there at the age of twenty. The boy's name was Timothy S. Mayer.

After our happy collaboration on *Utopia, Limited* the year before, Tim had little trouble persuading me to join him at Highfield. The season was to feature eight operettas, four of them directed by Tim himself. *Patience* was to be the first. This florid comic romance was W. S. Gilbert's cheerful satiric swipe at Oscar Wilde and nineteenth-century aestheticism. Tim cast me as Bunthorne, Gilbert's patter-song stand-in for Wilde himself. Opposite me, he cast Jean Taynton as Lady Jane. Tim Mayer had thus unwittingly cast *himself* in the extremely unlikely role of Cupid.

From the beginning Jean and I were an odd couple. If I was a six-foot-four string bean, she was a five-foot-two brussels sprout. In *Patience,* our physical incongruity made us a hilarious pairing, a kind of Edwardian vaudeville team whose scenes were the comedic high points of the show. With Jean's herky-jerky dance moves and a deep contralto singing voice emanating from her compact little body, she outdid even W. S. Gilbert in mocking the conventions of Romantic light opera. For my part, the *Utopia, Limited* experience had liberated the zany song-and-dance man in me. As Bunthorne, a foolish popinjay in a floppy beret and purple faux-velvet, I hurled myself into my role with campy, loose-limbed enthusiasm. Every night for a week I leapt around the stage in that stuffy, sweltering little playhouse, soaked with sweat. Months later I learned that at the end of the show's run (as with every other show that summer), the wardrobe crew had held a ritual burning of my fetid costume.

Patience was such a ball that Jean offered to stay on at Highfield for the summer and play several more roles. Stirred by the exuberant fun of our onstage hijinks and by a long list of overlapping enthusiasms, we became inseparable pals and, within weeks, curiously mismatched lovers. To my youthful eyes, Jean was a blend of effervescence and gravitas, of girlishness and maturity. This duality showed in everything she did. Her bubbly nature concealed a strain of caustic wit. She was a serious, compassionate teacher who spearheaded weekend games of coed touch football. She had an abiding passion for classical music and the Old Masters, yet her great hero was Bill Russell of the Boston Celtics. Her piping voice verged on baby talk, and yet she held forth with penetrating intelligence on poetry, fiction, philosophy, and psychology. I was nineteen years old when we met. At that age, a six-year age difference is enormous. Yet Jean presented a wide-eyed, Peter Pan version of grown-up life that, for mysterious reasons, seemed to be just what I was looking for. When the Highfield season ended, she returned to Cambridge to her teaching job, I returned there for my junior year of studies, and she became my off-campus girlfriend. After two years at Harvard, my social life had barely gotten under way. Now it was pretty much over with. As for the great youth revolution known as "The Sixties," it had started without me.

A good friend named Tim Jerome was also an actor at Highfield that summer. Recently he came across a candid photo from back then and sent it to me. The photo showed him and me forty-five years younger. We are shirtless and winded, having been tossing a football. I am pale, rawboned, and painfully thin. My hair is long and Byronic. Seeing the photo in the present day was a shock. I barely recognized myself. In my memories, I was a strapping, confident young man that summer, with the world on a string—nothing like the callow schoolboy who stared out at me from that photo. My heart sank at the sight, and a harsh question formed itself in my mind:

"Who in the world does that kid think he *is*?!"

I was a deeply confused young man and I didn't even know it. Having successfully navigated a childhood of constant, disruptive change, and having turned myself into a roaring furnace of compensatory creative output, I had ended up with delusions of adulthood. Everywhere I went I was a whirling dervish of artistic enterprise, hailed as a kind of Midas-like talent. But the pride and pleasure I derived from all of my projects masked a troubling truth: I was sublimating like crazy. I had conveniently ignored an essential stage of my emotional development. I had dispensed with adolescence. In my mind, I was socially and artistically complete—a fully functioning adult and the second coming of Orson Welles. On both scores, I was woefully mistaken. And that misperception of myself was to be the root cause of a world of troubles in the decade to come.

For starters, there was "The Great Road Players."

The Great Road Players does not rate a footnote in anyone else's history, but it is a significant chapter in mine. Halfway through my college career, subconsciously reenacting my father's youthful exploits, I hatched a plan for my own summer theater. My growing list of stage successes at Harvard, both as an actor and as a director, had boosted my confidence, inflated

MAN IN CHARGE: John Lithgow, son of Arthur Lithgow, McCarter Theatre's executive director, will guide the activities of The Great Road Players during the 1966 summer season.

my ego, and spurred me on to this next step. When the idea was still barely embryonic, I happened upon an eager confederate. A sharp young New York actor named Paul Zimet showed up in Cambridge one day in late autumn of 1965. He was visiting a woman friend of his, a dancer who was appearing in one of my Loeb productions. I met Paul at an off-campus party after he had seen the show. A gentle soul with the dark good looks of Montgomery Clift, I liked him immediately. The fact that he had loved my show inclined me to like him even more. In the intense conversation that followed, I aired my ideas to him for a theater workshop the following summer. That very night we decided to team up, plotting the workshop together. I don't recall having the slightest doubts about our partnership or feeling for a moment that I was acting with precipitous haste.

That night of crazed optimism was the starting point of a journey that, several months later, would end in irredeemable disaster. With zero experience as an actor-manager and with a producing partner I barely knew, I proceeded to make just about every bad decision I could have possibly made. To begin with, I picked the wrong setting. Instead of Cambridge, the scene of all my recent triumphs, I set my sights on my hometown of Princeton, New Jersey. And as a mentor and shadow executive producer, I chose my father.

By this time, Dad was in his third year as artistic director of the McCarter Theatre. I looked to him for advice, for logistical support, and for protective cover. Distracted by the continuing pressures of his own job, he listened to my grand scheme with an aloof, abstracted air. If he had any doubts, he didn't show them. He signed on to the idea and breezily guided me through the basics of institution building. He helped me enlist a board of directors, composed mostly of Princeton boosters with their roots in community theater. He put his McCarter staff at my disposal to help me with such matters as press releases and brochures. And he accompanied Paul and me as we checked out possible performance spaces around the town. Through it all, he maintained a kind of bemused indulgence, with nary a whiff of skepticism or devil's advocacy. His own history was checkered with cautionary tales of ill-advised theatrical ventures, some of them downright catastrophic. But he shared none of those tales with me.

We found a beautiful theater. It was the brand-new, barely used auditorium of The Princeton Day School, a tony private school ten minutes outside of town. The school's administrators were proud as pink of their new facility, flattered by our interest, and tickled by the notion of presenting plays to the public on their remote campus. With a heedless naïveté that I am sure they have never displayed since, they put the space at our disposal as summer tenants. On our first trip out to the school, we passed a signpost en route. The signpost bore the name of the country lane where the school was located. It was called "The Great Road." As we drove back into town a few hours later, flushed with success, we had both a home for our new company and a name. We dubbed it The Great Road Players.

A recent graduate of Columbia, Paul was one of a vital group of recent Columbia alumni whose adventures in college theater had closely paralleled my own. Outside of the protective cocoon of academia, he had barely dipped his toe in professional New York theater. He and his Columbia pals had attached themselves to various avant garde troupes in downtown Manhattan. They had also joined a class in Shakespeare performance led by a charismatic English émigré whom I'll call Tony Boyd. Paul and I intended to form our company by recruiting an equal number of fellow actors from the Harvard and Columbia theater communities. So I traveled down to New York one weekend to confer with him and meet all of his Columbia friends. During the visit, I even visited Mr. Boyd's Shakespeare class and watched them all at work. As actors they were a completely different species from me and my Harvard gang—impulsive, improvisational, and barely disciplined. But their talent was obvious, I liked them all, and I persuaded myself that our differences would lead to exciting work onstage.

Paul and I picked a slate of four plays derived from work that both of us had already done. Our plan was to follow the model of my dad's old Shakespeare festivals—to open one production at a time, then to perform them all in rotating repertory, offering subscription tickets to the public. The titles were an arty, eclectic mix, and extremely challenging for a young company. Ominously, they were even more challenging for a pool of Princeton theatergoers looking for light summer fare. Paul was to kick things off by directing *Woyzeck* (the Büchner play that I myself would direct the following year at Harvard). As a curtain-raiser to that gruesome tale, we would also stage an absurdist take on T. S. Eliot's dialogue poem "Sweeney Agonistes." I would follow with an evening of Molière one-act farces (including *The Forced Marriage*, which I'd already done twice). The third offering was perhaps our only safe choice (though hardly a piece of cake), Shakespeare's *Twelfth Night*. I honestly cannot remember what the fourth show was intended to be. It doesn't really matter. We never got that far.

In the months leading up to our start date, things got a little strange. At the very time that I had begun to cook up a summer theater in Princeton, Tim Mayer had had the much more sensible idea of starting one in Cambridge. Quite naturally, Harvard actors flocked to Tim's company. As a result, I was hard put to lure anyone to mine. By the time Paul and I had finally assembled our core group, he had enlisted six stalwarts from his New York crowd. I had brought aboard only one actress and a stage manager (the fiercely loyal Vicki Traube). And the Harvard-to-Columbia ratio was about to become even more unbalanced. In the middle of the recruitment process, Paul phoned me from New York with what he considered sensational news. His revered Shakespeare mentor, the great Tony Boyd himself, had agreed to join our company as an actor, and had even condescended to direct our production of *Twelfth Night*. Despite a growing sense of unease, I accepted Boyd's offer with bovine submissiveness.

The debacle known as "The Great Road Players" unfolded like a ten-car pileup. Sadly, it took much longer.

With Tony Boyd in the title role, *Woyzeck* badly misfired. Its curtain-raiser, "Sweeney Agonistes," was bewildering. Hardly anyone showed up.

Our board of directors, who had been expecting a palatable season of Shaw, Wilde, and Kaufman and Hart, treated us with withering scorn. They never showed up, either.

The Molière one-acts were diverting and fun, but still nobody came. I took to making curtain speeches, begging the sparse crowds to tell their friends about us.

Staffers from The Princeton Day School angrily complained as we began to leave our messy mark on their pristine theater.

Despite our paltry budget, subsistence salaries, and grab-bag sets, red ink flowed like a river.

The living room of my parents' home became a crowded war room for our embattled staff. My mother, playing hostess to a second generation of theater lunatics, approached the breaking point.

Tony Boyd revealed himself to be a wildly inconsistent actor and a contempt-spewing megalomaniac. The notion of him directing us in a play was inconceivable to me. I fired him.

I quickly learned that Boyd's presence in the company had been the principal reason that his devoted students had signed on. When I fired him, they were enraged.

My father offered to bail me out by taking over *Twelfth Night*. I presented the idea in a meeting of the full company. The Columbia contingent mutinied. They screamed invective at me and stormed out.

Two actors got other job offers (or claimed they did) and blithely walked away.

I called a halt to the season with two productions to go. Our tiny pool of subscribers were livid and demanded their money back. What money?

Word reached me from Cambridge, where, in the meantime, Timothy Mayer's Harvard Dramatic Club Summer Players were in the midst of a triumphant inaugural season.

Until that summer, everything I'd attempted as an actor and as a director had been kissed by success. Not The Great Road Players. It was a total fiasco. Its failure stunned and stupefied me. But it should not have surprised me. In retrospect, the project was fated to collapse. The odds were heavily stacked against us from the outset. I was woefully inexperienced. I had no sense of the challenges of creating a new institution or cultivating an audience. I had no support system beyond a well-meaning but distracted father. I had no leadership skills. I tried to accommodate everyone and recoiled from confrontation. When I hired people, my instincts were abysmal. When I fired them, I waited far too long. These failings, of course, would characterize virtually all twenty-year-old young men, and very few of them would ever put themselves in a position of such responsibility and stress. But I had no such perspective that summer. When The Great Road Players clumsily folded its tents, I could not forgive myself. And if the experience does not quite qualify as a major trauma, it certainly left its mark. I never again attempted to start up a theater company, nor aspired to run one.

By then, Jean Taynton had been my girlfriend for a year. She had accompanied me to Princeton that summer. She'd even played a small role in our first show. Through all of my Joblike agonies she had been staunchly in my corner. At that harrowing company meeting when everything fell apart, she was there to witness the insurrection. She even spoke up in an attempt to cool hostilities, bringing down upon herself a volley of angry insults. After the meeting, the two of us sneaked off to lick our wounds, benumbed by all that had gone before. We drove out of town, heading for the Jersey shore. We ate supper in a restaurant and went to see Cary Grant and Audrey Hepburn in *Charade*. We did all that we could to put The Great Road Players out of our minds, at least for one evening. I felt comforted, grateful, and deeply attached to her. I'd left my own mother back in Princeton, but I was enfolded in Jean's maternal love. And eight weeks later, in an Episcopal church service in Philadelphia, with fifty guests in attendance, including the two stricken parents of the groom, I married her.

14.

Three Lincolns

At some point, every skinny six-foot-four American character actor is asked to play Abraham Lincoln. I've been asked three or four times. The only time I actually did it was in the summer of 1967, when I was twenty-one years old. I had graduated from Harvard and was heading to London in the fall to study acting on a Fulbright grant. I'd decided to stick around Cambridge for the summer prior to my departure, as a member of the Harvard Summer School Repertory Theatre. This was a company run by the professional staff of the Loeb Drama Center and made up of recent graduates of several college drama departments. After the runaway turmoil of the summer before, this job was comfortable and risk-free. (Tim Mayer's far more raffish and daring troupe, now in its second season, was at the tiny Agassiz Theatre, across the street.) Our Loeb company presented four shows. The last of them was a new play about Abraham Lincoln called *White House Happening*. The writer and director of the play was, surprisingly, the larger-than-life impresario of the New York City Ballet, Lincoln Kirstein. And in Lincoln's play, I was Abraham Lincoln.

Lincoln Kirstein was a mighty figure in American arts and letters, particularly in the world of dance. Over many years he had poured his titanic energies and his considerable fortune into the creation of the New York City Ballet and its feeder institution, the School of American Ballet. He had lured the great choreographer George Balanchine to New York, inviting him to create the repertory of ballets that continues to define the company's artistic identity. But since I knew precious little about the Manhattan arts scene, and even less about the world of ballet, I'd never heard of Lincoln Kirstein. Months before starting work on his play, I was sent to New York to meet him. It was like making the acquaintance of a turbulent, fast-moving human storm system.

First of all Lincoln Kirstein was big. At six-four, he was my height, but a solid, top-heavy 250 pounds. His wardrobe rarely diverged from a kind of uniform, made up of a navy-blue double-breasted suit, white shirt, black shoes, and dark tie. He was bullet-headed, with his silvery hair clipped to a prickly bristle. His posture was erect but he led with his chin, and his impatient gait always seemed to be just shy of a trot. His intense eyes glinted under a knit brow, and his smile was a grimace, giving him a mischievous, almost satanic air. That year he was sixty years old and at the height of his powers. On my visit to New York he briskly squired me around town, keeping up an animated running commentary on every conceivable subject, ranging far beyond his play. The highlight of the trip was an evening at the New York State Theater at Lincoln Center. I sat next to Kirstein for a program of four ballets performed by his company. He was like an emperor proudly displaying his private treasure. At each intermission, he led me backstage, introducing me to the dancers as if they were beloved adopted children. At every moment he was an effusive host, the master of all he surveyed. I was awed and mystified by him in equal measure.

A couple of months later, Kirstein arrived in Cambridge to take charge of rehearsals for the world premiere of his *White House Happening*. The premise of this overheated historical drama is far-fetched and provocative. It proposes that Abraham Lincoln carefully plotted his own assassination. His motive, according to the playwright, was his conviction that the American North needed to make a blood sacrifice to the South to heal the wounds of the Civil War. Kirstein himself seemed utterly convinced of the truth of this wild hypothesis. His play takes place in the White House on the day of Lincoln's fateful visit to Ford's Theatre. Surrounding Lincoln is a cast of characters that mixes historical fact and fiction: his wife, a raving-mad Mary Todd Lincoln; his head of the Secret Service, a hand-wringing George Chatterton; his two earnest young aides, John Hay and John Nicolay; and a voodoo-spouting Creole housekeeper. Finally, there is a character that lends a whiff of historical scandal to the proceedings. This is a young mulatto man working as a steward in the White House. The young man is Abe Lincoln's illegitimate son, born of a long-dead slave girl whom the morose president recalls with moony longing and lip-smacking sensuality. This unsavory historical stew was to be stirred by our writer-director Lincoln Kirstein, who had never directed a play in his event-filled life.

Lincoln directed with the wide-eyed delight of a child with a new toy. He had no conception of the rudiments of staging, and half of our rehearsal time was given over to his long, irrelevant tangents. But none of this mattered to us actors. Nobody could resist the man's charm, his charisma, and his enthusiasm for the project. Among the cast was Tommy Lee Jones, playing the role of John Hay. Tommy and I were good friends by this time and we watched Lincoln at work with wary admiration and slightly conspiratorial bemusement. Neither of us had ever seen anyone like him.

As the weeks passed and we counted down to our first performance, strange things started to happen. We all watched with growing concern as Lincoln became progressively manic. As the play evolved from its halting first rehearsals to a polished imitation of reality, it seemed to touch some deep well of anxiety in him. One day things reached a tipping point. We arrived for rehearsal that morning, but Lincoln was nowhere to be seen. One hour passed, then two. He finally arrived, bursting into the room with volcanic energy and carrying an open bottle of vodka. He was an alarming sight. His clothes were disheveled, his face was flushed, and his eyes were wild with excitement. He immediately launched into another of his rambling speeches, but this one was fueled by a crazed intensity. As he spoke, he dispensed with his jacket, his tie, even his dress shirt, leaving only a T-shirt covering his massive torso. Every few minutes he swigged from the vodka bottle, emptying it as his company of young actors sat there watching, mute and incredulous.

Lincoln's speech was wild and disjointed, but we gradually caught the gist of it. *White House Happening* was not about Abraham Lincoln. It was about Lincoln Kirstein. He rattled off the play's connections to his own life. The mad Mary Todd was his wife, Fidelma; Hay and Nicolay were his extramarital gay infatuations; his black son was Arthur Mitchell, the New York City Ballet dancer whom Lincoln had made into the first great African-American ballet star. And Abraham Lincoln himself was the playwright-director, a haunted, torn, self-destructive creature, struggling to contain his demons. As the production of Lincoln's play had inexorably taken shape before his eyes, its metaphorical reflection of his own life had become almost unendurable to him. It was pushing him toward a severe psychotic collapse. Listening to his long, tortured outpouring that day, I began to sense how complex my onstage and offstage roles had become. I was Abraham Lincoln, Abraham Lincoln was Lincoln Kirstein, therefore I was Lincoln Kirstein. And in Lincoln Kirstein's fevered mind, he was gradually losing track of any distinction between the three of us.

Lincoln had lost control. He had been accompanied to Cambridge by an attentive male companion, a man close to his own age named Dan Malone. But not even this kind, solicitous soul could help Lincoln through this terrible crisis. The big man was bewildered and disoriented but full of ferocious, undirected energy. That afternoon he took to the Cambridge streets like an escaped animal, padding around barefoot in that same soiled T-shirt and trousers, with Dan doing his best to steer him clear of trouble.

The following day, we witnessed the full force of Lincoln's mania. We were due to rehearse for the first time on our monumental set. The poor, pitiable man showed up in time for rehearsal, but he looked worse than ever. He was still barefoot, wore the same clothes, and by all appearances had not slept since the day before. When the cast assembled onstage, he ordered us to sit out in the house. For four weeks, we had been performing for him. Now he performed for us. Like a cartoon version of a madman, he acted out a frenzied pantomime. He barked, bellowed, and darted about. He seized a prop knife and whittled away frantically on a wax candle. He dashed behind the scenery, then stuck out his hand, his foot, or his head with jerky, percussive movements. The entire "performance" was agonizing to behold. Tommy Lee and I sat side by side in the theater, stealing looks at each other. No one knew what to do. But something definitely had to be done.

Lincoln appeared to have lost all sense of his own ego. Reminding myself that I was playacting the part of Lincoln Kirstein, I gingerly decided to take on the role of his other self. I stood up, walked forward, climbed up onstage, and spoke quietly to him.

"Lincoln."

He looked at me as if I had suddenly come into focus.

"Yes?"

"Why don't we call Dan on the phone?"

"Yes."

"He can take you to the hotel, and you can have a nap."

"Yes. Yes."

His massive body seemed to slump with relief. I got him to the phone, Dan got him to the hotel, and an hour later he was fast asleep. We didn't see Lincoln again until near the end of the run of his play, about five weeks later. In the meantime, we had learned a bit about his psychological history. Apparently he had experienced a few episodes like this in his adult life, though none nearly as severe or painful. When he reappeared he had lost weight, his hands trembled, his temples were marked with purple bruises, and his manner was tentative, muted, and sweet. Curiously, after all he had been through, he didn't seem that interested in his own play. But he was grateful and generous to each of us when he came backstage afterwards. Knowing that I was heading off for a year in England, he handed me a stack of letters of introduction to his London friends, including Irene Worth, Cecil Beaton, and Sir John Gielgud.

The director of the Loeb Drama Center had taken over *White House Happening* and we had managed to open with no further mishaps. Despite the passion that Lincoln had poured into the project, it ended up a fairly unremarkable evening in the theater. But for me the experience was overwhelming. It taught me a frightening truth: creating theater, even not very good theater, is like working with volatile chemicals. And in the wrong combination those chemicals can burn you. For the first time I had seen a soul in agony, and that agony had arisen directly from his own emotional investment in the creative process. I had glimpsed real madness, not the pretend kind. And it was all the more poignant and pitiable to see it afflict such a warm, powerful, seemingly indomitable man. This was an acting lesson that couldn't be taught.

Because of Lincoln Kirstein's high profile in the cultural landscape of the nation, his play attracted far more attention than it probably should have. Critics flocked up to Cambridge to cover it, and so for the first time in my career I was reviewed in the national press. Lincoln's notices were mostly dismissive, treating his play as something between a curiosity and a vanity project (to this day, it has never had a second production). As for me, I got one bad review and one good one. The description of me in the pages of *Newsweek* introduced me to the word "neurasthenic." And the first mention I ever received in the *New York Times* appeared in the last sentence of a negative review written by Daniel Sullivan, their second-string critic:

"The role of Abraham Lincoln is played by John Lithgow, a young man with a future in the theatre."

15.
This Scepter'd Isle

Halfway through my last year of college, I told my father that I was going to audition for a Fulbright grant to study acting in London. His face fell as if I'd just told him I'd contracted a terminal disease. This was hardly the response I'd expected. I had spent four summers working for him, I had played a dozen parts, I had built props, run lights, pulled curtains, and mopped the stage. I had developed friendships among his adult company members that were deeper and more lasting than any friends of my own age. My father had directed me, acted with me, and watched me perform huge roles in school plays. He'd been surprised and increasingly pleased at my growing skill and confidence. By this time, any fool could see that I was heading toward a career in the theater. I was practically addicted to it.

But confronted with the reality of my choice, Dad was completely blindsided.

If my decision was a surprise to him, his disappointment was a surprise to me. Each of us had completely misread the other. In that instant, father and son experienced twin shocks stemming from two sources: his withholding nature and my blinkered naïveté. The stricken expression on his face stuck in my memory. It told of anxiety, struggle, and debilitating self-doubt. In my eyes, the theater had always been exotic, seductive, and fun. Each of my father's companies had seemed a magical circus, with him as its insouciant ringmaster. Suddenly that image was turned on its head. I saw that a life in the theater had been harrowing for him and that he feared the same fate for me.

In the halting conversation that followed, he tried to articulate those fears. He painted a picture of the desperate insecurity of an actor's life, the scarcity of steady work, the difficulty of providing for a family, and the unending anxiety of being subject to the whims of producers, directors, critics, and fickle crowds. He told me that, in fact, he had always imagined me as a producer-director, beholden to nobody and immune to the constant rejection that all actors must endure. If you must go into the theater, he advised, be the person in charge and acquire the skills to do it right. He confessed to his own sense of inadequacy as a theater manager, how inept he felt at the essential tasks of fundraising, budgeting, and personnel management. But all of this, he claimed, need not be a problem for me. It was acquired knowledge. I could master it as he never had. As a follow-up to my newly acquired Ivy League education, he suggested an altogether different direction.

"Why not go to business school?"

Business school? Where on earth did *that* come from? It was a suggestion that completely floored me. It was the first piece of direct advice my father had ever given me. It was succinct, sensible, even wise. But to me it was a message from another planet. It was like advising a poodle to become a pit bull. My brain was exploding with the absurdity of the notion, but I betrayed none of this to him. I listened, smiled, and nodded as if the idea intrigued me. But . . . business school? It was never going to happen. Without a word of defiance, or even skepticism, I proceeded to utterly ignore my father's counsel. In the coming weeks and months, I perfected a speech from *Richard II*, I traveled to New York, I auditioned before a blue-ribbon Fulbright panel, I landed a grant, I sailed to Southampton with my wife on the second-to-last ocean crossing of the RMS *Queen Mary*, and I set foot for the first time on the green and pleasant land of England.

England!

Can you imagine a more thrilling time to go to England? And to go there for the very first time? In September 1967, I arrived in London, dizzy with sensory overload. This was the London of the young Rolling Stones and Pink Floyd, of Carnaby Street and Portobello Road, of James Bond, Stanley Kubrick, and *Blow-Up*, of the young Harold Pinter, David Hockney, Julie Christie, and Albert Finney. Gielgud, Guinness, Scofield, Ralph Richardson, and Maggie Smith were showing up regularly on the stages of the West End. Laurence Olivier was running the National Theatre. Peter Hall was passing the torch to the twenty-seven-year-old Trevor Nunn at the Royal Shakespeare Company. Peter Brook had not yet decamped for Paris. And although John and Yoko had found each other, *the Beatles were still together*!

And the backdrop to the electric bustle of Swinging London was the stately grandeur of Great Britain herself. Suddenly I found myself hungry for all things British. I had been studying the history and literature of England for the preceding four years, but I learned more about its society, culture, and geography in the first week that I was actually there. I had known all about characters named Cornwall, Gloucester,

Northumberland, and Kent from Shakespeare's plays, but I'd never bothered to look at a map to find the counties that bore their names. I had spouted a hundred place names in the lyrics of Gilbert and Sullivan, but I'd never seen any of them, nor even knew where they were. On crisply painted row houses in leafy squares all over London, round blue ceramic plaques marked the former residences of notable figures from centuries of British politics, arts, and sciences. Charles Dickens! Benjamin Disraeli! Alexander Pope! Every hour of every day seemed to crackle with such discoveries. And at night the plummy accents on BBC broadcasts lent an air of elegance and exoticism to even the most humdrum reporting. I would avidly soak up news of a cricket test match at Lord's, a brawl in the House of Commons, or a by-election in West Walthamstow. It barely mattered that I had no idea what any of it was all about.

My main passion, of course, was London theater. I was over there to study acting, but I saw immediately that my most vivid lessons would be delivered to me in a theater seat. My first days in London were filled with the logistical tasks of finding a cheap flat, opening a bank account, mastering the London Underground, and mustering for my first classes (and in Jean's case, sniffing out job prospects in London schools). But no matter how packed our days were, the nights were given over to theater. With a hectic pace we were to maintain for the next two years, we sprinted around town, taking in plays like children on an Easter egg hunt.

Mainly I was drawn to the National Theatre and the Royal Shakespeare Company, the two mighty magnetic poles of the British stage. At that time, the National was housed at the Old Vic, and the RSC's London home was at the Aldwych. On a typical morning I would stand in line outside the Old Vic at 7 a.m. to buy cheap same-day tickets for that evening's performance. I would then run across Waterloo Bridge to pick up a fistful of tickets for upcoming RSC shows. And that evening, after a long day at school, Jean and I would be right back at the Old Vic, perched in our favorite seats in "the gods," craning toward the stage.

In those first weeks, I saw the National's *Much Ado About Nothing*, *Rosencrantz and Guildenstern Are Dead*, *The Three Sisters*, and *A Flea in Her Ear*, in thrilling productions featuring such actors as Joan Plowright, Derek Jacobi, and the very young Anthony Hopkins. Over at the RSC, I squeezed in three or four productions of Shakespeare, brought down to London after a summer season at Stratford-on-Avon. Sprinkled throughout that company were young actors whose names would one day become household words all over the world, including Judi Dench, Patrick Stewart, and Helen Mirren. The fervent pace of my theatergoing, combined with the relentless, unaccustomed cold and damp of the English climate, sent me to bed wracked with influenza, causing me to miss an entire week of school just after classes had gotten underway. For days I alternated between raging fevers and bone-rattling chills, with Jean hauling sweat-soaked sheets to the coin-op laundry and ministering to me in our dismal little bed-sitter in Courtfield Gardens. It was the sickest I'd been in my life. But the tradeoff was the finest theater I'd ever seen. I barely minded at all.

At some point in that autumn avalanche of playacting, I saw Laurence Olivier in Strindberg's *Dance of Death* at the Old Vic.

It has always mystified me that some stage performances live on in your memory as if you had seen them the night before, whereas so many others are completely forgotten. Olivier as Edgar, the tempestuous, tyrannical army captain locked in a diabolical marriage, was one of the indelible ones. During my time in London, I probably spent a hundred evenings in different theaters, opera houses, and concert halls. If I had seen only *Dance of Death*, it would have been worth the trip.

I'd never witnessed such power onstage. Olivier's military strut, his trumpet bark, his satanic humor, and his scary flirtation with madness were all woven together into the best piece of stage acting I'd ever beheld. Most compelling was the soaring arrogance of the character and, seemingly, of the actor playing him. The National was a company virtually created in Olivier's godlike self-image, and when he was onstage there was no question who was number one. And in taking on the role of Edgar, Strindberg's savage and self-lacerating despot of a husband, Olivier had cast himself to perfection. His Edgar was a roaring lion of a man, exchanging verbal body blows with his equally ruthless wife, Alice (Geraldine McEwan). But as Olivier played him, Edgar's manic savagery alternated with a whiny, strangulated insecurity. Marriage was driving the man crazy.

But Olivier's audacity extended beyond the brilliance of his bravura performance. At that time it was common knowledge all over London that he was fighting a prolonged battle with cancer and continuing to perform in spite of it. His muscularity and titanic energy onstage belied any infirmity, but the fact of his cancer undeniably hung in the air. As a consequence, at every performance of The Dance of Death, there was a palpable sense in the audience that they might be watching one of his last performances. It is unimaginable that Olivier was not aware of this fact. And in one scene in particular, he had clearly chosen to exploit it to the hilt.

It is the play's signature scene. Alice sits at the piano downstage right and plays a snappy mazurka. Her husband Edgar dances to the music with martial crispness, wasting not a single step or gesture. He grins maniacally and his black boots flash, a figure out of the acid ink drawings of George Grosz. Alice's piano playing grows more percussive, almost violent. She quickens the tempo and Edgar dances faster. And faster. It becomes a contest between them, a marital fight to the death, music versus dance. At a certain point, Edgar appears to be losing his breath. He dances upstage, heading toward a sofa. Suddenly a seizure hits him like a thunderbolt. He pitches forward awkwardly, banging to the floor behind the sofa like a fallen horse, and then lying there inert. Witnessing this on the stage of the Old Vic, every member of the audience gasped audibly. Suddenly this was not Strindberg's *Dance of Death*. This was not Edgar. This was the great Olivier, mortally stricken before our very eyes. We sat there frozen in shock. Seconds passed. Olivier staggered to his feet. The play lurched back to life and we regained our composure. Once again, we were just an audience in a theater. We had seen a dazzling, deeply disturbing piece of stagecraft, executed by a genius of manipulation. As my heartbeat slowed, I felt a crazy mixture of feelings, enthralled and bamboozled, in equal measure. Sitting in the darkness, I silently addressed myself to Laurence Olivier, my new hero:

"You *bastard*! You knew *just* what you were doing!"

The following morning I spoke to a friend about *The Dance of Death*. He was an English acting student, one of my newly acquired school acquaintances. I was still under the spell of Olivier's performance and spoke of it with worshipful effusiveness.

"My god," I said. "What a great actor!"

"Yes," he replied, with withering scorn. "He's a great actor. A great 1945 actor."

What was this? Was my new hero old hat? It was my first insight into the fact that, between English and American actors, the grass is often greener on the other side of the pond. I had traveled to London to study acting, pricked on by the sense that classical English acting was the high-water mark in English-speaking theater. I would soon learn a surprising truth: I came from America, home to an acting tradition that my new English friends envied, to an even greater degree than I envied theirs. In days to come, I myself would lose patience with the decorous manners of the English stage (and even tire of Olivier's bag of tricks). But for now, it was everything I wanted. In West End playhouses I was gorging myself on a steady diet of plays, like so many sausages in the pubs of southwest London. And in the classrooms and studios of my new school, I was learning how the sausages were made.

16.
D Group Days

In the world of British theater, "The London Academy of Music and Dramatic Art" is too much of a mouthful. They just call it LAMDA. When I enrolled there in 1967, LAMDA had been around for a while, but it still had the air of a breakaway, upstart institution. Situated in the unprepossessing neighborhood of Earls Court, the academy was crammed into a musty, three-story gray-brick building, referred to with wistful grandiosity as "The Tower House." Today LAMDA boasts a sterling reputation with a long list of renowned alumni. But in those days it was the second choice for most young English applicants, far less prestigious than the Royal Academy of Dramatic Art (RADA), its venerable Bloomsbury rival. RADA, after all, had produced Gielgud, Finney, Courtenay, Caine, and

Rigg. The best-known fact about the more proletarian LAMDA was that the boisterous Richard Harris had been kicked out of the school for unruly behavior and dirty fingernails.

But for aspiring American actors looking to travel to London for a heavy dose of British academy training, LAMDA was the place. LAMDA, you see, had the D Group. This was a special one-year program offered to fifteen "overseas students," many of whom had already had a couple of years' experience in the profession. In a typical year, a dozen of the fifteen D Group kids were Americans. Of that dozen, one actor and one actress were there on a Fulbright grant from the U.S. Government. And that year, I was the Fulbright actor.

The D Group year was a kind of British drama school horse pill. It was LAMDA's entire three-year curriculum squeezed into one. Our group worked from nine to five every weekday, a regimen as taxing as preseason training in professional sports. Every morning, we would run a gauntlet of intensive classes and every afternoon we would rehearse for one of five productions, spaced out over the year. In my year we performed two plays by Shakespeare and one each by Shaw, Chekhov, and Congreve, directed by a mixed bag of staff teachers and veteran London actors.

Shakespeare, of course, was at the heart of our curriculum. And Shakespeare was spoon-fed to us by an extraordinary teacher named Michael MacOwan. Michael was our Yoda. He was in his late seventies, a stringy little man just over five feet tall, with a booming, gravelly voice seasoned by a lifetime of cigarettes. He was colorful and endearing but prone to crankiness and sudden inexplicable rages. Around the school his quirks and foibles were legendary. In recent years, he had occasionally forgotten where he had parked his car, angrily insisting that it had been stolen. He had been the longtime principal and guiding light of LAMDA, but by the time we arrived he was in semiretirement. His only students were the Shakespearean neophytes of the D Group.

Three times a week, Michael led us in an hour-long scene study class. His teaching method was simple but idiosyncratic. He would assign each of us a speech from Shakespeare. One by one, we would deliver our assigned speech, listen to him hold forth about it, then speak it again. He would grunt and grumble as we spoke, chuckling with pleasure when his notes bore fruit. His head would bob with palsy as he stared intently at each of us in turn, his dark-brown eyes magnified by horn-rimmed spectacles. In his rambling responses to the speeches, he would tease out the meaning, emotion, and music of the verse. He would sprinkle his talk with tales of fabled productions and performances, tossing off nicknames like Larry (Olivier) and Johnny G. (Gielgud) as if they were old friends (which they were). He would educate us in the vast range of Shakespeare's knowledge, dissecting even the most obscure references, images, and metaphors. And on a Saturday in autumn soon after we started classes, he took us on a field trip to Penshurst, the grand manor house and gardens in Kent. On our way home in the late afternoon, he treated us to supper in a centuries-old country pub. He thrilled us with the fact (or possibly fiction) that the building had once been a hunting lodge belonging to Henry V himself. We arrived back in London after dark, his adoring disciples. The whole glorious day was Michael MacOwan's notion of a young actor's education. No one could truly understand Shakespeare, he said, without experiencing the gentle splendor of the English countryside.

Besides the gift of his wisdom, one day Michael did me an enormous favor. The favor was unsolicited and unintended. Indeed he was never even aware of it. A few years before, when he was still LAMDA's principal, a certain acquaintance of mine had been a member of his teaching staff. This was none other than Tony Boyd, the crazed martinet who had made my life so miserable back in the States during the summer of The Great Road Players. When I learned of Boyd's tenure at LAMDA, I disingenuously asked Michael about him. Michael wearily shook his head as he answered.

"Tony was a brilliant teacher," he said. "Very energetic. Very original. The students loved him. But he was a difficult man—chippy and bull-headed. We had a few too many run-ins. It was a messy business. I'm afraid that in the end I had to let him go."

At these words a wave of relief broke over me. In my mind, I had shouldered all the blame for the Tony Boyd fiasco for two long years. Michael had unwittingly unburdened me. He must have been considerably taken aback when I blurted out, *"So did I!"*

If Michael MacOwan's Shakespeare tutorial was the heart of our LAMDA training, the rest of our classes provided its blood, bone, and gristle. These classes included movement, voice, diction, historical dance, choral singing, stage fighting, and even tumbling. Our half dozen teachers ranged across a broad spectrum of English eccentricity. At one end of this spectrum was Elizabeth Wilmer, the prim finishing-school headmistress of a certain age who spent an entire diction class teaching us the difference between the formation of the words "blow" and "blue." At the other end was

B. H. Barry, our furiously energetic young fight instructor (now one of the premier fight arrangers in American theater). In Barry's class we learned to fence, box, fling each other to the floor, impale each other with knives, and deliver hideously convincing blows to the face, gut, and nape of the neck. Somewhere in the middle of this spectrum was Anthony Bowles, our choral singing teacher. Appropriately nicknamed "Ant," he was a wiry, febrile little man with a mocking wit who, by some mysterious magic, coaxed sublime close-harmony madrigals from a chorus of young acting students that included not a single decent singing voice.

This wildly varied teaching crew shared a single coordinated mission: to tear us down and build us back up, and to do it with patience, kindness, and good humor. Layer by layer, they peeled away the facile habits and manners that I had accumulated in my short, packed career onstage. In performing Shakespeare I had long ago fallen into a tight, singsong imitation of John Gielgud, probably the result of listening a few times too many to a scratchy LP recording of his *Ages of Man*. My LAMDA teachers were determined to put an end to this. In voice class I learned to completely relax from my waist up, to reflexively fill up my diaphragm with air, to loosen the tense tangle of muscles in my neck and throat, and to produce an easy, natural sound, more Lithgow than Gielgud. On account of my height I had always tended to unconsciously slouch to the eye level of whomever I was acting with. This question-mark posture constricted not just my body but my voice as well. In movement class, I learned to straighten my spine and stand up to my full height, to vocally stand and deliver.

Finally there was the deceptively simple business of making dramatic sense of what I was saying. Gielgud's Shakespearean speech favored music over meaning. For all its glories, it was a throwback to a much earlier, near-operatic stage tradition. Under Michael MacOwan's penetrating gaze, I learned to tilt the balance back toward meaning, to fall a little less in love with the sound of my own voice. He was teaching me lessons that I had spent the last several years ignoring. In his patient prodding, I occasionally heard echoes of my father's voice back home:

"Just speak the words."

I loved the D Group. It remains the only formal acting training I've ever had. The months I spent in LAMDA classrooms and London theaters were challenging, exciting, formative, and fun. But the LAMDA experience had its distinct drawbacks. It saddled me with two heavy burdens that I would carry with me like twin millstones when I finally joined the American acting profession.

First of all, I became far too English. I had thought that studying acting in the company of a dozen other Yanks would inoculate me from this curious affliction. I thought I could take what I needed from English academy training and then go home with my red-blooded American actor's identity intact. I was wrong. Osmosis, it turns out, is a powerful thing. I came home with a fruity British accent that I didn't even realize I had acquired, complete with lilting inflections and arch locutions. Old friends would look at me askance when I'd chirp "Bob's your uncle," "spend a penny," or "a bit how's yer father." My own sister Robin wouldn't speak to me until I dropped "that awful English accent!"

"Wot acksnt?" I asked, puzzled.

She refused to answer.

I was . . . well, gobsmacked.

For my first year back in the States, I eminated Englishness like cheap cologne. At the end of that year I was subjected to a kind of radical therapy that finally purged it from my system. I was cast as Andy in Neil Simon's trifling sixties comedy *The Star-Spangled Girl*, in a summer-stock production at the Bucks County Playhouse in New Hope, Pennsylvania. I have long since forgotten the name of the show's director, an unsurprising memory lapse since he barely directed it at all. But during rehearsals he taught me an invaluable lesson. I failed to appreciate it at the time. Indeed, I bridled against it. But it was just what I needed.

In the play, Andy is a sanitized, Simonized hippie, the youthful editor of a radical San Francisco magazine. The boy is an American—"an *American,* dammit!"— and my director was determined to rid me of any trace of an English accent in the role. As we rehearsed, he sat behind a table with a tiny bell in front of him. Every time he heard the slightest English inflection from me he would ring the bell. In the first few days of work he was ringing that damned bell every ten seconds. It was absolutely infuriating. I couldn't believe that, a year after coming back from England, I still sounded *that* English. But by the last rehearsal, the bell had stopped ringing. The show was godawful and I was pretty dreadful in it. But I was an American again. I was cured.

The second problem was not so easily remedied. LAMDA turned me into an insufferable Shakespeare snob. Until I went off to England, American productions of Shakespeare's plays had suited me just fine. I had loved to act in them and I had loved to watch them. They were my birthright, after all, and my father's abiding passion. I had adored their reckless energy, broad comedy, and high spirits. By the late 1960s, the American style was virtually defined by Joseph Papp's free Shakespeare at the outdoor Delacorte Theater in New York's Central Park. I had always savored every visit to the Delacorte, a pastoral oasis in the midst of a clamorous city. My heart had swelled at the populist spirit of those shows, with their raucous, grateful audiences and their tossed salad of acting styles, accents, and ethnicities. The crowds never seemed to understand half of the lines (and, for that matter, neither did a lot of the actors). But it didn't matter. This was Shakespeare at its most joyful and exuberant.

England dulled my enthusiasm for it. My taste was now defined by everything I had seen and done over there. For me, the bar had been set impossibly high. Oh, certainly I had seen plenty of bad Shakespeare in London and Stratford. Some productions were stagey and predictable, some woefully misconceived. But the good ones had been amazing—Peter Brook's *Lear* and *Midsummer Night's Dream*, John Barton's panoramic *Troilus and Cressida*, Clifford Williams' daring all-male *As You Like It*. And no matter how good or bad the productions were, the standard of acting had always been uniformly high. There are at least a dozen characters in every Shakespeare play, so every production requires at least that many actors capable of handling the particular challenge of Shakespearean speech. To my overly trained ear, half the actors in every American production of Shakespeare were either miscast or inept.

This was ridiculous, of course. English actors were just as judgmental of their own countrymen as I was of mine (remember my snotty friend's contempt for Lord Olivier?), and they tended to be far more tolerant than I of Americans playing Shakespeare. Shortly after I returned to the States, CBS televised A. J. Antoon's brilliant Central Park production of *Much Ado About Nothing*, set in Teddy Roosevelt's small-town America. When the BBC aired the show in England, it caused a sensation. All those Brits were delighted to see that old Shakespearean chestnut completely reimagined, with all the freshness, energy, and innocence of its all-American cast.

I loved that production too, but from my high horse I regarded it as the rare exception to the rule. In my view, American Shakespeare just didn't cut it. In hindsight, I suspect that this arrogance was probably colored by an Oedipal reaction to my father's long history with Shakespeare and by my unconscious desire to break free of it. True or not, it is an arrogance that has only slightly diminished over the years. It is one explanation for a surprising fact: after appearing in some twenty Shakespeare plays in my first twenty years, I appeared in only two in the following thirty-five. These two productions (the last in 1975) were arguably the worst shows of my professional career. This was all the evidence I needed to support my Anglophiliac bias. Over the years, I have turned down a long list of stupendous Shakespearean roles, among them Angelo, Bottom, Falstaff, Hamlet, Prospero, and Lear. Listing them fills me with wistfulness and regret. But I couldn't help it. My snobbery made me do it.

Perhaps all of this will explain why I finally returned to Shakespeare a few years ago, at the age of sixty-two. After spurning all those job offers for three decades, I finally received an offer I couldn't refuse. In the summer of 2007, the Royal Shakespeare Company invited me to come back to England and join them for three months at Stratford-on-Avon. They asked me to play Malvolio in *Twelfth Night*, to reprise the role I'd played as a teenager in Ohio all those years ago, in junior high school assemblies and National Forensic League meets. This was my chance to tread the very boards where I had seen Judi Dench as Hermione, Helen Mirren as Cressida, Kenneth Branagh as Berowne, and where, in its most recent season, Patrick Stewart had played Antony and Ian McKellen had unveiled his King Lear. Forty years after my full-immersion Shakespeare training, here was a chance to finally put it to work. And, more significantly, Malvolio at Stratford was the perfect way for me to memorialize my father, three years after his death.

I took the job in a heartbeat.

And so began my *Twelfth Night* adventure, the most intense déjà vu experience I've ever had. On a morning in mid-July, I showed up for London rehearsals at the RSC studios in South Clapham and entered a dreamlike time warp right out of science fiction. Forty years had wrought vast changes in me, but England in 2007 was far more similar than different. And so was the business of putting on plays. From the outset, I felt as if I were reliving an earlier chapter of my own life. The morning tube rides, the drafty rehearsal rooms, the yoga mats, the rehearsal skirts, the chatty green room, the sugary tea, the pints at the pub, and the impulsive evening dashes to West End shows—all of it brought back the sights, sounds, and smells of my days as a young drama student in London, unburdened by the humbling weight of years.

We rehearsed for six weeks in South Clapham before moving up to Stratford, led by our endearing, exotic, comfortably camp director, Neil Bartlett. The first several days of work were given over to exercises, theater games, and improvisations, many of them conducted by RSC voice teachers and movement coaches. For the first two weeks, barely a minute was spent on the play itself. The days virtually duplicated my old LAMDA regimen. It was as if I had never left the place. This was not exactly good news. I began to secretly wonder why I had ever taken the job—wasn't I a little old for drama school? But if the rehearsals smacked of theatrical boot camp, none of the other company members seemed to mind. Most of them were terrifically talented young actors, willing and eager to try anything. But even the old-timers were game for whatever Neil threw at them. Bit by bit, they brought me around. Neil's work started to pay off, and my doubts evaporated. I realized that this was exactly what I'd signed up for. Our cast evolved into a strong, sprightly, mutually responsive ensemble, worthy of the company that had hired us. And at last we were ready for Shakespeare.

Twelfth Night at Stratford was a glorious time for me. During the run of the show, I lived in a tiny row house in Stratford's "New Town," two blocks from Shakespeare's burial place, in Holy Trinity Church. Every day I strolled around town, nostalgically retracing my footsteps from a dozen visits, forty years before. After every show I caroused with the cast at The Dirty Duck, the RSC's traditional pub of choice. I rented an ancient Morris sedan and spent free afternoons idly exploring the quaint towns and rolling countryside of the English Midlands. I hosted friends, family, and Brit actor pals who trekked up to Stratford to see the play. I even engineered a sentimental sibling reunion with my brother and two sisters, complete with Cotswold picnics, midnight suppers, tipsy reminiscences, and maudlin toasts to our mother and to the memory of our dear, departed dad.

And the production itself? I was crazy about it. Neil had chosen to set *Twelfth Night* in a late-nineteenth-century *Gosford Park* kind of world. The severe black

dresses, swallowtail coats, top hats, and starched collars of the period created an atmosphere of constriction from which the play's sexual energy and drunken high jinks strained to break free. The comedy was there, of course, but it was shot through with anxiety and pain. As a result, the longing and melancholy of the characters had an unexpected depth. I loved working in these dark colors. Neil's concept made Malvolio into a stern, dictatorial Edwardian butler, obsessed with protocol and coldly ambitious, a character torn from the pages of Trollope. I embraced this portrait wholeheartedly. My Malvolio was arrogant, judgmental, and sexually repressed, but with a prurient fantasy life. I had little trouble unearthing such strains, buried in my own Puritan nature. When Malvolio is gulled into giving vent to his fettered passions, the moment is wildly comic. But in our version, the joke went much too far. By the end, he had become a broken, vengeful creature, a figure of both pity and danger. Calibrating the stages of this complex comic story was, for me, a fascinating process with a thrilling payoff. After we opened, posters and ads for the production trumpeted a quote from Charles Spencer, the exacting critic from the *Daily Telegraph*. It proclaimed that "the American actor John Lithgow turns out to be one of the greatest Malvolios I have ever seen."

Every actor savors a rave review, of course. But the *Twelfth Night* experience led to another tribute that I prize even more. By tradition, one of the rooms in The Dirty Duck is informally set aside for actors currently in residence at the RSC. Displayed on the walls of this room are fifty or sixty signed black-and-white photographs. These are portraits of the major actors and actresses who have performed with the company over the last few generations. The photos range from faded, yellowing shots of the young Michael Redgrave and Peggy Ashcroft to more recent glossies of Jeremy Irons, Miranda Richardson, and Ralph Fiennes. Toward the end of my run in Stratford, the owner of The Duck drew me aside and asked me for a signed picture to hang with the others. I was ecstatic. Next morning I urgently sent home for a photo. It arrived the day before we closed. I signed it and ran it over to the pub. I haven't been back to Stratford since, but I've left my mark: mine is the only photograph of an American actor to grace the walls of the Actors' Bar at The Dirty Duck.

17.
Getting Out

I n 1968, war was raging in Vietnam, and in the
United States all hell was breaking loose. On March
31 of that year, Lyndon Johnson withdrew from the
presidential election. Four days later, Martin Luther
King was shot, setting off riots in every major city. In
June, Bobby Kennedy was shot, too, and in August
the Democratic National Convention roiled Chicago.
American society was being torn asunder by violent
forces of revolution and counterrevolution. This epic
drama was fueled by the passions of Black Power and
radical youth. Its soundtrack was acid rock and it
played out in a haze of tear gas and pot smoke. And
there was I, sitting with my wife in a South Kens-
ington mews house and watching all of these dire
events being reported in British accents by befuddled

newsmen on the BBC. I stared at the evening news every night with a combination of lefty rage and the impotence of a self-exile. What the hell was I doing in *England*?

But my sense of political anger and dislocation wasn't the only thing unsettling me.

During that time, most young American men in London fell into two groups: the ones who had gotten out of the draft and the ones who hadn't. The boys in the first group were full of manic, subversive energy. Each had his draft-dodging story to tell, a story that got more elaborate and darkly comic with each retelling. The boys in the second group didn't laugh at these stories. To them, the draft was not the stuff of comedy. A sullen, haunted look would cloud their faces whenever it was mentioned. Most were in London on student visas for a year of graduate studies. They were serious students, to be sure, but many of them also had an unspoken secondary agenda. They were relying on their studies to keep them out of the army. But the war in Vietnam continued to escalate, and student deferments were not going to last forever. A day of reckoning was approaching for these boys, even the fey young *artistes* in London drama schools. And the draft lay on their shoulders like a heavy weight.

I was in this second group.

In the spring of my D Group year I applied to renew my Fulbright. I couldn't stay on at LAMDA, as there was no point in repeating a one-year program. But that didn't stop me from submitting an application. By chance I had spent a few hours in RSC rehearsal rooms during my school year, teaching American accents to the likes of Michael Hordern and Peggy Ashcroft for Peter Hall's production of Edward Albee's *A Delicate Balance*. For my Fulbright renewal application, I spun this piddling part-time gig into a proposal to work as an intern or assistant director with London's major theater companies. Extend my grant, I declared, and I'll make good use of it. It was a pretty feeble case for renewal, and I didn't expect it to work, but it was worth a shot. If the U.S. government was willing to continue supporting my studies in England, I figured there was no way it would send me to fight in Vietnam. To my amazement, my Fulbright was renewed. To my dismay, halfway through my second year in London, I was drafted anyway.

I had registered for the draft in Trenton, New Jersey, when I was eighteen years old. At that time, only a tiny fraction of the U.S. population had ever heard of Vietnam. I had filled out a form that included a question asking if there was any reason I should not serve in the American military. I had loftily written that I "disapproved of war as a means to settle disagreements between nations," or words to that effect. This had been my only gesture toward earning myself conscientious-objector status. And four years later, at the height of the Vietnam conflict, with 500,000 American soldiers stationed there and thousands more being conscripted every day, that arch sentence had clearly made no impression on the Trenton draft board. A formal notification arrived at my London address, forwarded to me by my parents. It ordered me to report for a draft physical in Trenton, assigning me a date and time a few weeks hence.

I was barely ruffled. I fired off a letter to the draft board in response, confident that it would get me off the hook. The letter was bold and indignant, but my arguments against being inducted were absurdly thin. I firmly stated that I could not possibly show up in Trenton on the date assigned. I was in England, after all, on a U.S. government grant. I told them I was an assistant director on an important new play at the Royal Court Theatre in London, working with a core group of disciples of the great Peter Brook. On the ridiculous assumption that the name Peter Brook would mean anything at all to the Trenton draft board, I enclosed a letter from him claiming that I was "indispensable" to the project (this, notwithstanding the fact that I had never met the man). I even reminded the board of my

watery antiwar protestations, written on that registra-
tion form six years before. In retrospect, I picture a
table in an office in Trenton, New Jersey, surrounded
by staffers from the Selective Service System, reading a
letter out loud from a Fulbright scholar in England and
sharing a good hearty horselaugh before tossing it in
the wastebasket.

Shortly afterwards I heard from Trenton again.
Once again I was given a date and time for my draft
physical, but this time I was told to report to a U.S. Air
Force facility, situated on an RAF air base just outside
of London. This time I was scared.

In desperation, I decided to fake my way out of the
army. With a combination of political self-righteousness
and creative zeal (and a healthy dose of fear and
cowardice), I set out to forge my most challenging,
complex, and subtle performance to date. I would play
the role of John Lithgow, but I would play him as an
unrecruitable psychological basket case. For this particular piece of playacting, I would put aside the rigorous precepts of my LAMDA training and adopt my
own half-baked version of the Method. I would forsake
stage technique for sense memory and emotional truth.
And I would play my part as if my life depended on it.

My basic approach was to create a heightened version of my darker self. In the week leading up to my

physical, I lived the life of another person. Everything I did was a perversion of my customary behavior. I barely ate and barely slept. I went unshaven and unbathed. I picked my face and peed on my own fetid undershorts. One afternoon, I sat in the dark in a near-empty Soho strip club with a couple of furtive old men, staring at the desultory, sexless performance of a po-faced stripper who might have stepped out of a Diane Arbus photograph. By such means, I struggled to induce in myself a feverish state of anxiety, depression, and near-madness. And it worked. On the morning I reported for my physical, I was an ashen, quivering, foul-smelling mess. I had scrupulously rehearsed for a week, and now I was ready to perform.

My goal was to fool the military into thinking I was unfit for service. In fact, circumstances made it far easier for me to achieve this goal than I could have hoped. Since the physical was being conducted at an Air Force facility by Air Force personnel, no one had any particular stake in whether or not I was inducted into the U.S. Army. Everyone involved in my exam seemed bored and offhand, making no effort whatsoever to see through my act. My red eyes drooped with fatigue and my hands trembled as I filled out forms. I even fainted dead away when my blood was drawn. But none of this artifice raised the slightest suspicion among my examiners, or even much interest. They simply wrote down a description of whatever they saw, ready to send it back to Trenton as observable fact.

After completing my battery of tests, I was singled out for one more interview. I was ushered into the office of an Air Force psychiatrist. He was the only person I dealt with that morning who appeared to be seriously engaged in his duties. He was kindly and soft-spoken, an earnest young man with a distinctly unmilitary aura of compassion about him. He gently questioned me about my psychological state, and I was ready for him. In the weeks leading up to this interview, I had created a detailed psychological profile of myself. I now laid it out for this young man without making a single false statement. I had taken mildly neurotic aspects of my own nature and inflated them into full-blown psychosis. My garden-variety shyness was now pathological fear. My tendency to avoid confrontation was now a phobic terror of violent conflict. My scanty sexual experience was now a tormenting doubt about my manhood. When he asked me straightforwardly if I was homosexual, I obliquely replied that, in spite of my marriage, I often thought about my college roommate. As we spoke, he took down detailed notes, entirely persuaded. I was acting for an audience of one, and he had no idea that I was acting. This made my session with him the most convincing performance I'd ever given. A triumph! But I took no joy in it. The man was filled with such empathy and understanding that I actually felt bad for him. My self-contempt bloomed like a poisonous flower. Ironically, this only deepened my performance.

A month later, another letter from the Trenton draft board was forwarded to me in London. The reviews were in. I was a smash. They classified me 4-F. This was the Holy Grail of the antiwar generation. I would not be drafted.

That year, Arlo Guthrie's "Alice's Restaurant" was a huge hit in the United States. The song was a loopy anthem for the antiwar youth of America. It tells the story of Guthrie's attempts to get out of the army by faking his way through his draft physical. It is a farce version of exactly what I went through in London that very year (and, by coincidence, much of it was set in Stockbridge, Massachusetts, one of my many home-towns). The tone of the song is comical and carefree. For Guthrie, dodging the draft was a clownish lark, a cause for celebration, and the raw material for a hit song. This was not my experience. I never regaled any-body with my draft story, nor ever dreamed of mak-ing it a public entertainment. Indeed, this is the first time I've ever told it. A sense of shame stayed with me for years and has never entirely disappeared. Some of that shame had to do with the appalling suffering caused by the Vietnam War, suffering that I so conveniently avoided. Some of it had to do with the fact that I showed so little courage and conviction in protesting the war and that I spent two of its most turbulent years leading a comfortable, fun life in swinging London.

But somewhere deep down there was another source of my shame. I didn't get out of the army by acting. I got out by lying. There is a difference. When you act, you do it for a willing audience, ready and eager to be tricked into belief by a crafty imitation of reality. There is an unwritten pact between an actor and his audience: I will deceive you but I will do it for your delight, your edification, or your illumination. And I'll only do it if you so desire. On that Air Force base I was violating that pact. Until then, I had always thought of acting as an art—a slightly tainted, highly suspect art perhaps, but an art nonetheless. The events of that morning troubled me deeply. If acting was an art, I had abused it. The concerned face of that Air Force shrink stayed with me. He wrote down my fake ailments without a trace of skepticism or doubt. As he did so, I was overwhelmed with relief. But at the same time, shame was churning inside of me.

18.

Coming Home

In 1968, my wealthy, childless Uncle Bronson announced that he would make a gift to each of his nieces and nephews of a safe, reliable automobile of our choice. The news of this gift reached me in London. I chose a sturdy, navy-blue VW station wagon, purchased through a dealership in Mayfair. With an eye to the future, I requested a model with its steering wheel on the left side. When I finally sailed home from England on the brand-new *QE2*, my new car was ferried home, too, on a separate vessel. That car would figure prominently in my first weeks back in America.

I was ready to return. The London chapter of my life had been rich, vivid, and fulfilling, and my wife had been gainfully employed there for the entire length of our stay. (Jean, in fact, had found a new vocation:

working at a school called "The Word Blind Centre," she had proved herself to be a wizard at teaching dyslexic children to read.) But not for a moment did we ever consider staying on. In spite of the glories of England, the pleasures of London theater, and the distinctly British coloration of my drama school education, I had a growing sense that an actor was meant to perform for his own native audience. I was desperate to go back and get started. From across the Atlantic, news had reached me of the daring work of Sam Shepard, John Guare, and Megan Terry; of Ellen Stewart's Café La MaMa and Joe Papp's Public Theater; of the Living Theatre, *MacBird!* and *Hair.* In fact, the Living Theatre had turned up in London on an international tour. I saw them perform *Frankenstein* at the Roundhouse in Chalk Farm and it blew my mind. Theater like this seemed inextricably tied up with the rush of events back home, and the urgency of those events made me feel more American than ever. The opening words of Buffalo Springfield resonated in my head:

There's something happening here.
What it is ain't exactly clear.

"Here" did not refer to England. It was time to go home.

On my return, I didn't exactly dive into the trenches. I went right to work for my father. Several months before, halfway through my second year abroad, I had slipped home to Princeton for a month to direct *As You Like It* for Dad's McCarter Theatre Repertory Company. On that visit I had come loaded with directorial ideas and rehearsal techniques cribbed from my favorite London productions. The show was the hit of the McCarter season. For me, it had served as a highly successful audition: the company loved performing it, audiences had received it warmly, and I had comfortably navigated the twin challenges of nepotism and overweening youth. As a result, my father was emboldened to offer me an entire season of work at McCarter, his seventh as the company's artistic director. A letter from him arrived at our London flat. In a quaint blending of formality and fatherly affection, he laid out his terms:

January 29, 1969
Mr. John Lithgow
61 Onslow Gardens
London S.W. 7
ENGLAND

Dear John,

Your letter home has bugged me into writing an official sort of communication that I have been too slow in getting off.

In the first place, the production of As You Like It has been a great success at many levels. The general public and the student public has been delighted. The Shakespeare Establishment on the faculty seem ecstatic (after all, the obscure material on the allowed fool has remained uncut, unlike most productions). And, most rewarding perhaps, the Company loves to play it. Furthermore, our august Committee itself has initiated enquiries about your availability for next year.

Naturally, I have never entertained any doubts about your artistic and productive capabilities. Indeed, my main concern about my own dilatoriness was what I have thought the likelihood that you would be making commitments to the theatre there in London which would obviate a possibility here at McCarter.

While there are good psychological reasons why you should go off on your own for your next professional step, thoroughly objective good sense can be found in offering you an important rank on the McCarter artistic staff next season. The particular

emphasis in acting, design, and directing, the de-
tails, the draft problems or its interference—all of
these can wait upon conversations. You can go on
the payroll as early as July 1ˢᵗ, if certain assignments
are attractive, and you could count on at least
$150.00 per week.

At any rate, give us an opportunity to compete
with other offers which might be upcoming for
you. I'd be interested in a structuring of your own
particular interests at this time.
Affectionately, but officially,
Dad

In subsequent conversations, my father outlined
his plans for me. He proposed that I direct and design
two productions and play major roles in several others.
It would be my first time working under an Actors'
Equity contract, an eight-month job that perfectly
suited my triple-threat ambitions. Considering my age
and inexperience, it is inconceivable that any other regional theater producer would have made me such an
offer, but I ignored the implicit favoritism. My father
asked and I accepted. I rushed home in midsummer,
1969, to help him staff up for the coming year. Jean
stayed behind in London for another month to finish
her teaching commitments, and I went right to work.

My first McCarter assignment was a solitary one. At the wheel of my newly imported blue station wagon, I drove out of Princeton to visit summer-stock companies all over the Northeast. The trip was to be a random search for young talent, with special attention paid to set designers. I hit the road with a list of theaters, a pocketful of McCarter cash, and no specific itinerary. This proved to be unwise. For days I wandered New England like the Ancient Mariner, clocking hundreds of miles and nodding through woefully inept summer-stock shows in sweltering, barnlike playhouses, fanning myself with my program and ducking the nosedives of the occasional bat. The only designer prospects I spotted were "highly desirables," long since committed to other jobs.

After my first few stops I became convinced of the futility of my mission. But I pressed on anyway. In fact, I was having a pretty good time. New England was green and gorgeous in the mid-August sunshine, and I reveled in my solitude. I was still in a transitional mode between two worlds, reacquainting myself to the States. Having been away for two long years, I was a twenty-three-year-old Rip Van Winkle, keenly attuned to how much the country had changed since I'd left. Radicalism was being subtly incorporated into the culture. The long hair, torn jeans, head bands, beads, and tie-dyed T-shirts of the hip young had created a new aesthetic, very different from the Kings Road modishness of London. Images of smiling, assimilated African-Americans were all over TV and billboard advertising, an astonishing change from two years before. The car radio blared with the exuberant defiance of Hendrix; Joplin; Crosby, Stills, and Nash; and Country Joe and the Fish. These were the sights and sounds of a changed America, and I drank it all in. But if I felt the giddy excitement of a returning prodigal, that excitement was tempered by the nagging awareness of all that I'd been missing.

On a Thursday, I left the town of Stowe, Vermont, having sat through a threadbare production of *The Apple Tree* there the night before. Heading south, I had chosen the Taconic Parkway, a route that took me through upstate New York, alongside the Massachusetts border. I was thinking that I might catch an evening performance of the American Shakespeare Festival at Stratford, in southern Connecticut. But I hadn't decided for sure, and I was in no particular hurry. When I stopped at a café for lunch, I overheard a conversation at the cash register about a three-day music festival that was just getting underway in the area. Back in the car, I heard even more about it from a radio disk jockey. Several of the very groups I had been listening to were expected to perform. I began to notice a proliferation of VW microbuses on the road, spray-painted in rainbow colors and packed with funky, long-haired young people. I surmised that they must be heading to that festival I'd been hearing about.

"This might be interesting," I thought. "Maybe I should go."

I sized up my situation. My wife was on the other side of the ocean. I'd spent hardly any of my expense-account money. I had no set schedule and no immediate obligations. My talent-scouting trip was yielding no results. I could easily spare three or four days. And even if I couldn't find a place to stay, I could always sleep in the back of my station wagon. Jimi Hendrix? Richie Havens? Joan Baez? The Grateful Dead? The Who? "Three days of peace and music"? Sounds great. Why not?

. . . Naaaah!

I kept driving that day. By evening I was sitting by myself in a stuffy crowd, watching *Henry V* in Stratford, Connecticut. A few days later I was back in Princeton, reporting dutifully to my father on my fruitless mission. I thereby missed out on one of the most pivotal moments in the history of rock and roll, three days that would come to define my generation. I missed Woodstock.

What if I'd made an abrupt right turn and headed to Max Yasgur's farm that afternoon? What if I'd heard all that music, smoked all that dope, and done all that acid? What if I'd danced in the rain, played in the mud, and screwed stoned-out girls in the back of my car? What if I had rebelled against the careful orderliness of my life—my tidy marriage, my dutiful job, my accommodating father, my "art"? What if, for one weekend, I had broken loose? Such speculation is pointless, of course. I would never have done any of those things. It simply wasn't me. My orderly life was a response to the disorder of the years that had gone before. The only moments of rebellion I allowed myself were playacted moments onstage, with all my lines written out for me. I would rebel all right, but it wouldn't be for several more years. And when it happened, it wouldn't be at a music festival.

19.
The Triumph of Nepotism

Lenny in *Of Mice and Men*? Were they crazy? When I was cast as Lenny at McCarter, I thought the idea was insane. I was still scarecrow thin, and still affected the dandified airs of a fresh-faced LAMDA alumnus. These were hardly the qualities anyone would associate with Lenny, the lumbering, feeble-minded San Joaquin Valley migrant in John Steinbeck's Depression-era yarn. The role was first played onstage in 1937 by Broderick Crawford, a beefy, beetle-browed character actor who couldn't possibly have been more different from me. But there were no Broderick Crawfords on hand at McCarter that year, so who else were they going to cast? I was half a foot taller than the next-tallest actor in the resident company, so with height as my only asset, the role of Lenny fell to me.

I'd never dreamed of playing such a part. The notion scared me to death. But I was about to learn a lesson that would echo repeatedly throughout the coming years: the most exciting acting tends to happen in roles you never thought you could play. Writers, directors, and producers tend to picture you differently than you picture yourself. They sometimes have more faith in you, and more imagination. This can be a very good thing. An actor is often much better off as the subject of other people's brainstorms. When I was cast as Lenny, I was the only person in the building who didn't think I could handle the part. Surprise! It ended up being my best performance yet.

Of Mice and Men was scheduled to open in tandem and run in repertory with George Bernard Shaw's *Pygmalion.* The Shaw was to open first. In that show, I was on more familiar ground: I was cast in the chatterbox role of Henry Higgins. The virtuosic double act of the flighty Higgins and the earthbound Lenny saddled me with a backbreaking workload. But there was more to come. The third offering of the season was to be Shakespeare's *Much Ado About Nothing,* which I would both design *and direct.* With a swiftness and confidence that verged on the foolhardy, my father had made me a major player in both the acting ensemble and the directing staff of his company.

Barely pausing to look this gift horse in the mouth, I dived right in.

So began the first official chapter of my career in American theater. It might have been titled "The Triumph of Nepotism." But if Dad had given me the meatiest, most coveted assignments of any member of his company, the other actors didn't seem to object. With fond memories of my production of *As You Like It* the year before, they warmly welcomed me back into their midst. Or at least they appeared to. In retrospect, I suspect that this courtesy was merely skin-deep and may have masked a considerable degree of show-me skepticism. I had two enormous parts to learn and a big production to design, so I wasted no time worrying about their envy or doubt. But when I lost my voice and the opening night of *Pygmalion* was cancelled (an inauspicious start to my professional career), my fellow company members could have been forgiven for feeling a sweet, collective rush of schadenfreude.

Of Mice and Men suffered no such setbacks. It was a remarkable journey from beginning to end, full of startling, revelatory moments. The production was staged by a journeyman actor-director several years my senior named Robert Blackburn. Bob had first known me years before when he was acting

for my father at the Antioch Shakespeare Festival. I was seven years old at the time. Directing me in a leading role must have been an odd adjustment for him. But if he still saw me as that skinny kid hanging around rehearsals, he managed to get past it. He rolled up his sleeves and methodically set out to transform me, piece by piece, into the hulking Lenny. He ordered up padding from the costume shop to add heft to my torso. He had me wear elevator insoles inside my heavy work boots to make me loom even larger. He prescribed a regimen of weightlifting to make my upper body ache and to slow my movements. He attached weights to my ankles to hobble my gait. As the rehearsal days passed, my thought processes gradually slowed down. So did my speech. Henry Higgins' crisp chatter gave way to Lenny's stammering plainsong drawl. I stepped out of Shaw's Wimpole Street parlor and into Steinbeck's dry Dust Bowl world. I felt like Lenny to the life.

The two shows opened within weeks of each other. They were well received by critics and crowds alike, and company morale was high as we began to perform both of them in repertory. For me, alternating between two such different roles was exhilarating, especially since the challenge had seemed so insurmountable when I had begun. Best of all, I keenly sensed that, long after I'd left school behind, I was learning more about acting than ever. Creating a believable Lenny, so distant from me in every conceivable way, had been a thrilling breakthrough, broadly expanding my sense of what I could do. But the biggest lessons I would take from *Of Mice and Men* were yet to come. And those lessons would come from an extremely unlikely source.

McCarter Theatre, you see, had student matinees. This was a tradition begun by my father a decade before, in his job as McCarter's education coordinator. The program had expanded considerably over the intervening years. Still booming today, it is now named after him, and a plaque in McCarter's lobby memorializes his early commitment to it. Then as now, thousands of high school kids from all over New Jersey arrived in bright yellow school buses throughout the season, to attend matinees of all the McCarter productions. Of the theater's yearly offerings, familiar chestnuts and high school English-class standbys tended to be the plays most heavily scheduled. One of these, of course, was *Of Mice and Men*. And we were slated to do a dozen performances of it for teenage kids.

By the time we faced our first student audience, we'd already performed the show several times for adults. Puffed up by rave reviews and loud ovations, we were pretty full of ourselves. If grown-ups are so moved by *Of Mice and Men*, we thought, just imagine the response of sensitive young kids. They will love this! There won't be a dry eye in the house! We were about to see fresh evidence of just how thoroughly actors are capable of deluding themselves.

The play, of course, is the story of Lenny and George, two itinerant fruit pickers in a work gang on a California truck farm in the bleak 1930s. The two are a symbiotic pair, traveling and working together year-round. Lenny is big, powerful, and retarded, with an infantile weakness for anything soft and furry. Like a child in his parent's care, Lenny is lost without George. His shy, childlike nature makes him a touching, gently comic creature, but it conceals a scary, almost unconscious capacity for violence. George is constantly alert to this, and has learned to control Lenny by feeding him fantasies of a farm of their own, "with rabbits." But on a couple of occasions, Lenny's violence comes out. He kills a puppy when it won't stop barking. He crushes the hand of a taunting foreman named Curly. And in a horrific scene near the end of the play, he strangles Curly's wife when she resists his innocent attempts to stroke her soft, golden hair. Knowing that Lenny is doomed once he is apprehended, George administers a nighttime mercy killing in the final seconds of the play. As Lenny kneels in a dry riverbed, dreamily intoning his ritual description of the farm they will someday own, George stands behind him and fires a bullet into his head.

It is a play full of tenderness, melancholy, and horror. The first time we performed it for kids, they thought it was screamingly funny.

And Lenny was the most hilarious thing they'd ever seen. I was literally laughed off the stage. I'd always adored the sound of laughter from an audience, and by that time I'd heard plenty of it. But I'd never heard the jeering, mocking, ear-splitting laughter of those kids. It rained down on me in torrents and drowned out the play. They laughed loudest at the moments I had considered the most delicate, tender, and moving. Rabbits? Hysterical. A dead puppy? A riot. Curly's wife? A hoot! And at the end, when George held the pistol to Lenny's head, some class clown out in the darkness shouted, "Go 'head! Shoot 'im!" and a crowd of a thousand teenagers exploded. It was a moment of horror, all right, but not the one we had been looking for.

The shrieks of laughter carried over into the curtain call. After my last grudging bow, I stormed into the wings and stood there in the darkness, shaking with humiliation and rage. As I listened to the happy jabber of the kids clambering out of the theater, I cursed every last one of them at the top of my lungs. Then an appalling thought abruptly silenced me:

I have to do this *eleven more times*!

I wouldn't have to wait long. A few days later we performed our second *Of Mice and Men* matinee for kids. I had been anticipating it with misery and dread. But at the same time a gritty determination had set in. There was no way out. I had to face the screaming mob. But this time, I was determined to avoid another cascade of taunts and guffaws. I decided to challenge the teenage audience to a kind of theatrical chess match. More by instinct than calculation, I set out to make tiny adjustments every time I came to a moment that had triggered laughs the last time around. I overlapped

cue lines, rushed through pauses, mumbled some pro-
voking phrases and buried others altogether. The process was like tiptoeing through a minefield or plugging
leaks in a dike where laughter had gushed in. Only a
few of these strategies worked. There were still plenty
of moments where the young audience got away from
me and ran roughshod over a scene like an unbroken
horse. But it happened less often. There were fewer
laughs, I was less cranky, I had a clear sense of where
the trouble spots still lay, and I had begun to savor the
challenge.

In each succeeding student matinee, I eliminated
a few more unwanted laughs. I also discovered a few
laughs that were worth keeping. Adjusting the humor,
pathos, and horror of the play became a game of strat-
egy and intrigue. Each show was an onstage laboratory
where the experiments became increasingly complex
and daring. I began to realize that kids—so spontaneous, restless, and impudent—were the ideal focus group
for a piece of theater. If you are inauthentic, excessive,
or boring onstage, an adult audience will rarely protest.
Out there in the darkness, they will cough, shift in their
seats, stare at their programs, roll their eyes, or nod
off. The only way they register their displeasure is by
merely applauding at the curtain call with slightly less
enthusiasm (when did you last hear someone actually

boo an actor?). But kids? When kids think something is dull, fake, corny, square, gauche, or inept, they'll let you know it. They'll riot. But if you can keep their attention and reach into their hearts, you know you've really achieved something.

By our last *Of Mice and Men* matinee, we had learned to cast a spell over an audience of teenage kids. They laughed all right, but only when we wanted them to. And when we wanted them quiet, you could hear a pin drop. They followed every turn of the plot, every ebb and flow of emotion. They listened intently and leaned forward in their seats to hear every syllable of every scene. All through the final terrible moments of the play, we could hear muffled sobs out in the house. And when George raised his pistol behind Lenny's head, we would once again hear the occasional cry. But now the cry was "Don't do it, George!" shouted out through tears. This time, it was a cry from the heart.

And here's the point. During those weeks, we also performed *Of Mice and Men* several times in the evening for grown-up crowds. By the end of our run, the show had greatly improved. And I believe it was the student matinees that had improved it. We hadn't learned all that much from the adults who had come to see us, but those kids had taught us volumes.

20.
Much Ado

So what was it like, working for my father? It was complicated. *He* was complicated. But because Arthur Lithgow presented himself to the world as such a warm, witty, genial man, I didn't even glimpse those complications (or begin to understand them) until I myself arrived at adulthood.

I was lucky. All through my childhood there had been far more contact between Dad and me than between most parents and children. I had been a happy hanger-on, an eager volunteer, cheap labor, and local non-Equity talent for every one of his theater companies. Like an attentive student, I had watched him at work for days at a time. He had directed me in several roles, and I had acted alongside of him. We had shared dressing rooms and makeup tables. We had been at the same cast parties and company picnics. We had played chess together backstage during shows—in a moment of shared hilarity, he even missed an entrance once as a result. In all those years, there was never a harsh word between us. I idolized him and strove constantly to please him. But despite all of that companionable warmth and congeniality (or perhaps because of it), I never quite noticed that there was a dimension missing in our father-son friendship.

It could be argued that there is an element of performance in the interpersonal dealings of all entertainers, and that, in fact, their struggle with real relationships may be what drives them to perform in the first place. Whether or not such a generalization holds up in every case, it certainly characterized my dad. When I came back from England and worked for him on a professional footing, I began to see clearly what I had only hazily perceived up until then: for all his wit, wisdom, and jocularity, both as the head of a family and the head of a theater company, he had a lonely, self-doubting side, like the dark side of the moon. This unseen dark side prevented him from fully engaging with the most important people in his life. It was almost certainly tied to the loss of his own father when he was four years old and with his black sheep status within his own family as he grew up. Consciously or unconsciously, he had devised strategies to deal with these demons. He entertained other people to lift his own spirits. Creating theater was, for him, an ingenious and exhilarating way of coping with an indefinable emptiness inside himself. As a result, he was a charming, funny, deeply likable man. But when it came to the thorny realities of life, he could be aloof to the point of invisibility.

This was the missing dimension. Unquestionably, my siblings and I had a wonderful father. He loved to read us stories, tell us jokes, show us magic tricks, and impart to us great chunks of his endless supply of quirky, eclectic knowledge. He loved to entertain us, and we loved to be entertained. But when I was growing up, there were countless moments when his paternal guidance was virtually nonexistent. The trauma of starting seventh grade in a new town halfway through the school year? Not a word of reassurance. The chaotic arrival of puberty and the onset of feverish sexual urges? Not a scrap of information. The worrisome notion of marriage at the tender age of twenty? Little more than disgruntled silence. And worse was to come: halfway through that season of plays at McCarter Theatre, I experienced the first genuine tragedy in my life. Jean gave birth to a son nine weeks early. For a few hours the little boy struggled for life and then gave up the ghost. It was a devastating loss

Pickup Before: 4/21/2012

JENCKES

4409

for both of us. My mother was deeply comforting. My little sister wept compassionate tears. Actors in the company clasped me in long, heartfelt embraces. I honestly cannot remember my father registering the slightest reaction.

In good times my father was effusively present. In hard times he was bafflingly absent. But I never judged him harshly for his abstraction and aloofness. How could I? In so many ways, he reminded me of *me*.

So what happened when this father and this son, these two genetically connected souls, faced hardship together?

When I set out to direct *Much Ado About Nothing* for my father that autumn, I had a problem on my hands. As with every production in McCarter's repertory, the play was cast entirely from members of the resident company. At its best, this system leads actors to stretch their abilities and discover new strengths. At worst they simply end up miscast. Sadly, the latter case applied to the actor playing the role of Don Pedro in my McCarter production. In the play, Don Pedro is the commanding officer of a band of returning soldiers. The role is a little thankless but extremely important, since he sets in motion the entire comic machinery of the plot. An avuncular figure with a devilish streak,

Don Pedro devises an elaborate prank to trick the caustic, quarrelsome Beatrice and Benedick into a passionate love for each other. Beatrice and Benedick are the flashiest and funniest roles in the play. But without a strong, stylish Don Pedro functioning as their impish puppet master, their comic romance doesn't stand a chance. In London the year before, Albert Finney had played the role.

My Don Pedro was no Albert Finney. I'll call him Biff Richards. Biff was a very nice guy. He was tall and rangy, with an easygoing masculinity and movie-star good looks. Rare among rep actors, he seemed destined for screen stardom. He had already gained a certain prominence in the business: everywhere he went he was recognized for a series of TV commercials he had done. In these ubiquitous ads, he smoked a stogey in dramatically lit close-up while someone else's resonant off-camera voice extolled the virtues of a certain cigar. My father had been delighted to land such a splendid figure of a man for his company, blithely disregarding Biff's meager list of stage credits. At first this enthusiasm was justified. Early in the season, Biff was broodingly effective in the role of Slim, a plainspoken mule skinner in *Of Mice and Men*. He played the part without a trace of artifice or histrionics. Neither was there a trace of nuance, variety, emotion, humor, or even energy. No one seemed especially bothered by this. No one but me, that is. I was sick with worry. After all, *Much Ado About Nothing* was just around the corner. I would be in charge, and Biff would be Don Pedro.

As we gathered for the first rehearsal of *Much Ado*, everyone felt the first-day-of-school giddiness that accompanies the start of any new production. Lots of chatter, lots of coffee, then we all took our places around a long table. I expounded at length on my concept of the play—its late-nineteenth-century setting, its airy high spirits, its sexual sparring, its Mediterranean machismo, its military culture under assault by dizzy small-town romantics. I had a word or two to say about every character, right down to the clownish members of the Night Watch (one of whom was played by an eager sixteen-year-old local boy named Christopher Reeve). I passed around reference materials and costume designs. I unveiled a model of the set. I did everything I could to project my own enthusiasm and bring the cast on board. Everyone seemed charged with anticipation.

After a break, we launched into a read-through of the text. Halfway through the first scene, the soldiers make their bravura entrance. The first of them to speak is their commanding officer Don Pedro:

Good Signior Leonato, you are come to meet your trouble: the fashion of the world is to avoid cost, and you encounter it.

Uh-oh.

These were the words of William Shakespeare as spoken by a mule skinner named Slim. A dense fog of unease slowly descended on the whole company. None of them looked up from their scripts. They didn't have to. The sound of that monotone voice told them all they needed to know: Biff was going to weigh down the show like a flatiron. But their distress was nothing compared to mine. As I listened to the poor man struggle through his lines, an appalling thought took hold of me. Not only was I saddled with Biff in the role of Don Pedro. Later in the season I was set to direct William Congreve's *The Way of the World*, a Restoration comedy that's fiendishly difficult to perform, even by trained English actors. And who was already cast in the huge role of Mirabell, the dashing leading man with the voracious libido and the quicksilver wit? This well-intentioned lug, this sodden no-talent, this latter-day Tom Mix. Biff Richards.

For the next few days of rehearsal, I struggled mightily to raise Biff's energy level and help him through the tricky syntax of Don Pedro's speeches.

Nothing worked. Every time he spoke, the energy would leak out of his scenes. As a result, the play felt like a dirigible that stubbornly refused to leave the ground. My anxiety was shared by everyone in the company—everyone, that is, except Biff. He was cheerfully oblivious to all the eye-rolling, foot-tapping, and teeth-grinding around him. He was having a fine time.

More days passed. A catastrophe was slowly unfolding in front of me. I continued to go through the motions of directing the play, but inside I was in agony. A few weeks hence I foresaw a disastrous opening night of *Much Ado About Nothing*. I couldn't even bring myself to *think* about *The Way of the World*. Something had to be done. For everyone's sake (including his own), Biff Richards had to be replaced. I had to speak to the boss. I had to go to my father. I didn't have to go far. He was playing Friar Francis.

When I broached the subject of firing Biff, Dad was hardly surprised. He convened a meeting of the directors of the season's remaining plays. After all, each of them had a vote. Biff was cast in their shows, too (albeit in much smaller roles), so whoever replaced him in my two productions would be replacing him in theirs. Within minutes the five-man meeting had reached a rueful consensus. Biff would have to go.

To replace him, we settled on an actor named John Braden. All five of us loved the idea. Johnny was spirited and reliable. He was a seasoned character man who had worked with half the actors in the company. My father left the meeting to track Johnny down by phone. Within an hour he came back with great news. He told us that he'd spoken with Johnny and found him game to join us for the rest of the season. The directing staff was delighted. We assured Dad that if he made an immediate change, we would back up his decision before the entire company.

But my father chose to proceed more gingerly. He enjoined us to secrecy. His plan was to personally deliver the bad news to Biff at the end of rehearsal on the Wednesday afternoon before Thanksgiving. John Braden would report for work at 10 a.m. on Saturday, two days later, and the cast of *Much Ado* would be introduced to their new Don Pedro. Dad reasoned that, if the news of Biff's firing got out and caused any alarm in the rest of the company, there would be forty-eight hours and the distractions of Thanksgiving to dispel it. The change would be a *fait accompli,* the production would be back on track, and the cast would lose barely a minute of rehearsal time. The directors deferred to my father's judgment. I returned to the rehearsal room with my confidence restored. My problem was solved.

A couple of days of pretense and I was home free. I was elated.

I got through to the end of the Wednesday rehearsal with affable good humor. The actors gaily dispersed for their Thanksgiving break, not remotely suspecting that one of them was getting the ax. With two full days off, most were heading home to New York. Out of the corner of my eye I watched Biff leave the room, blithely unaware that my father was waiting to intercept him. I felt bad for him but my regrets were swept away by my relief. The next day I joined the family for Thanksgiving dinner, with something new to be thankful for. On Friday I rested and regrouped after the stressful week that had gone before.

I headed for rehearsal Saturday morning bursting with renewed optimism. Most of the cast had already arrived, greeting each other in high spirits. In walked Johnny Braden. His arrival sparked surprise and excitement—everyone knew in an instant what his appearance meant, and everyone was delighted. Three or four of his old friends greeted him with hearty bear hugs and introduced him to the others. I looked on with undiluted pleasure. Everyone was happy. Things were going better than I could have hoped.

Then Biff Richards walked in.

I looked around wildly for my father. He was no-where to be seen.

Where was he?

It turned out that, unbeknownst to me, Dad had ar-rived late to the rehearsal room that Wednesday and missed his chance to speak to Biff. Unaided by cell phones or email, he had set off to overtake him. First, he had hurried over to Biff's rented Princeton apart-ment. Not finding him there, he had left a letter at the door giving him notice. Biff, meanwhile, had headed straight to the Princeton train station and had missed my father's letter. Worried that this might have hap-pened, Dad had sent a copy of the letter by messenger to Biff's New York home and had left messages with his answering service. Biff, meanwhile, had spent Thanks-giving with his girlfriend and had received neither the second letter nor the messages. Anxious that *this* might have happened, Dad had raced over to the Princeton bus stop on Saturday morning desperately hoping to intercept Biff. Biff, meanwhile, had arrived by train and had walked directly to rehearsal, where the cast, John Braden, and I had all gathered to resume work on *Much Ado About Nothing* without him.

When Biff appeared in the rehearsal room, there was a ghastly moment of confusion. A few of the actors looked darkly in my direction. I strode over to Biff, took him by the arm, and led him into an adjoining hallway. I informed him that he had been replaced and that his replacement was standing with the others in the next room. I said that my father was supposed to have broken this news to him two days before but that clearly something had gone dreadfully wrong. I attempted to explain the reasons behind the decision but my mouth was dry and my words sounded hollow. Inside my head, a voice was screaming, "Why do *I* have to do this? Where the hell is my *father*?!" Biff went pale as I spoke. Then he flushed crimson as incomprehension began to give way to humiliation and blind rage. Finally my father arrived, his face a mask of anxiety. I flatly informed him that Biff had already been told he was fired, then turned on my heels and walked off, letting him deal with Biff while I dealt with the cast. They were waiting for me in silence, poleaxed by what had just happened.

It was awful.

It wasn't so great for my dad either, of course. He must have spent the preceding two days in a state of mounting dread, and the last hour must have been worst of all. He had wanted to let Biff down easy, he had hoped to ease his company through a difficult transition, and he had intended to protect me from the wrath of a jilted actor. But for all his kindly intentions, he had made a terrible mess of things—for Biff, for Johnny, for the company, and for me. And the strangest aspect of the whole episode was his reticence. For two days, he had heard nothing from Biff to acknowledge his dismissal. By Saturday morning the silence must have been deafening. Dad must have been sick with worry. And yet in that entire time, including a long, leisurely family Thanksgiving full of laughter and festive good cheer, he hadn't betrayed a hint of that worry to me.

My father was a remarkable man of the theater. There has probably never been an American repertory theater director as civil and gentlemanly. He was gracious, generous, humorous, and deeply intelligent. He gave a leg up to hundreds of young people, signing many of them to their first professional jobs. These were qualities that made him a charismatic, beloved teacher when he was occasionally forced into that fallback line of work. I am constantly approached by people with grateful tales of my father changing their lives, in a classroom, a rehearsal studio, or a school play. He was deeply lovable, not an adjective often applied to your boss when you work in the theater.

But it is possible that his finest traits as a person were the very things that hobbled him as a theater manager. He was missing a key son-of-a-bitch chromosome, the quality that would have helped him make short work of

Biff Richards. In creating his companies, he typically sought out theater talent that was just as easygoing and companionable as he was. He valued niceness overmuch. Often he would hire happily married couples to strengthen the social dynamic of an acting troupe, ignoring the fact that one of the partners was dead weight. By the same token, he steered clear of the blazing talents, the prima donnas, the edgy, challenging stars-in-embryo that light up the stage and magnetically draw audiences into theaters. These preferences extended to actors, directors, and designers alike. He refused to believe that such ego-driven behavior was an essential element in great theater. To him, it was not worth the trade-off.

Maybe he was right. Right or wrong, it was his inescapable nature. In retrospect, I revere him for it. But in those days I was a young Oedipus. I was hungry. I was impatient. I wanted to be involved in the best theater out there. I wanted to work for the best directors. I wanted to go up against the best actors. I didn't give a damn for niceness. Bring on the tyrants! The monsters! The sons of bitches! I wanted to work for people who would settle for nothing but the best.

That McCarter season continued until the following May. My two productions came off well enough.

I acted in two or three others. My father and I had a perfectly good working relationship. We never exchanged a word about the Biff Richards mess. This was a little weird, but it never seemed to cause us undue strain. In the summer, Jean and I kept our Princeton apartment while I acted and directed at the Bucks County Playhouse, a half hour's drive away. Dad offered me another season at McCarter. He even proposed making me his associate director. I turned him down. I told him I needed to strike out on my own, to test myself in the marketplace, to audition and compete, to perform without a net. I needed to go to New York. He said he understood and he gave me his blessing, but he was probably more disappointed than he let on. By September, Jean and I had moved into an apartment on the Upper West Side of Manhattan. With her usual resourcefulness and alacrity, Jean found a job. I assumed the long-running role of an unemployed New York actor. There was work waiting for me in Princeton but I wouldn't even consider it. Was this naked ambition on my part? Was it Oedipal pigheadedness? Did I have too high an opinion of my own abilities? Too low an opinion of my father's? Whatever the reasons, I never worked for him again.

That McCarter season continued until the following May. My two productions came off well enough

21.
Reality

How stupid can you get? That September I arrived in New York City a jobless twenty-four-year-old with no savings, and no income, only to learn that I had blown my chance to collect unemployment insurance. During the long McCarter season, my canny actor friends had advised me to contrive a fake New York address and apply those eight months of rep work in New Jersey to my record of earnings as a resident of New York State. That way I could start collecting unemployment as soon as I moved into town. "Unemployment is our biggest source of income," my friends had proclaimed. "It's the closest thing there is to state support for the arts. No actor in New York can survive without it!"

But alas, I am my father's son. With the airheaded heedlessness that has always characterized my financial dealings, I barely heard their advice. I arrived in New York with no official work history whatsoever. This was an appalling strategic lapse. My first week there, I walked into the Unemployment Insurance Office at Broadway and Eighty-ninth to make a claim. I stood at a window as a weary, contemptuous woman informed me that, as far as New York State was concerned, I had never earned a salary in my life. Go out and accumulate twenty weeks of work, I was told, or you can't collect a penny. Listening to her testy, offhand words, I was seized with money panic. My knees were like water, my face was ashen, I was clammy with sweat. I had turned my back on Princeton, eager to perform without a net. And I was already in free fall.

I also had no idea how to get a job. Unemployed in New York, I was the victim of an absurd irony. A Harvard degree, a Fulbright grant, two years of study in London, and a year in my father's employ—all of this had given me a substantial head start in the profession. But it had also spoiled me rotten. I had never had to scramble for work. I had learned nothing of the gritty, fiercely competitive dogfight that is New York theater. Having abruptly left my father's protective cocoon and moved into the city, I suddenly found myself lagging far behind every other actor in town. Reality hit and it hit hard.

Jean was now a teaching specialist in Westchester County and was essentially supporting the two of us. Her job required a daily forty-minute commute up the Saw Mill River Parkway. She couldn't drive, so she got a learner's permit and set out to learn. Seated beside her in the passenger seat of our VW wagon, I became her driving in-structor. I squired her to and from her job in White Plains with my heart in my throat, five times a week. For all in-tents and purposes, this was the only work I could get. The rest of each day was spent chasing my tail in a parody of the clueless neophyte New

York actor. I printed up résumés and glossy photos, I sat through frosty meetings with B-list agents, I pored through issues of *Backstage*, I sat for hours at Equity open calls, waiting for a two-minute interview with the assistant stage manager of a show I would later learn had already been cast. Day by day I was learning the most basic hardship of the acting profession: getting rejected by people of no consequence.

On a good day I would land a commercial audition at one of the big Madison Avenue ad agencies—Young & Rubicam perhaps, or Doyle, Dane, Bernbach. This was the golden age of television advertising, with terrific character actors in stylish little mini-comedies pitching every conceivable product. To sell Alka Seltzer, a heavyset man in a T-shirt sits on the edge of his bed and moans, "I can't believe I ate the whole thing," and the sentence enters the cultural lexicon overnight. A woman in a flowing white gown sits under a tree and, when she is told that she has tasted Chiffon margarine and not butter, her response becomes a catchphrase for passive-aggressives everywhere: "It's not *nice* to fool Mother Nature!" Lay's Potato Chips even reeled in the great Bert Lahr. In a commercial for Lay's, Bert donned a hokey devil's costume and stood in red light with hellish smoke surrounding him. Holding a bag of potato chips, he comically growled Lay's famous tagline: "Bet you can't eat just one!" Ads like this were classy, clever, and extremely lucrative. Landing them was hardly where my larger ambitions lay, but I tried desperately to get one.

Bert Lahr's memorable ad may have lent an extra measure of excitement when I got an audition for another Lay's Potato Chip spot. This one was to be a parody of *Mutiny on the Bounty*. I was set to read for

the Fletcher Christian role. In the ad, Captain Bligh
tortures the crew of the ship by insisting that they be
limited to only one Lay's potato chip. "But, Captain,
that's impossible!" Mr. Christian exclaims. "Everyone
knows *you can't eat just one!*" Waiting to audition, I sat
with a gang of Christians and a band of Blighs, spot-
ting among them some of the best character men in
New York. I was called in to audition with one of the
Blighs. Scrutinizing us were the director, the writers,
the admen, and the fretful folks from Lay's. When I
read the ad copy, this group seemed to like what they
saw. I was called in again and paired with another
Bligh. Then another. By the third time through I was
performing off book, confident and cocky. Finally I
was thanked profusely by all the parties and sent on
my way.

I waited at the elevator, giddy with optimism. The
elevator doors opened, disgorging a gabbling crowd
of salty, grizzled men in bell bottoms, striped nauti-
cal T-shirts, and tam o'shanters. One had an eye-patch,
another clenched a corncob pipe in his mouth. These
were the actors auditioning for the *Bounty's* crew,
summoned from one floor below. Their entrance was
hilarious, their high spirits infectious. I rode the elevator to the ground floor, laughing out loud the whole
way. I stepped out of the building and onto Madison

Avenue, golden in the midday autumn light. "I got the gig!" I thought to myself. "I'm sure of it!"

But no. I didn't get it.

I didn't get any others, either. The same story was repeated fifty times that year. I just couldn't land a commercial. I began to think that something else was at work, that subconsciously I didn't really want these jobs, that I thought they were beneath me, and that all those admen and their clients sensed my veiled contempt. I tried to cultivate my own indifference, to persuade myself that being turned down for commercials was a good thing. This way, I figured, I could pretend to stand on principle. I could loftily claim, for the rest of my life, that, no, I don't *do* commercials. No one need ever know how hard I tried to get them. Of course this comforting rationale did not prevent me years later from hawking insurance companies, credit cards, telephone services, and Campbell's Soup on TV with the best of them. It's easy to stay uncorrupted, you see, if you're never asked.

But if no jobs came my way, I was far from discouraged—at least at first. New York was full of old friends, most of them in the same boat I was in. They hailed from all walks of my recent life: Harvard, LAMDA, Ohio Shakespeare, McCarter repertory, Bucks County Playhouse, Highfield Summer Theatre, even The

Great Road Players (my friendship with Paul Zimet survived that debacle). All of us lived on the cheap and dealt with the futile pursuit of work with fatalistic gallows humor. Like them, I was determined to stay positive. I may have had no income, but to fend off gloom I kept myself frenetically busy. I did satirical skits for the radical radio station WBAI-FM. I acted in an off-off-Broadway workshop production in a church basement. I directed a completely incomprehensible new play in a studio on East Fourth Street where, at each performance, the five actors outnumbered the audience. I tried to convince myself that all of this was leading somewhere, but it was becoming a hard sell. I was just about to admit defeat, to return to McCarter Theatre with my tail between my legs and direct a production of *Macbeth* for my father, when something amazing happened.

I got a movie.

22.
Induced Insecurity

A movie?! Until that moment, I never dreamed I would ever be in a movie. Acting in movies was simply outside the context of my life. From before I could even remember, acting on the stage was the only acting I had ever known. Beyond the odd commercial or soap opera, none of the actors I had ever worked with had appeared on a screen. I loved movies, of course. Like anyone else, I had my favorite movie stars, and going to the movies was part of the rhythm of my life. But movie actors struck me as a breed apart. To me, it seemed they worked in a different profession. I never pictured myself in their company. I never envied them, coveted their roles, or thought I could do any better.

So imagine my astonishment when I got a phone call out of the blue asking me to come to a swanky townhouse in the East Sixties and interview for a major role in a Hollywood film. For months I had been pounding the New York pavements, looking for an open door into the acting game outside of the protective custody of my father. I had struggled with the ego-bruising reality that, apart from him, no one wanted to hire me for a paid acting job. And now a movie director was coming after *me.* How did this happen?

The seeds had been planted years before. By a sublime irony, it turns out that my good fortune had had its beginnings at the lowest point in my fledgling professional life. In the disastrous summer of The Great Road Players, a young filmmaker named Brian De Palma came down to Princeton to see his old Columbia buddies in that long-ago production of Molière one-act farces. I had directed the show and performed the part of a loony philosopher, maniacally spouting a stream of philosophical gobbledygook. I remember being onstage that evening and hearing a wild cackle rising above the titters of the sparse audience. That cackle was Brian De Palma. When I met him briefly after the play he was effusive in his praise; but with the weight of the world on my shoulders, his compliments barely registered. I never heard of him again until a few years later when his anarchic low-budget film comedies *Greetings* and *Hi, Mom!* came out.

I had forgotten Brian, but he had not forgotten me. And when another young filmmaker named Paul Williams was looking for someone to play a patrician Harvard undergraduate dope dealer, Brian De Palma told him to track me down. It didn't hurt that Williams was a Harvard alumnus himself and remembered my glory days on the stage of the Loeb Drama Center. These two fleeting connections from my past steered me to that townhouse and got me that role. It was not the last of Brian De Palma's favors. In the years to come he was to hire me more often than any other film director. By then he had become known as "the Master of the Macabre." Each time he hired me, I was his villain. In three of his classic psychological suspense thrillers, I was the psychological suspense.

And what about the movie itself?

Does *Dealing: Or the Berkeley-to-Boston Forty-Brick Lost-Bag Blues* ring a bell? Probably not. You will find almost nobody who has seen or even remembers the title of my first film. But for me it was huge. It introduced me to the magical, mysterious, nutty world of filmmaking. On location in Toronto within two weeks of that townhouse meeting, all the rigorous rules and protocols of theater were tossed out the window. For me, making a movie was like entering an altered state of consciousness. This was particularly true of *Dealing*, since the subject of the film and the process of making it were both suffused with the smell of pot smoke. *Easy Rider* had exploded on the scene only a year before, and the Hollywood studios were scrambling to duplicate its runaway success. Every one of them was throwing money at stoner filmmakers with reckless abandon. *Dealing* was Warner Brothers' entry in this drug-addled cinema horse race. I'd never made a movie and I'd never been much of a pot smoker, so the entire *Dealing* enterprise was almost surreally new.

Any stage actor recruited into films has shared my experience of the first time on a movie set. Nobody tells you *anything*. Who knew that a two-minute scene could take ten hours to shoot? Who knew that you would perform it sixty times (half of them off-camera) before it was in the can? Who knew the difference between masters, panning shots, two-shots, over-the-shoulders, and close-ups? Who knew the precise roles of operators, focus-pullers, key grips, dolly grips, gaffers, and best boys? Who knew the particular challenge of husbanding your physical and emotional resources, and keeping yourself fresh and spontaneous until your very last shot of the day? Typically the novice actor arrives on the set and is promptly flung into the deep end, left to discover all these mysteries for himself. On *Dealing*, this precipitous learning curve made me feel like I was learning the craft of acting all over again, and in the slow learners' group at that. Never the most confident of actors, I found myself in the grips of an insecurity as acute as a chronic low-level fever.

My big breakthrough came when I realized that insecurity is the prime currency of film acting. In a sense, induced insecurity is exactly what you strive for. This was a major shift from what I was used to. In theater acting, you work to overcome your insecurities. In weeks of exhaustive rehearsals you carefully craft a performance, polishing it like a gemstone. You work at it until you're finally "secure" in your role. You rely on technique to sustain you and keep you consistent over the length of a run. That run can be weeks, months, or even years long. Your challenge is to sustain the illusion of the first time, for yourself and for the audience, from the first performance to the last.

In the movies, you only need to achieve that illusion *once* and you're given lots of chances to get it right. When shooting a single scene, the camera captures the trial-and-error process that a stage actor goes through during weeks of rehearsals. Only a tiny fraction of what's shot eventually appears on film. In the course of several takes, all sorts of happy accidents can happen in front of the camera, completely uncalculated. The best of these accidents are like lightning in a bottle. They are flashes of artless reality born of your induced insecurity—your fear, your pain, your longing, your nervous laughter. They have a close-up truth that can't be faked. Hence, when you're shooting a film you must recklessly put your emotions into play. You must induce your own insecurity, ignoring all constraint (a plausible explanation for the on-set misbehavior of so many film and TV actors, luridly recounted by the tabloid media). Emotional accidents are a film actor's most potent tools. You don't actually need a stage actor's skills to achieve them. You just need the willingness to let accidents happen and enough technique to put them to work. Indeed, the more polished your performance the more you risk losing its truthfulness. Happy accidents are at the heart of the best film acting. You offer them up to a filmmaker and hope that he or she will make good use of them. And as a general rule, those accidents make up your best work on film.

Dealing was not my best work on film. It was a listless caper movie, lacking both comedy and suspense. A caustic viewer might have remarked that everyone involved had smoked a little too much weed. This did not dissuade me from thinking that we had made a masterpiece, destined for blinding success. That it opened to resounding silence and disappeared without a trace was a lesson that I would learn over and over again in the years to come: when you're shooting a movie, you really don't know what you're doing. The process of making a film has a way of persuading you that it's going to be great, often against all evidence to the contrary. Work that hard on something and it just *has* to be good, right? Not necessarily.

With movies, you're curiously unmoored from reality. While you're shooting, you have no audience on hand to hold you to their demanding standards and validate your work. You're flying blind. How else do you explain so many bad films by so many good filmmakers and so many bad performances by good actors? Of the many films I've done, a painfully small number have been as successful as I had expected them to be, or even as good. And the rule applies in reverse. In the mid-eighties I did five days of shooting on location in Nebraska on a film that was clearly out of control and destined for obscurity. How was I to know that it would be hands down the best film I have ever appeared in? It was called *Terms of Endearment*.

But if *Dealing* was not the second coming of *Easy Rider*, it delivered in other areas. I gained my sea legs on a movie set (once the paranoia wore off). I befriended a great character actor named Charlie Durning (with whom I would twice compete for an Oscar). I got myself an agent (the William Morris Agency assigned me a rookie named Rick Nicita, who would represent me for the next thirty-five years). And I got my first look at the West Coast. Because I needed to loop a couple of scenes during postproduction, I was flown out to Los Angeles by Warner Brothers. I parlayed my round-trip plane ticket into a month-long visit and ventured into yet another undreamt-of world. For the first time I beheld the sun-baked, pastel-tinted, tacky, wacky, glorious lotusland called Hollywood.

If the learning curve on the set of *Dealing* was steep, in Hollywood it was downright vertiginous. Not since those traumatic days as the new kid in school had I felt so disoriented and out of place. I had barely adjusted to tough, abrasive New York City, and here was a scene that was entirely different in every conceivable way—languorous, narcissistic, and cynical, with feigned sincerity raised to the level of a fine art. But if the world of Hollywood confused and unbalanced me, I didn't dislike it. Indeed, I plunged into it with the zeal of a convert. I eagerly shook hands with my cabal of broadly smiling new William Morris agents. I sat stoned on Trancas Beach with the West Coast *Dealing* contingent. I drank vodka at poolside at the Sunset Marquis with all the other deracinated and paranoid visiting New York actors. I even had lunch with Brian De Palma and Raquel Welch at the Polo Lounge of the Beverly Hills Hotel as part of Brian's (failed) plot to get me approved for a movie he ended up not directing. *Me?* Playing comedy sex scenes with *Raquel Welch?* Had the world gone crazy? It was as if I had fallen down the rabbit hole.

I thanked my lucky stars for my sister Robin. Within a few years of her graduation from Barnard, she had married an artist named Tim Rudnick. They had settled down in Tim's home town of Los Angeles. Robin would soon begin a teaching career there which, years later, would place her at the head of arts education throughout the vast L.A. school system. But for now she and Tim were living with their baby daughter Anya in a bungalow-style house near Venice Beach, savoring the last heady days of the hippie era. During my dreamlike sojourn in Hollywood, they opened their home to me and showed me the essential Los Angeles as only natives can. If they hadn't been there to lend a dose of reality to those dizzying days, I would have been a goner.

My Hollywood month passed in a flash, like the sweep of a klieg light outside a movie premiere. Despite the unending stream of shallow praise and the glib promises of fame and fortune from a whole army of agents, casting directors, and studio flacks, I never got a whisper of work. This didn't really bother me. I hadn't expected much, and no role had appeared that I really wanted. Indeed, I would have been much more surprised if somebody *had* hired me. In that brief month I never got beyond the feeling that I didn't really belong out there. Except for some wonderful times hanging out with Robin and her family, it had been an arid, desolate time, my self-respect ebbing away by the hour. I missed New York, I missed my wife, and I was ready to go home.

Then finally something happened. Two days before my plane was scheduled to depart, William Morris called. They wanted me to meet a director for a film. They told me his name. My heart leaped. He was Terrence Malick, the brooding genius whose daring first film, *Badlands*, was already causing a tremendous stir, even before being released. Clearly this was a dazzling new talent for Hollywood to reckon with. But I had an even bigger reason to be excited. Terry had been a friend at Harvard and a fellow resident of Adams House, my undergraduate dorm. A taciturn Texan with a Buddha-like air and a razor-sharp mind, he studied philosophy at Harvard and Oxford, and taught it at MIT. Even among Harvard brainiacs, Terry had been regarded with awe verging on reverence. But despite his aura of complex brilliance, he had always been a gushing fan of my acting. I hadn't seen him since our Harvard days, but I had heard the surprising news that he had changed gears and become a filmmaker. He was already moving on to his next film, called *Days of Heaven*. It would be a period piece set in the vast grain fields of the American plains. It would feature a romantic triangle of which one character was a severe, silent homesteader. Terry was looking for the right actor for this part, and he wanted to meet with me.

I showed up for my 5 p.m. appointment in the offices of William Morris breathless with anticipation. I sat in a lobby with two or three other actors (severe, silent types), waiting to meet with Terry. Having heard that I'd arrived, he suddenly bolted out of an office and greeted me with a completely uncharacteristic bear hug.

"The hell with this!" he cried. "Let's not sit in an office! I'm housesitting for George Segal at his place in Coldwater Canyon. Come on over for a drink at, whaddya think, six-thirty? Then let's go someplace for supper!"

The other actors looked on balefully. An assistant scribbled directions for me and set about booking a table at Scandia on Sunset Boulevard. Terry went back into the office to wrap up his interviews and I took off, avoiding eye contact with any of my dour rivals. I drove around for an hour through the leafy avenues of Beverly Hills north of Sunset, browsing the garish mansions as if they were so many baroque paintings in a museum. It was an unimaginable display of affluence. At the appointed time, I pulled up to George Segal's Tudor-style manor and rang the bell at the massive wooden door. Terry lugged the door open and greeted me again, as warmly as the first time. He led me into a spacious, gorgeously appointed living room where a handsome German shepherd lolled on the ample sofa. Terry told me to pour myself a drink and to give him ten minutes. He was just finishing a meeting with his casting director, Lynn Stalmaster, in the next room. When he was done, he said, he would bring Lynn out and introduce us.

Lynn Stalmaster! I didn't know much about Hollywood, but I knew about him. The dean of movie casting directors, Stalmaster's name was attached to several of the best films the industry had produced in recent years, the closest thing there was to a superstar in his arcane field. And in a few minutes, Terrence Malick, the hottest young director in town, was going to squire him in to meet me, in the living room of George Segal's house. I poured myself a crystal tumbler of scotch and settled into the soft cushions of the sofa, stroking the German shepherd affectionately like the lord of the manor. This was unbelievable. I had reached the sensual core of Hollywood success. I had drawn a full house. All I had to do was play my cards right.

Terry strode in. With him was Lynn Stalmaster, a slight, spiffy man in white shoes, white pants, and an aqua shirt.

"Lynn," said Terry, "I want you to meet John Lithgow. He's *the best actor I've ever seen in my life.*"

My heart swelled. The whiskey shot pleasurably to my brain. I goofily deflected the lavish compliment. Lynn Stalmaster was impassive.

"So what have you been doing recently?" he asked blandly.

I had heard this question forty times in the past month. It was the standard casting directors' opening. The information requested was secondary. Mainly they just wanted to see what happened when you actually talked. It was the equivalent of a horse breeder examining the teeth of a thoroughbred. I launched into my practiced reply, exuding suavity and confidence.

"Well, there's *Dealing*, of course. I'm out here doing some ADR for it and meeting a few people, but mostly

I've been doing theater in New York, blahblahblah-blahblah . . ."

Terry beamed with pride, like the owner of a prize-winning whippet at a dog show. Stalmaster stared at my eyes implacably. As I gabbled on, my mind raced with dreams of glory and with the pragmatic matter of whether I could change my flight back to New York without paying a penalty. Things couldn't possibly have been going better.

And then something horrible happened. The German shepherd lumbered off the sofa and walked to my side, hungry for more affection. He batted my hand with his snout and I scratched his ear, stupidly thinking that this manly gesture would only enhance my performance. The dog rubbed his shoulder against my knee. I continued my patter. Terry and Lynn continued to listen and nod, gazing at me attentively at eye level. The dog became more ardent. Clearly I had befriended him far too much. He wrapped his two front legs around my thigh and with all his considerable strength proceeded to hump against it. His slick pink phallus made an alarming appearance. My efforts to push him off seemed only to heighten his ardor. Through all of this I kept on talking, but my polished narrative became halting and fragmented, and my forehead bubbled with sweat. Both men seemed totally oblivious to the humping dog. Their expressions turned quizzical, then concerned as if they worried that perhaps I had suddenly taken sick.

Terry finally took notice of the sex-mad canine's rape attempt and summoned a houseboy to haul him out of the room, the retreating dog scrabbling madly along the marble tiles of the foyer. The hound was gone but I was rubble. My dream casting session had ended up a nightmare. Lynn Stalmaster excused himself, unimpressed. Terry ushered him out with the air of a man who had given a broken toy to a child. Later that evening, dinner at Scandia involved six other strangers. I contributed barely a sentence to their manic babble. I drank too much and drove back to Venice Beach, weaving along the Santa Monica Freeway in a state of woozy self-disgust. Two days later I was on a plane back to New York with the strong sense that I never should have left in the first place. As for *Days of Heaven*, it came out seven years later. By that time I had long since repaired the Hollywood-inflicted dents in my battered ego. The film was magnificent, yet more evidence of the brilliance of my old friend Terry Malick. My part was beautifully played by the severe, silent playwright Sam Shepard. Up until then he had never acted in a movie in his life.

23.

A Fork in the Road

I was back in New York. *Dealing* was behind me and
I had descended from the hallucinatory ether of Hollywood. I'd come home to no work and no prospects, as
if none of the heady promise of the movies had ever
existed. And this time, unemployment brought a whole
new set of complications. My wife was pregnant.

A pregnancy has a way of grabbing your attention. It
was a cause for celebration, of course, and for enormous
relief as well, since we had barely recovered from the
loss of our firstborn child. But Jean's pregnancy also
considerably ratcheted up my anxieties about money
and jobs. The two of us had been living simply in a
small apartment at West End Avenue and One Hun-
dredth Street. We had good friends, good times, and
a few occasional inexpensive luxuries. Our economic

status was far from dire. But we were ill-prepared for parenthood. Our Upper West Side life was entirely supported by Jean's modest salary. In an era that predated the concept of paid maternity leave, that salary would shortly disappear. And besides that scary prospect, our one-bedroom home barely accommodated the two of us, let alone a family of three. The gauzy unreality of moviemaking quickly gave way to the hard facts of joblessness and impending fatherhood. I *had* to find some work.

By this time I was a little more seasoned in the New York job market. I had an agent. I knew some key casting directors. I'd learned not to bother with *Backstage* and Equity open calls. But in terms of actual results, things hadn't gotten any better since I'd traveled north for my movie and west for my Hollywood baptism. Sifting through my own history of that period, it is startling to recall that, in over two years, I never got a single acting job in New York City. Movie meetings were infrequent and fruitless. Ad-agency clients continued to spurn me. New York theater, on Broadway and off, was a closed shop. I couldn't even manage the most likely entry-level job: despite my LAMDA pedigree and all the Shakespeare in my lengthy résumé (or perhaps because of them), Joe Papp's New York Shakespeare Festival showed no interest. My hardships, of course, were not unique. Acting jobs in New York were hardly abundant. They never are. But the ones that came along always went to a tiny cadre of actors who never seemed to be out of work. Try as I would, I couldn't break into that circle. Envy and disappointment clung to me like a bad smell.

So I took stock and began to think strategically. I looked farther afield. I made a short list of all the notable regional theater companies within striking distance of New York City. The list included Arena Stage in Washington, D.C.; the Shakespeare Festival in Stratford, Ontario; Long Wharf Theatre in New Haven, Connecticut; and several others. McCarter Theatre was the only one I left out (I was determined not to swim back to that nepotistic safe haven). To each of the targeted companies, I sent a picture and a résumé. I also included a cover letter. It stated that I was heading their way, that I would like a general audition, and that while I was there I would like to buy a ticket for their current production. Intent on not seeming too eager, I waited for a week after I calculated that each letter had arrived. Then I telephoned the office of each theater's artistic director to follow up on the letter. I rarely spoke to this person, but in most cases there was someone on the staff who would make arrangements for me. Off I would go in my aging VW station wagon, trying my best to treat each long-shot outing as a colorful adventure. Some of them were major treks (it took me nine hours to reach southwestern Ontario), and none of them yielded immediate results. But I met a lot of directors and I saw some pretty good theater. And, most important, the trips left me with the feeling that I was doing something, *something* to plant a seed and make a green shoot sprout in the unyielding soil of the acting profession.

In between these out-of-town jaunts, I continued to scratch around for other ways to make a little cash. A bunch of Princeton undergraduates hired me to stage a Mozart chamber opera for $500 (which was quickly swallowed up by gas and tolls on the New Jersey Turnpike). I solicited group sales on commission for dance programs at the Brooklyn Academy of Music (I never sold a single ticket). With two friends, I cooked up a moneymaking scheme to perform Chekhov's one-act farce *The Marriage Proposal* in city schools (we performed it exactly once, for no pay). I even got my medallion and tried my hand at driving a taxi (long enough to discover that nobody measuring six-foot-four could sit in the front seat of a New York City cab for a ten-hour stretch without crippling himself for life). And on what was possibly the cheesiest program ever produced in the early days of cable television, I earned fifty dollars for narrating a TV tour of Robert Redford's home in the mountains of Utah. Oh, the indignity!

Such desperate measures yielded meager returns and cost me dearly in ways that had nothing to do with money. As Jean drew closer and closer to her due date, my confidence and self-esteem were trickling away. At what should have been our most hopeful, life-embracing moment, I was drooping with pessimism. But if nothing else, I was at least learning about the inane vicissitudes of my chosen profession: all of this desolate demi-prostitution was happening within months of sipping whiskey in George Segal's living room and having lunch at the Polo Lounge with Raquel Welch.

Finally, three months before the baby was due to arrive, I got a proper job. But, true to the nutty illogic of show business, it wasn't the job I was looking for. I was asked to direct a play. A year before, I had put a director's résumé into circulation. I had sent it to many of the very same regional theaters I had since approached for acting work. One day I got a call from a man named John Stix. An intense little gnome with a mane of wiry gray hair, Stix was the artistic director of Baltimore's Center Stage. My year-old director's résumé had caught his attention. For a December slot

in his upcoming season, he had scheduled *The Beaux'*
Stratagem, a late Restoration comedy by George Far-
quhar. When Stix had perused my credits on the résumé, *The Way of the World* at McCarter had jumped
off the page. It placed me on a very short list of American directors who had directed a Restoration comedy.
So Stix summoned me to his dingy New York office
on the dark and dusty top floor of the Lyceum Theatre on Forty-fifth Street. At the end of an interview
punctuated by long, inscrutable pauses, he hired me
on the spot. I packed my bags for a month-long stay,
said goodbye to my pregnant wife, took a train south
from Penn Station, and for the first time acquainted
myself with the city of Baltimore, Maryland, and with
the resident company of its estimable little repertory
theater.

As it turned out, *The Beaux' Stratagem* was a tremendous success, both for Center Stage and for me
personally. It was the first time I had marshaled the
forces of a large professional artistic staff under some
aegis other than my father's. Working with excellent
costume, lighting, and set designers, I devised a show
that managed to be both spare and lavish, both contemporary and true to its period. In the course of four
weeks of rehearsal, I rushed the cast through a brisk
boot camp of Restoration language and high style, and

worked closely with them to invent all sorts of bawdy stage business. The finished product was a Hogarth painting brought to life, with all the hilarity and high spirits of Tony Richardson's great film version of *Tom Jones*. It burst upon bleak, wintry Baltimore like a brightly colored Christmas present (the review in the *Baltimore Sun* was every bit as glowing as my own).

The play features a classic comedy plot involving a clash of landed English aristocrats and their rustic, countrified neighbors. To project this duality I came up with a nifty theatrical device, thrilling in its simplicity. The setting was a bare, raked platform with a symmetrical seventeenth-century pattern covering its floor. Suspended above this platform were four large panels, each mounted vertically on a pivoting central axis. One side of each panel was covered with rough-hewn planks. On the other side were elegantly carved bas-relief moldings in the style of Grinling Gibbons. Every time the setting shifted between rustic and aristocratic, the panels would swivel 180 degrees and the stage would be transformed in an instant. Simultaneously members of the cast would sweep across the platform, changing the furnishings and props as they went, to a lush torrent of Henry Purcell's incidental theater music. Often these set changes would fold right into the action. For example, when highwaymen stormed the manor house, the actors changing the furniture would shriek out "Thieves! Thieves!" as they rushed wildly on and off the stage in their nightclothes.

The Baltimore audiences lapped up the production, the Center Stage board was ecstatic, and even the taciturn John Stix managed a furtive smile. As for the actors, they were in heaven. For them, the show was pure pleasure. They even loved doing the set changes. Incredibly, several of them even volunteered to stand in the darkness backstage and man the long poles that made the big panels swivel. Onstage, their performances were uniformly fine—expert, witty, and heartfelt. The names Wil Love, Henry Strozier, and Fran Brill may have rung few bells in New York theater circles, but their wonderful work in *The Beaux' Stratagem* was ample evidence of the talent and commitment of American rep actors, happily toiling away in the vineyards.

But on the morning after our opening night I was in a lousy mood. I sat on the train heading back to New York with a heavy heart. I was in the grips of postpartum blues. I'd labored through a month of hard work and worry, savored a single evening's flash of triumph, and then relinquished to the actors the fun of performing the show. The production belonged to them now. They no longer needed me. Indeed, when I revisited the show a few weeks later, they were demonstrably uninterested when I offered them my notes. They had each other and their audience. I was no longer a part of the equation. Far from being welcomed back into the fold, I was now a meddling uncle, fondly remembered but merely tolerated and indulged. Every time I've directed a play, this phenomenon has left me with the same sharp sensation of letdown and loss. I've always suspected that most stage directors go through some version of this peculiar actor-envy whenever they launch a production and depart the scene. But surely they never feel it as keenly as I. After all, they're not actors.

But when my work was done in Baltimore, there was plenty to come home to. A month after the play opened, my son Ian was born. All the anxiety and feverish striving of the previous months were instantly eclipsed by that one gigantic event. There is no clearer demarcation in a man's life than the birth of his first child. It is the bright line between not being and being a father. I felt as if a new dimension had been added to my being, as if I had cast a shadow for the first time. The magnitude of the moment was not lost on me. I was throttled with a complex mix of intense emotions, ranging from ecstatic joy at Ian's arrival to heart-stopping fear that something might happen to him. It was the best possible cure for an unemployed actor's solipsistic self-absorption: suddenly there was another person in my world more important to me than I was to myself.

Jean had left her job to care for the baby, and almost instantly we began to feel the economic pinch. Despite the deep sense of fulfillment at Ian's birth, the pressure to provide was like a steadily building drumbeat in the soundtrack of my life. True, I had gained perspective and a clearer sense of priorities. My career anxieties were now less about me and more about my family. But those anxieties were still there, and more crippling than ever. The sizzle of the city had turned to a sputter. Its economy was dire. Half the theaters on Broadway were dark. My prospects had never been bleaker. *Dealing* and *The Beaux' Stratagem* had begun to feel like aberrant blips in a desolate stretch of joblessness. And as if all this were not enough of a burden, parenthood was *hard*. For all its joys, caring for a baby in our tiny apartment was draining for both of us. Sleep deprivation left us bleary-eyed and bone-sore. But every morning I shook off my fatigue and hit the streets, hustling work with redoubled determination.

Though hardly a lifesaver, a curious job did present itself. Since moving to New York, I had sporadically volunteered at radio station WBAI-FM, performing sketch comedy and radio drama with a gang of similarly out-of-work actor friends. The station's management now offered me a steady (if part-time) job, doing more of the same. This meant writing and producing whatever I liked, on my own schedule. If the job was unlikely to advance my fortunes much in the entertainment business, at least it promised an intriguing challenge, a new creative direction, and a little anarchic fun. Most important, I would be paid. I was offered the lordly salary of $115 a week. I leaped at it.

These were the salad days for WBAI. Dubbed "an anarchist's circus" by the *New York Times*, the station was perfectly in tune with the activist cacophony of the radical left in the early seventies. Late night hosts like Steve Post, Bob Fass, and Larry Josephson gave voice to the caustic spirit of the city's lefty fringe. The staff was brilliant, cynical, contentious, and frequently stoned. In their midst, I was a goose among grackles, but from my first day there I had a ball. Before I knew it, I was doing full-time work for my part-time salary. I spent hours in the station's cluttered, dimly lit studios, housed in a rambling deconsecrated church in the East Sixties. Fueled by the manic energy of my stoned-out sound engineers, I churned out hours of programming for the station's unseen audience of New York hipsters.

Stealing blatantly from *Beyond the Fringe*, *The Goon Show*, and *Firesign Theatre*, I cooked up daffy parodies of game shows, newscasts, beer ads, NASA astronauts, Chekhov, Mister Rogers, and Martin Buber (because of his funny name). I recruited actor friends to record plays by Shakespeare, Shaw, Wilde, and Thomas Middleton. I perfected a dead-on audio impersonation of Richard Nixon and aped him mercilessly. Everything I did was flung out over the airwaves with never a word of editorial input or constraint.

Our mother lode, of course, was political satire. I had never been very vocal politically (nor have I ever been since), but the everyday politics of that era presented me with a subject too good to resist. I would arrive in the morning with a couple of willing, unpaid confederates. We would step over to the Reuters teletype in the station's newsroom and pore over the printed pages that were rattling out of it. I would always have a couple of half-baked comedy sketches in hand, but on a good day I would jettison them in favor of up-to-the minute satirical commentary on the day's events, fed to us by Reuters.

Our finest (or most infamous) moment came on May 2, 1972. We arrived at the station that morning and headed to the teletype. A major item of breaking news supercharged us. J. Edgar Hoover, the longtime head of the FBI, had died in his sleep. Hated and feared by every major public figure, the despicable Hoover had been miraculously transformed overnight into a beloved national hero in the public press. Reverential tributes were pouring in from statesmen of all stripes, every one of whom Hoover had terrorized with compromising information about their private lives, right up until the night before. The hypocrisy of these tributes elated us. We immediately set about providing a different perspective. We would create our own version of a J. Edgar Hoover memorial tribute, and we would put it on the radio.

As we saw it, Hoover was a creature of a bygone era. So to memorialize him we hit on the notion of parodying a 1940s "News on the March" featurette. Working at a feverish pace, we dragooned people from all over the station. We put the sound engineers to work collecting audio effects and heroic forties-era music. We hit up the news staff for arcane biographical facts. These guerrilla journalists were uncannily well-versed in all sorts of damning information about Hoover that the public was not to learn about for years—his ruthless use of blackmail, his racism, his drunkenness, his prurience, his gay companion Clyde Tolson, even his transvestitism. Armed with all of this, we wrote a five-minute script that raced from scene to lurid scene of

Hoover's shady life, mercilessly lambasting him while maintaining a gleefully ironic tone of public canonization. And the title for our venomous little screed? "J. Edgar: A Desecration of the Memory of J. Edgar Hoover."

The WBAI staff was so thrilled with the sketch that they chose to air it at 6:25 p.m., immediately preceding their evening newscast. Seconds after it ended, the actual news came on. The lead story, of course, was Hoover's death. It was announced in sober tones not unlike my stentorian narration of the "News on the March" parody that had gone before. The effect was like an underground nuclear blast. Until that moment I had never had a sense that anyone out in the world was actually listening to anything I produced. When you perform on the radio, you hear neither cheers nor jeers. But that night I found out just how far my voice reached. For several hours after the Hoover piece hit the airwaves, the switchboard at the station was lit up like Chinese New Year's. We had managed to scandalize hundreds of thousands of people. A huge segment of WBAI's listenership, the most left-wing audience in the entire nation, was appalled. To our merry band of newsroom anarchists, this was an undiluted triumph. They celebrated as if their soccer team had just won the World Cup.

The episode was the high point of my WBAI days and typified the whole crazy enterprise—raucous, reckless, politically charged, a little dangerous, and deliriously fun.

But $115 a week?!

Despite all the high times at the station, I knew that they weren't meant to last. In terms of the hard realities of life, my low-paid radio job was barely better than unemployment. It was leading me nowhere professionally, it was never going to sustain my family, and in spite of its part-time status, it was affording me precious little time at home with my wife and baby son. At WBAI, I was just marking time until something better came along. And late that spring, just as I was reaching the end of my tether, something better *did* come along. John Stix called again.

Apparently *The Beaux' Stratagem* had left its mark. On the strength of its success, Baltimore Center Stage had created the post of associate artistic director and was offering it to me. Although I didn't betray the fact to Stix, I was less than ecstatic about the offer. It meant a long-term commitment to life in Baltimore and a partnership with an enigmatic man with whom I'd had an oddly strained professional relationship. Worst of all, I was being asked to give up on acting. Stix intended for me to co-manage the company with him and direct at least two productions a year. It was clear to me that he regarded my lingering acting ambitions as whimsical at best and a distraction from my intended job definition. Over the years I had taken a lot of pleasure and pride in directing. I'd had a lot of success and felt convinced of my own abilities. Associate artistic director was a title that virtually guaranteed a quick ascendancy and a blooming career. But was I ready to throw in the towel as an actor? Could I embrace a future in the theater devoid of the joy of performing? I wasn't sure.

I had a child. My wife had supported me long enough. I was broke. I took the job.

Everyone at Center Stage was delighted. Jean was game. A press release was sent to the *Baltimore Sun* and a glowing article appeared. Packets arrived describing the pleasures of Baltimore life. Real estate agents sent apartment listings and condo brochures. Stix ran titles by me for the following season's productions. I did my best to put an enthusiastic face on all my dealings with him and the rest of the Center Stage staff. Inside I struggled to persuade myself that, in time, the enthusiasm would be genuine.

I gave my notice at WBAI. On my last day at the station, a couple of wags from the news department asked me to record a radio sketch they'd written. It was based on a trifling news item from the night before.

The sketch was a parody of the old *Mission: Impossible* TV show. It used that show's familiar musical theme and its famous catchphrase: "Your mission, should you accept it . . ." The script featured a single voice, heard over the telephone. It was the voice of Attorney General John Mitchell. In the role of Mitchell, I instructed a silent operative to break into the offices of the Democratic National Committee in Washington, D.C. The offices were in a building called the Watergate. I didn't know it at the time, but that morning was the dawn of the best year for satire in the history of American politics. But the sketch was the last piece of political satire I ever did. I was on my way to Baltimore.

I never got there. A few weeks later I received yet another phone call. I recognized the cheerful voice. It belonged to a man named Arvin Brown. I sensed immediately that one of the seeds I had planted months before on one of my meandering theater junkets had finally sprouted. Arvin Brown was offering me an acting job. This time it was a job that I unequivocally wanted. Arvin was the director of New Haven's Long Wharf Theatre. Of all the theaters I'd sought out in my travels that year, Long Wharf was the one where I most wanted to work. Under Arvin's leadership, the theater had routinely produced shows that were lavishly praised in the New York press. When I'd auditioned for him, I'd found him to be funny, sweet-natured, smart, and self-possessed. On that visit, I'd seen his brilliant production of *The Iceman Cometh*, Eugene O'Neill's monumental portrait of New York dead-enders and alcoholics. In Arvin's hands the play had shimmered with humor and passion, and its four hours had sped by. I sat in the audience that night and ached to climb up on the stage and join that company of marvelous actors.

And now Arvin Brown was inviting me to do just that. He was offering me a season of six roles in six terrific plays. I told him I would get right back to him. Within twenty minutes I abruptly changed the entire course of my life. I called Center Stage and, withstanding a blast of vindictive fury on the other end of the line, I withdrew from its associate artistic directorship. I called back Arvin and told him he had hired a grateful actor. In the weeks to come, Jean and I gave up our New York apartment. We relocated to Branford, Connecticut. I became a member of the Long Wharf Theatre's resident company. I was perfectly prepared to work there for the rest of my life. But this was not to be. Long Wharf was to be my springboard to other, even more wonderful things. I began rehearsing my first Long Wharf production that September, some forty years ago, and I have barely stopped working since. I've often wondered about the other fork in the road, what life might have been like if I had been directing plays all this time. But I've never thought about it with any regrets.

What I really wanted to do was act.

24.
Naked

Why do all of us want to hear stories? Why do some of us want to tell them? As long as I've been an actor, I've puzzled over those two questions. The questions are so basic, so stupidly simple, that it rarely occurs to us to even ask them. We hear about a show, we buy tickets, we file into a theater, and we sit in the darkness with a bunch of total strangers. The lights go down, the curtain goes up, and we stare at the stage, full of eagerness and hope. Why are we there? What are we looking for? What do we want? It's a little easier to answer such questions when it comes to comedy. Everybody loves a good laugh. But what about drama? If some event in your everyday life were to make you sob uncontrollably, it would be the worst thing you ever lived through. But if something onstage made you cry that hard you would remember it as the best time you ever had in a theater. Why on earth do we subject ourselves to that? Even long for it?

Simply put, we want a good story. We want emotional exercise. We want theater to make us laugh, but we want it to make us cry too. We want to feel pity, fear, anger, hilarity, and joy, but we want these emotions delivered to us in the protective cocoon of a playhouse, and we want to experience them in a more heightened way than we ever do in our humdrum day-to-day existence. We want to be persuaded that we are intensely *feeling* beings. Why we want, need, and love such emotional exercise is a mystery. But one thing is clear: none of us can do without it.

The whole business is equally mysterious up there onstage. Hundreds of times, in mid-performance, I've been struck by the absurdity of my situation. All those strangers out there in the darkness are staring at me. They are all bound by some strange, unwritten contract. They must focus their eyes in reverential silence on me and my fellow actors. They must only laugh or applaud when they sense that it's appropriate. If anyone should break this contract—if he should speak out loud, answer a cell phone, crinkle a candy wrapper, or, God forbid, *fall asleep*—he earns the stern reproof of everyone around him, while those of us onstage are peevishly indignant. And why have we agreed to this ironclad contract? It allows for a two-hour performance that the spectators all know is a completely false version of reality, but which might, just *might* provide them with a few spasmodic rushes of feeling. It is as if the actors have made an unspoken promise from the stage: You hold up your end of the bargain and we'll hold up ours. It's our job. We'll make you laugh. We'll make you cry. We'll give you emotional exercise.

The Changing Room is a play written in the early 1970s by the British playwright David Storey. Its subject is a semiprofessional rugby team in the North of England on the dark, rainy afternoon of a match. The setting is what we would call the team's locker room but what the Brits call a changing room. Act I of the play takes place in the half hour before the match, Act II during the halftime break, and Act III immediately following the team's victory. The cast is made up of twenty-two men. Fifteen of them are the players on the team. The rest include the coach, the trainers, the club owner, the club secretary, a referee, and an ancient janitor. *The Changing Room* is a near-documentary look at the lives of these twenty-two men during a four-hour span of their gritty lives. It is a play with virtually no plot, but as a portrait of a living, breathing, twenty-two-person social organism, it is hypnotic and moving. A year after the play's first production in England, the Long Wharf Theatre presented its American premiere. I had just joined the Long Wharf resident acting company for a season and *The Changing Room* was our second offering. The play opened on November 7, 1972. If there was any opening night that could be said to have launched my career as a working actor, that was it.

Although he was not the production's director, Arvin Brown had cast me somewhat arbitrarily in the role of Kendal. Kendal is a forward on the team. He is a big man with the stolidity and limited intelligence of an ox. As with every other role in the play, Kendal's dialogue reveals almost nothing of his life outside that room. From the moment he enters, his only outward preoccupation is a newly purchased electric tool kit that he proudly shows to a couple of his teammates. Nonetheless, his character is vivid and indelible. All through Act I, Kendal is the butt of numerous jokes from his taunting teammates. The jokes sail right over his head. They obliquely hint that Kendal's wife is a loose woman and that a few members of the team have already cuckolded him. But the earnest and unperceptive Kendal seems completely innocent of this knowledge. Reading the play, I instantly fell in love with the part.

In the play's middle act, halfway through the match, the team bursts back into the changing room like a herd of panting cattle. They are covered with mud, numb with cold, and gasping for breath. They are losing the match, and this makes them foul-tempered and quarrelsome. They guzzle water bottles, nurse cuts and bruises, and endure the hectoring pep talk of their coach. Then they pull themselves together and roar back out for the second half of play. A little time passes with only the janitor left on the empty set, listening to occasional muffled phrases from the game's announcer over a crackly speaker in a corner of the room.

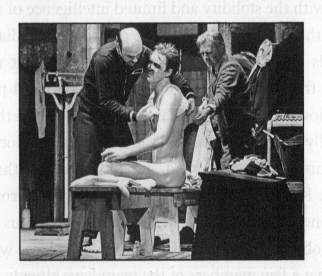

Suddenly one of the players is brought back in, having just been seriously injured on the field. He bays with pain. His nose is broken and streams with blood.

His eyes are so swollen he can barely see. He struggles so violently that his coach and two trainers must pin him to the training table. They tend to him with ointments and cotton swabs. One of the trainers helps him into an adjoining room, where he bathes himself in a big communal tub, unseen by the audience. After a couple of minutes, the trainer helps the injured player back onstage. He is naked, disoriented, and glistening with bathwater. The trainer sits him down on a bench and ministers to him. In a long, virtually wordless scene, with only the distant roar of the crowd filling the air, the trainer towels the player down from head to foot, dresses him like a helpless child, bundles him up, and steers him toward the door, returning him to the desolation of his bleak life. Just before he reaches the door, the injured player remembers, through the fog of his addled mind, something he has left behind in the changing room. It is his electric tool kit.

The injured player is Kendal. My part.

And by a happy chance, so typical of the serendipity of our profession, the trainer was to be played by my good friend, the former McCarter Theatre "Don Pedro," John Braden.

We'd been given four weeks of rehearsal. Our director was Michael Rudman, a sardonic Texan who had long since emigrated to England. By yet another stroke of serendipity, Michael had been the man who hired me to coach American accents at the RSC in London, three years before. Under his deft direction, our sprawling production took shape. He tapped into the testosterone coursing through the veins of a twenty-two-man ensemble. He sent us off to a park to play touch football together. He brought in a Yale coach to dispense the basic rules of rugby. He steeped us in the guttural molasses of North Country accents. He showed us David Storey's rugby film *This Sporting Life*. He noted the competitiveness, showmanship, insecurity, and physical jeopardy in the lives of both actors and athletes. Cannily drawing parallels between the two professions, Michael unleashed us, forging a show that surged with masculine energy.

Nudity, of course, was an essential element of the staging. Professional athletes don't enter and exit a locker room on the day of a game without twice taking off all of their clothes. But Michael was intent that nudity should not be the play's titillating main event. He wanted it to emerge as part of the overall texture of the production, so frank and realistic as to pass virtually unnoticed. As he saw it, this openness needed to characterize even the rehearsal process. Notwithstanding the presence of Annie Keefe, our attractive young stage manager, all traces of hesitancy or self-consciousness had to be banished. In this, Michael had an eager confederate in the horse-faced Rex Robbins. Rex was a veteran character man with a dry, winning manner and a readiness to try anything onstage. He played the part of Fielding, the oldest player on the team. On our second day of work he casually shed every stitch of clothing, striding around the rehearsal room as if it were the most natural thing in the world and startling everyone with the size of his softball-shaped scrotum. Rex's insouciance had the desired effect. In no time at all, the rugby players in the cast went from giggly and self-conscious to offhand and swaggering. Some moved right on to flat-out exhibitionistic. Weeks later, at our drunken opening-night party, most of the company strutted around with a newfound, cocksure manliness. The rest giddily sprinted out of the closet. One or two did both.

Similarly, the larger concept of onstage nudity evolved in our minds over the course of the rehearsal period. Initially the subject of embarrassed laughter, we began to see nudity as the most potent theatrical expression of vulnerability and naked truth. Serious acting is a constant effort to illuminate, expose, and unlock emotion. There is no escaping its essential pretense, but actors are always striving to make that pretense invisible, to present life with such honesty that members of the audience momentarily forget that they are watching a play. And what is more honest than a naked body? Of course the use of nudity onstage needs to be handled with great care. A naked person standing in front of hundreds of other people is such an unfamiliar, unsettling event that it is just as likely to make an audience recoil as to disarm them. But supported by a superb play and a deft, deeply felt production, we had the growing sense that, with *The Changing Room*, we were about to work a minor theatrical miracle.

In the days leading up to our first performance, Michael presided over the obligatory technical and dress rehearsals. For long, tedious hours, the cast shuffled through the staging while he carefully adjusted all the tech aspects of the production around us. He calibrated the sounds of the crowd that emanated from the offstage rugby pitch, the rain that streaked the grimy windowpanes, the harsh glare of the overhead lamps, and the slate-gray daylight outside the windows as it gradually faded to darkness. Every visual and aural detail was calculated to create the superrealistic illusion of that room on that day in that part of northern England. Even odors came into play: all through Act I, as we prepared for the match, we rubbed wintergreen onto our bare thighs so that its astringent smell would fill the theater for every performance.

One naturalistic detail was utterly unique, especially to American audiences. This was the large offstage bathtub. Communal bathing after an athletic event was unheard of in the U.S. (and has since disappeared in the U.K. as well). But it was *de rigueur* in the time and place of *The Changing Room*. Although Michael placed the tub out of the sight of the audience, he made it a vivid part of the action of the play. As with every other aspect of his production, he didn't want the unseen bathtub activity to betray a hint of artifice. In Act III he wanted the audience to hear the players sloshing around and braying their bawdy songs as they bathed together. He wanted cascades of bathwater to splash into the open doorway and onto the duckboards on the changing room floor. When the players entered from the bath, he wanted their pale bodies dripping wet and flushed pink from the hot water. And of course there was that key scene in Act II: Kendal exits the stage covered in mud and blood, plunges into the offstage tub, and reemerges a few minutes later, washed clean.

In the rehearsal room, we had merely gone through the motions of bathing. At the first tech rehearsal, the crew filled up the tub and we bathed in earnest. The effect was sensational. None of us had ever felt so goddamned *real* onstage. But after the first few hours, reality struck back. The tub sprung a leak. The crew drained it immediately, let it dry out, coated the seams with thick layers of caulking, then let it dry out again. The whole process took a couple of days. In the meantime, we pressed on with our tech rehearsals, minus the water and the mud, pretending to bathe just as we had in the rehearsal room.

In my Act II scene, stage manager Annie Keefe had to calculate exactly how much time it would require for me to take an actual bath. Hence, when the moment came, I staggered offstage in my uniform, hastily cast it off, jumped down into the empty tub and began a bizarre bath-pantomime. Except for the absence of water, it was accurate in every detail. I crouched stark naked in the tub, pretending to scrub myself clean. I dipped my head under invisible water, ran my fingers through my dry hair, and frenetically rubbed imaginary mud and sweat off every inch of my body. Three or four fully clothed crew members stood above me in the semidarkness, watching indifferently. One of them was Annie Keefe, holding a stopwatch and timing me. I was a naked man in an empty plywood box in an empty theater on an October afternoon in New Haven, Connecticut. I was the main character in a strange, surrealistic dream. For a fleeting moment, my brain departed my body. It floated above me and looked down at this naked, ludicrously contorted young man. A conscious thought formed itself, one that has passed through my mind a hundred times since:

What am I doing with my life?

I was acting, of course.

And not just acting. I didn't know it at the time, but I was also preparing for my first major breakthrough in show business. And by glorious good fortune, that breakthrough was linked to a stunning work of dramatic art. *The Changing Room* fulfilled the promise of theater like nothing that I'd ever been in. It had an overwhelming impact on our audiences. On several occasions, spectators needed to be literally helped out of their seats. As emotional exercise, it was visceral and cathartic. The show was an instant success at Long Wharf and the subject of glowing national press. Lavish praise was heaped on the play, the production, and the entire company. I was one of the few actors singled out. For the first time I was mentioned in the pages of *Time* magazine, where I chose to ignore the fact that I was referred to as "George Lithgow."

We began our run at Long Wharf with the sense that, for nearly all of us, this was the finest piece of theater we had ever been a part of. But the best was still to come. After one of our last performances, we were summoned into the empty theater. An elegant, expansive man named Charles Bowden introduced himself to us. He grandly announced that he had assembled a team of producers to transfer the show, exactly as we were performing it, to the Morosco Theatre on Forty-fifth Street in New York for the following March. *We were going to Broadway!*

The notion of acting on Broadway had been almost as foreign to me as acting in movies. Years before, I'd filled out my application for a Fulbright grant. One of the questions on the form asked how I would apply my experience if I were to study abroad. I had written three words: "American repertory theater." This was the world I'd come from and where I intended to return. At the time it represented the extent of my ambitions. My one vainglorious flirtation with the movies had done little to broaden those ambitions. My career at Long Wharf was only a couple of months old, but I'd felt no need to seek a better setting elsewhere. It felt like home. And now one of my very first Long Wharf productions was propelling me to another level of the business, one that I had thought I would never attain. I was astonished and I was elated, in equal measure.

The next few months passed quickly. The timing of our projected Broadway opening allowed me to perform in two more Long Wharf shows. Several actors from *The Changing Room* acted in those shows as well, so for all of us the air was charged with electric anticipation. Jean and I retooled for another big move. Most of the company showed up at our Branford apartment for a pre-matinee brunch celebrating Ian's first birthday. In February the *Changing Room* cast regrouped in a New Haven rehearsal studio. It was Valentine's Day and, by chance, Michael Rudman's birthday. Charles Bowden and his producing team were on hand with an enormous birthday cake. Bowden had secretly slipped the actors sheet music for "My Funny Valentine" and we surprised Michael with a hearty rendition of the song. Spirits were soaring as we set about putting the show back together for New York.

Jean, Ian, and I took up temporary residence in the Upper West Side apartment of a touring actress friend. Under Michael Rudman's stewardship, the company installed the show in the venerable Morosco Theatre, where it looked better than ever. The Morosco has long since disappeared, making way for an enormous Marriott Hotel on Times Square, but back then it was a prime legit house in the heart of the midtown theater district. The old building resonated with American theater lore, having been the site of the first runs of such classics as *Our Town*, *Cat on a Hot Tin Roof*, and *Death of a Salesman*. That season our show was within shouting distance of *Pippin*, *That Championship Season*, and *A*

Little Night Music. Heady with excitement, we moved
into our dressing rooms, linked up with working pals
in adjoining theaters, and staked out our favorite restaurants and bars. We previewed. We opened. That
night we gathered at Sardi's after the show to celebrate.
The *New York Times* review was read out loud. We
were a smash.

Opening night was March 7, 1973. Less than three
weeks later, on March 25, in what was surely the short-
est period of time between a Broadway debut and a
Tony victory, I won that year's Tony Award for Out-
standing Featured Actor in a play.

Sure. Acting awards are trumped-up, corrupting,
meaningless, and unjust. They are anti-art. In a profession that relies on a collaborative spirit, they pit
artists against one another. They are the wellspring
of more envy, anger, resentment, and covetousness
than anything else in show business. Awards turn us
into appalling hypocrites. We airily dismiss their importance but we secretly long for them. When we
win them, we are often at our very worst. Our acceptance speeches are generally a graceless cavalcade of
pomposity, crocodile tears, and egregious false mod-
esty. An award winner is usually the only person in
the room who is genuinely pleased by his prize. By

varying degrees, everyone else is bitter, begrudging, and judgmental. Often this even includes the cast of a winner's very own show. All things considered, it is far better to never win an award for acting.

That said . . .

Winning a Tony Award was the happiest moment I'd ever experienced in a theater. Nanette Fabray opened an envelope and read my name. Applause exploded all around me. I lurched up the steps to the Imperial Theatre's stage in my rented tuxedo, my ruffled shirt, and my black velvet bowtie. I stared out at the brightly lit mass of beaming faces, my heart racing like a hummingbird's wings. By some miracle I managed to recite every word of my carefully wrought speech. Seeing a grainy tape of that moment a couple of years ago, I saw none of the elation I remember feeling. I looked like a tremulous, stammering schoolboy. And with the lingering traces of my unwitting British accent, I sounded like a pretentious fop.

Oh, but it was wonderful. All actors strive for that elusive moment when the quality of their work is matched by the measure of its success. Such an occurrence is all too rare. Many of us go through our entire careers without it happening once. And here it was, on my very first outing. Between a Broadway debut and a Tony Award, I barely slept for the entire month of March.

The twin events ushered in a springtime full of sparkly new pleasures. The city, so recently an impregnable fortress of rejection and failure, suddenly flung open its doors. I and my *Changing Room* cast mates became fixtures at Downey's, Lüchow's, Jimmy Ray's, and Joe Allen. The play won the New York Drama Critics' Circle Award and we hobnobbed with the likes of Clive Barnes, John Simon, and Walter Kerr. We formed an unbeatable softball team for the Broadway Show League in Central Park. Our press agent cooked up a publicity stunt pitting us against a squad from the star-studded all-female cast of *The Women* (Alexis Smith! Rhonda Fleming! *Myrna Loy!*). I was sprung loose from our show for three days for my network TV debut, appearing in a tiny role with the great Jason Robards in a Hallmark Hall of Fame production of *The Country Girl*. Blessings rained down on me.

One day halfway through our time at the Morosco, an envelope arrived for me at the stage door. It contained a kindly note from John Stix, from Baltimore Center Stage. Without a trace of sour grapes he congratulated me on *The Changing Room*. In particular, he complimented me for having made such a wise decision in choosing to accept an offer from the Long Wharf Theatre.

Once I settled into the run of the show, Jean and I sought out another temporary housing situation. Back in New Jersey, my parents were now living outside of Princeton, renting a farmhouse surrounded by soybean fields near the village of Plainsboro. There was plenty of room for my family of three, so we moved in. I commuted daily to New York for my shows. Every night I sat on the train and read the next morning's edition of the *New York Times*. It was filled with coverage of the Watergate hearings and of the epic downfall of Richard Nixon. The extended Lithgow family, like the rest of liberal America, basked in the warm glow of political schadenfreude. My parents loved our company. In the sunny New Jersey countryside, Ian was in toddler heaven. My father and I replayed every game of the historic chess face-off in Iceland between Bobby Fischer and Boris Spassky. On a day off from the show, the cast of *The Changing Room* traveled down en masse for a picnic in the expansive yard of the Plainsboro house. For Jean and me, it was the happiest time in our marriage.

But there was something seriously wrong with this picture. My mother, my father, and my little sister, Sarah Jane, had moved out of Princeton, having lost their university-owned apartment. My father was no

longer employed by Princeton University. He was out
of a job. During a sabbatical from his duties as artistic
director of McCarter Theatre, the Princeton adminis-
tration had seized the moment to unceremoniously fire
him. While my parents' pride might have spurred them
to move far away from the source of such an indignity,
they had a compelling reason to stay in the area. Having
lived in Princeton for eleven years, Sarah Jane was the
only one of their children to spend all of her childhood
in the same school system, the only one who had never
suffered the trauma of being the new kid in town. Mom
and Dad wanted to spare her that. They wanted her to
finish up at Princeton High School before they left. So
they had rented the Plainsboro farmhouse, doing their
best to put on a brave face, enjoy a far less stressful life,
and avoid all thoughts, as they surveyed the vast fields
surrounding them, of being put out to pasture.

When my father was let go from Princeton, the rationale handed down from above was that the quality of
the company's work had slipped. Arthur Lithgow, they
declared, was no longer achieving a sufficiently "exciting" level of theatrical fare. This explanation enraged
me, especially as it was couched in the fatuous phrases
of Ivy League doublespeak. What did a bunch of stuffy,
hidebound academics know about professional theater?
Who did they think they were? And what the hell did

they mean by "exciting"?! But beneath my indignation there was a hidden strain of guilt. My father had lost his job for many of the very reasons that I had chosen to stop working for him. Like his Princeton employers, I had wanted something better. I had left his company at the very moment when he most needed my support. And now my career had taken off like a rocket just as his had suffered a devastating setback. He was fifty-seven years old, eight years younger than I am as I write these words, and he had no idea where he was going next.

For both my father and me, it was a season of deep conflict and painful contradiction. Success was countered by failure, pride by guilt, soaring confidence by gnawing doubt. I suppose that my dad's circumspect nature stood him in good stead during that time. It was certainly a boon to me. I can only imagine his hidden feelings of injury and humiliation caused by his treatment at the hands of Princeton University. He must certainly have succumbed to occasional spasms of envy directed at Arvin Brown, and personal hurt that I had chosen Arvin's theater over his. But outwardly he remained his sweet and genial self. To my eyes his delight in the success of *The Changing Room* was warm and genuine. He welcomed the cast to his home with effusive good will. If the events of the preceding year had taken their toll on him, he never showed it. He never betrayed a hint of self-pity nor made the slightest bid for sympathy. He may have revealed his bitterness and disappointment to my mother, but none of us saw a glimpse of it. Only in retrospect have I come to see what a Herculean effort that must have been for him. By keeping his pain to himself, he allowed me my first undiluted taste of success in a profession that had treated him shabbily and without mercy. It was a father's selfless gift to a son. I love him for it.

25.
Mr. Pleasant

I t is not for nothing that an actor is said to "give a performance." At its essence, acting is a gift to an audience, whether that gift is delivered from a stage or a screen. An actor gives something to an audience and, with any luck, the audience gives him something in return. When this curious transaction is successful, everybody is happy. The audience is elated and the actor is fulfilled. Things get a little warped when the actor loses sight of his mission, when he forgets its essential generosity, when he feels that he is not getting his due, that his audience is not sufficiently responsive, grateful, adulatory. At such moments, another diva is born and unleashed on the world. All actors are susceptible to this syndrome. Every single one of us. Applause is a narcotic, and we're all prone to addiction. The great challenge is to always remember a simple truth: that acting is not about *us*, it's about *them*. I once worked with an actor who had forgotten that truth long before, if indeed he had ever known it at all.

I'm disinclined to defame this man, so I'll call him Rock. Rock Masters. I acted with him in a movie. I'll return to him in a moment.

After the heady success of *The Changing Room*, I spent an entire year on Broadway performing in a dopey play called *My Fat Friend*. This was a campy four-character British farce whose main plot line concerned the drastic weight loss of its portly young leading lady. The play was a forgettable trifle, considerably elevated by the blithe performances of two terrific actors, Lynn Redgrave and George Rose. In the role of their dour, young Scottish flatmate, I had

a great time playing second banana to these two expert comedians. I admired them both deeply and loved their bubbly comradeship. Besides, a year's salary on Broadway was an unaccustomed luxury. It allowed Jean, Ian, and me to set up New York housekeeping again, in a bigger apartment with a comfortable, predictable daily life. But due to an insecurity born of my earlier hard times in the city, I clung to the show for far too long. After an entire year on Broadway, I joined Lynn and George on tour to Detroit and Toronto. When that was over, I still couldn't let go. I soldiered on without them in a slapdash New Jersey stock production of the play at the Paramus Playhouse on the Mall. A year of weekly paychecks had created a severe dependency in me, and I desperately needed to break it. A change was long overdue.

Happily, a filmmaker friend of mine came calling. Him I will call Paolo. Paolo had dreamed up a deliciously lurid suspense film set in Europe. I'll call it *Interdit*. Shooting was all set to start and he wanted me to be in it.

Interdit was second-generation Alfred Hitchcock. The leading role in the film is a man who falls in love with a much younger woman. This infatuation pulls him out of a long period of his life during which he has grimly buried himself in his work. The man has a longtime best friend who appears to have grave doubts about the disturbing intensity of his old friend's love for the young girl. But true to the film's Hitchcockian antecedents, the friend's kind-hearted concern is not all that it appears to be. I played the devious best friend. The starring role was played by Rock Masters. Working with him would prove to be more than just a job. It was an education.

By this time in his career, Rock Masters was running on fumes. He was navigating the rough waters of a middle-aged leading man's faltering career. His genial manner was tinged with desperation. For him, starring in *Interdit* was a chance to regain some lost credibility in the movie business. The plot of the film paired the two of us in a complex psychological chess game, full of mystery, duplicity, and shocking revelations. It was a meaty on-screen relationship, the kind most actors would kill for. I had practically salivated when I first read the script. I suspect that Rock was pretty excited, too. But he could have been forgiven for feeling a little concerned when he learned that he would be partnered with an unknown, untested New York theater actor half his age.

When the film's cast and crew assembled on location in Europe, things started off promisingly enough. As so often happens in the odd world of filmmaking,

I met Rock for the first time at a tedious afternoon-long session of makeup tests. That very morning I had stepped off a plane after a red-eye flight from New York, having delivered my last performance of *My Fat Friend* back in Paramus only twenty hours before. I was stupefied with jet lag but I managed to strike up the beginnings of a friendly working relationship with both Rock and his young costar, a Gallic beauty whom I'll call Julianne Clement. The makeup tests were conducted under the watchful eyes of director Paolo and his cinematographer (call him "Laszlo").

A lot was at stake. The plot of the film cuts back and forth between two time periods. Rock was fifty and I was just shy of thirty, but we had to look the same age in every scene. Hence half the time I needed to look twenty years older than my actual years and the other half Rock needed to look twenty years younger. This is what made the makeup tests so tricky and time-consuming. Through the fog of my jet lag I heard long, urgent discussions among Paolo, Laszlo, and Rock. Appearances, it seemed, were going to be a big issue on this film.

Not just a big issue. A big problem. Appearances were at the heart of a fading film acting tradition to which Rock Masters still fiercely adhered. According to this tradition, good looks were everything. Years before, Rock had carefully constructed a distinctive screen persona. He wasn't about to diverge from it. Thus he had devised several strategies to ward off incremental signs of change. His hair had begun to turn gray and thin out. He dyed it jet-black and battled hair loss with implants. These were several-inch-long strands of hair. He wrapped them around his scalp like a turban, massaged them into a sculpted helmet, and instructed the film's hairdresser to stipple the underlying patches of bare scalp with inky black stain. To Laszlo's dismay, Rock had schooled himself in the art of movie lighting. Whenever the crew had finished lighting a scene, Rock would stride onto the set with a tiny mirror, hold it eight inches from his eyes, and instruct the gaffer to add a tiny spotlight, called an "inky," to lend an extra sparkle to his eyes. He was also inordinately concerned with appearing too short on film. Hence he wore inch-high lifts inside his shoes, insisted on standing on an apple box in every two-shot, and lagged back a step or two whenever he walked down a flight of steps with another actor.

And then there was that contentious issue of makeup. For years Rock had used the exact same bronzer to give him the manly face of a rugged, leathery cowboy. On every film he brought along his own supply. This had been the subject of the muttered conversations on the day of those makeup tests: Paolo wanted Rock to dispense with his beloved bronzer. The character had led a sequestered, office-bound life for twenty years, Paolo argued. It didn't make sense for him to look like The Marlboro Man. In test after test, Paolo coaxed Rock to use less and less makeup. Finally Rock relented and Paolo was satisfied. But a week later, on the first day of shooting, Rock showed up on the set having already done his own makeup back at his hotel. He'd used the same old bronzer, slathered on thicker than ever. He was as ruddy as Sitting Bull, as if all those makeup tests had never happened. Paolo fumed. Laszlo despaired. Rock won.

This was only our first day of shooting. There was much more to come. Day by day I began to perceive Rock's priorities. It seemed that film acting to him was not about building a character, shaping scenes, or relating to other actors, and it certainly wasn't about "giving to the audience." It appeared to be about the everlasting pursuit of his own close-ups. To this end he had invented a system of doling out his energies. In the coverage of any given scene, his acting would be wooden and monotone all through the masters and two-shots. Only when he was being filmed in close-up did his performance come alive. By this means Rock calculated that the director and editor would be forced to heavily favor his close-ups when it came time to cut the scene together. And it wasn't enough for him to supercharge his own close shots. When it was time for his fellow actors' close-ups, he would lifelessly mumble his lines off camera, giving them almost nothing to play off.

Sometimes Rock would go even farther. In one scene halfway through the script, he and Julianne were locked in a passionate embrace. It was first shot from an angle that favored Rock. His face was nicely framed as he embraced and kissed her. Next the camera and lights were reset for an angle that favored Julianne. As Rock embraced her with his back to the camera, he lifted his shoulder, covering half her face. Paolo cut the take and mentioned to Rock the little problem with the shoulder. Rock assured him that he would make an adjustment on the next take. The camera rolled again. Once again his shoulder rose up, and once again Julianne was blocked, tilting her face backwards as she struggled to be seen. Paolo repeated the same note. Rock cheerfully acknowledged it. Take three. Up went the shoulder. Another note, another nod, another take, and once again the shoulder went up. The three of them danced this little minuet five or six more times. The tension on the set approached the boiling point. Everyone felt it but Rock, who remained relaxed, affable, and eager to help out. At last Paolo gave up and moved on to the next setup. Another round had gone to Rock.

A year later when the film was released, there was that embrace up on the screen. It plays in only one angle, with Rock's ardent face nicely on display and Julianne seen from behind. You can see the editor's dilemma. Why feature a shot in which a beautiful young starlet looks like a drowning woman, struggling to come up for air?

As the shooting went on, I watched all of Rock's moves with a kind of queasy wonderment. I was a starry-eyed innocent with the scales falling from my eyes. Confronted with all of these elaborate mind-games I began to self-protectively develop a few of my own. I made myself into Rock's guileless disciple, peppering him with questions about his technique as if I had never set foot on a film set. I figured the more I was attentive to him, the less he would ambush me. For his part, Rock relished the role of crusty mentor. He would take me into his confidence and share with me his crafty wiles.

One day on a city street, Rock and I were shooting a scene where we simply walked out of a building and climbed into a car. Paolo was covering the two of us in a broad master shot, followed by a closer shot of Rock as he got behind the wheel. Rock wanted to be sure that the closer shot would end up in the final edit.

"Watch this," he told me.

As we shot the master, he would do something slightly wrong on every take. He would trip on the curb, drop his briefcase, bump the fender of the car, or fail on his first attempt to open the car door.

"You see?" he said.

"See what?"

"Now they'll have to use the closer shot."

"That's incredible, Rock!" I said. "What do you call this?"

Rock grinned and winked at me.

"Trickery," he growled.

Despite all of this on-set gamesmanship, Rock's demeanor was amiable, courteous, and masterfully disingenuous. Anyone visiting the set of *Interdit* would have envied us the privilege of working with such a gracious, considerate star. But movie crews are a cynical bunch. They've seen it all and they catch on fast. In no time they became aware of every hoary trick Rock was playing. He was fooling no one, least of all Paolo and his editor. By the end of the shoot, everyone on the set was referring to him behind his back by the pet name they had coined for him. They called him "Mr. Pleasant."

Interdit was released in the U.S. under another name. Its French title had not survived the rigorous market testing of its American distributor. It had a middling success in the States but did little to revive Rock Masters' career. It was the last substantial leading role he ever played in films. But I took no pleasure in his decline. I'd actually liked the man. In fact, I was pleased for him when he recently scored a modest triumph in his late seventies, playing a small role in a Hollywood sci-fi blockbuster. In retrospect, his strenuous self-aggrandizement during the filming of *Interdit* strikes me as sad, self-deluding, and almost poignant. He was clinging to a Hollywood that no longer existed. He was playing by rules that no longer applied. Teaching me those rules was his version of an actor's generosity. Working with him had been an education all right. But it was an in-depth tutorial in how not to act in a movie.

While we were on location in Europe, three of Paolo's friends paid him a visit. By chance these three men had gathered in a nearby city to work on the script for a film that they would shoot in New York City the following summer. One of these friends was a screenwriter, one a director, and one an actor. Among them they were in the process of reinventing American movies. Their film would be dangerous, disturbing, and brutally real. It would be one of a handful of 1970s films that would shake Hollywood to its roots. It would be called *Taxi Driver.* The screenwriter was Paul Schrader. The director was Martin Scorsese. The actor was Robert De Niro. Their presence made poor Rock Masters look like a dinosaur nearing extinction.

26.
Broadway Baby

For me, the 1970s was Broadway. From *The Changing Room* in 1973 until the end of the decade, I acted in a dozen Broadway shows. It feels as if half of my waking life in those years was lived within the ten square blocks of the New York theater district. To be sure, I occasionally worked elsewhere. I did a couple of plays off-Broadway, one in D.C., one in San Francisco, and another one back at the Long Wharf. I directed two or three more times. I played smallish parts in a few more movies, one of which even took me back out to Hollywood for a month. But Broadway was my gravitational center, and I spent the overwhelming majority of my time there.

How do you distill a decade of work on Broadway without sounding like a tedious windbag in a theater bar? Describing each one of those dozen plays would

John Lithgow in "Bedroom Farce"

be like describing all the marching bands after a parade has passed by. Each band may have its own distinctive look, sound, and personality, but in retrospect they all become one big clamorous blur. How can I persuade anyone that there was anything special about any of my twelve Broadway shows in the seventies, or that they were even worth seeing? Theater is of the moment. Breathless self-praise, no matter how descriptive, can never recapture its impact after the fact. Simply put, you had to have been there.

And yet each of those shows was a formative and memorable chapter in my own history. Those twelve directors, those half-dozen playwrights, those nine different playhouses, those scores of fellow actors, those endless hours of rehearsals, those hundreds of performances, those tens of thousands of spectators, that army of drama critics and their reams of theater reviews—all of these played a role in shaping me as an actor. I have always felt that my early Broadway years were an incalculable gift, a priceless part of my actor's education. By the end of that decade I knew who I was onstage. I had learned what I did well and, more to the point, what I did badly. I had my successes and my failures, my rave notices and my withering pans. But nearly all of this took place in the friendly confines of the theater district. My hits and misses were watched not by the vast American film and television audience but by a comparatively tiny population of demanding yet forbearing New York theatergoers.

To sum up my 1970s career—"Turning the accomplishment of many years / Into an hourglass"—let me offer a kind of scorecard of my Broadway credits during that time. It is a portrait in numbers, a list that tracks the gradual evolution of a stage actor's persona. From this shorthand history I emerge as a fully formed actor at the dawn of the eighties, ready for the famous and infamous showbiz events of my later life:

SIX BRITS

Of the twelve characters I played on Broadway during those years, six of them hailed from different corners of the British Isles. I was a North Country rugby player (*The Changing Room*), a Scottish cookbook writer (*My Fat Friend*), a Manchester milkman (*Comedians*), an Irish stoker (*Anna Christie*), a Belfast bicycle shop owner (*Spokesong*), and a shambling English suburbanite (*Bedroom Farce*). This string of heavily accented Angles, Saxons, and Celts was born of two factors. One was the wave of new British playwrights who were infusing and invigorating New York theater at that time. I acted in plays by David Storey, Trevor Griffiths, Stewart Parker, and Alan Ayckbourn, while neighboring marquees displayed the names of Harold Pinter, Simon Gray, Christopher Hampton, David Hare, and Peter Schaffer. Five of my six British roles in those years were in plays that had made their mark in London the season before.

The other factor, of course, was my recent stint in a London drama school, absorbing all things British. My two years' exposure to British accents, idioms, and manners had uniquely qualified me to take professional advantage of the British invasion. The half dozen Brits that I portrayed were among my first several performances on Broadway, leading most theatergoers to conclude, quite logically, that I was not an American actor at all. As entire years passed without a single week of unemployment, this didn't bother me in the slightest. At least not for a while.

SIX PREMIERES

Six of those twelve productions in the seventies were American premieres. That fifty-percent ratio between new and old material is roughly what I've managed to maintain for most of my stage career. To be sure, revivals are a much safer proposition. Great revivals make great theater. They do great business. Theatergoers love them. I love them myself. Indeed, they formed the core of my father's best work when I was growing up. The audience for a revival sits there in the risk-free confidence that they are watching a play that has withstood the test of time. It's *sure* to be good. The only question is will it be as good as the last two or three revivals of the same play?

This is not the case with new writing. Any new play is a breathtaking leap of faith. The odds against success are appalling. Taking a chance on new material is fraught with danger. It relies on courageous producers, daring actors, and smarter, more adventurous audiences. But even with all those elements in place, the danger is still present. The critics are ready with sharpened knives. Flops will always outnumber hits. But that very danger is what makes a new play so exciting. Besides, you get the privilege of working with the man or woman who actually wrote your lines. You are a vital part of his or her creative process. When Samuel French finally publishes the play, there's your name right next to your character. It is not for nothing that an actor is said to "create" a role when he premieres it.

But there is a more basic reason why new works have such an appeal for a stage actor. The illusion of the first time, the elusive goal of every moment onstage, is far more potent when the audience has no idea what they are about to see. My most thrilling experiences onstage have been at those moments when a new play was unveiled for the first time. Everyone knows how *Death of a Salesman* ends. However stirring the performances, the salesman always dies. But in 1988, when I appeared on Broadway in the world premiere of David Henry Hwang's brilliant play *M. Butterfly*, no one knew what they were in for. We pinned their ears back with the shock of the new.

THREE COMEDIES

Three comedies out of twelve plays is not much of a percentage, but those three comedies were a lot of fun. *My Fat Friend* was the first, early in the decade. Near the end of it, I was in Alan Ayckbourn's *Bedroom Farce*. I was one of an entire cast of American replacements who took over for the play's original cast, imported from the National Theatre of Britain. In that gloriously funny production, I worked under the direction of Sir Peter Hall. The comic climax of the play involved the collapse of a desk built from a do-it-yourself kit. In that scene, actress Judith Ivey and I managed to trigger the loudest laugh I've heard from any theater audience anywhere.

But the comedy that was sandwiched between those two shows was the great one. In 1978 I played George Lewis in *Once in a Lifetime*, by Moss Hart and George S. Kaufman. This was an extravagantly daffy production directed by Tom Moore at the Circle in the Square Theatre. *Once in a Lifetime* is a classic American comedy from 1930, the first of eight collaborations by Kaufman and Hart, and the subject of a substantial section of Hart's great theater memoir *Act One*. Acting in this play revealed to me the true genius of the American comedy tradition. It also revealed to me one of my own untapped strengths. For the first time I played a role that can best be described as a comic "holy fool." Perhaps the most likely archetype for this role is the character created by the great Stan Laurel. As the holy fool, I turned out to be a natural.

The inciting incident of *Once in a Lifetime* is the arrival of talking pictures in 1927. Three New York–based vaudevillians named Jerry, May, and George impulsively sell their comedy act and rush out to Hollywood to join the "talkies" revolution. Jerry and May are the wisecracking comics in the trio. My part was George, their dim-witted "deadpan feed"—the holy fool. In the first scene of the play, Jerry and May devise a scheme to make a fortune in Hollywood by teaching dramatic speech to silent film stars. As a part of their scam, they anoint George "Dr. George Lewis," a renowned speech expert, and instruct him to keep his mouth firmly shut wherever the three of them go. As the plot unfolds, Kaufman and Hart paint a zany portrait of the glittering frenzy of Hollywood in those days. In that insane world, the vaudeville trio are fish out of water, navigating the shoals of the movie business. With inexo-

rable comic inevitability, George, the dopey innocent, makes a series of colossal blunders in executive suites and soundstages. Every one of his faux pas is hailed as a stroke of genius by the panicky movie muckety-mucks. The holy fool ends up ruling Hollywood.

The play is a miracle of comedy engineering. Kaufman and Hart time their plot twists, cross-purposes, and comic reversals with the precision of rocket scientists. The laughs build exponentially to the point where the audience can barely take it any-more. Read the play sometime. At a certain point in the second act, George Lewis bellows a five-word line into the face of the scowling movie mogul Herman

Glogauer. The line is "You turned down the Vita-phone!" Out of context, the line means nothing. But at that point, in that scene, it ignites a nuclear blast of laughter. Night after night I would yell that line into the face of the formidable comic actor George S. Irving. The two of us would stand there, nose to nose, for as long as we wanted. The audience would only stop laughing when we decided it was time to shut them up. It was pure comedy joy.

Many years later I worked on another comedy. It also featured a group of fish out of water. This one was not a play, it was a television series. The series lasted six years on NBC and churned out 138 episodes. In effect, each episode was a twenty-two-minute one-act farce. Each was written by a two-person writing team, not unlike Kaufman and Hart. During the week of re-hearsals for each show, the entire fifteen-person writing staff would pitch in on rewrites. At the very beginning of our six years on the series, I met with the writers for the first time. We talked generally about the tone of the show, the essence of its comedy, and the comic inter-play among its four main characters. These four char-acters were a team of researchers embedded in an Ohio college town, trying to blend into the native population while masking their true identities and intentions. De-spite their great intelligence, the four researchers are clueless and naïve. They regularly make a godawful mess of things. But they always survive their self-made disasters and they often triumph. In other words, they are a team of holy fools. In that writers' meeting, I invoked *Once in a Lifetime* to the writing staff and urged them all to read it. Kaufman and Hart, I declared, would have been a perfect writing team for our show. If they were alive today, I said, they wouldn't be writing for Broadway. They'd be writing for us. Our show was called *3rd Rock from the Sun.*

TWO TIMES ABOVE THE TITLE

In the 1970s I was no Broadway star. In twelve shows, I was billed above the title only twice. Once was for *My Fat Friend* (below Lynn Redgrave and George Rose, and in letters half their size). The other was for Eugene O'Neill's *Anna Christie* (well below the name Liv Ullmann). In each of the other ten productions, I was a member of an unbilled ensemble. This suited me just fine. I loved the company spirit that prevailed in shows like *Comedians, Trelawny of the "Wells," Spokesong, Once in a Lifetime,* and Arthur Miller's *A Memory of Two Mondays.* Even my Tony Award for *The Changing Room* was for "best featured actor" in a selfless twenty-two-man ensemble. In all of those shows there was rarely a sense of hierarchy, rarely an ego trip, rarely a catfight over prerogatives. My memories of those ensemble shows are packed with episodes of the kind of company spirit and moist sentiment that can only be generated inside a theater. Every opening night was a flood of congratulatory gifts (by tradition, mine has always been an inscribed caricature of every member of the cast and crew). At every performance that fell on New Year's Eve, the cast linked arms at the curtain call and led the audience in "Auld Lange Syne." Every Christmas featured an elaborate backstage game of "Secret Santa." When we had to perform a matinee and an evening show of *Comedians* on Christmas Day of 1976, Rex Robbins (the beloved *Changing Room* alum with the enormous testicles) swung into action. He organized a potluck supper between shows for the entire cast and crew and their families. He decorated the basement under the stage of the Music Box Theatre. He even installed a Christmas tree. And he himself performed the role of Santa Claus for all the children. Of such moments, sweet memories and lifelong friendships are forged.

For me, that is the essence of the theater. For all the pleasures and perks of the movie business, it can never achieve the theater's sense of community or its ineffable *esprit de corps*. Neither can television. A sitcom like

3rd Rock bears a lot of resemblance to the world of the-ater—a long run, a tight-knit company of actors, a collaborative rehearsal process, a creative interaction with writers and directors, even a live audience. But it can't touch the theater for selflessness, ensemble teamwork, and generosity of spirit. A soundstage is nothing like a backstage. A wrap party is nothing like a cast party. The honorifics of the theater are quaint and archaic, with few price tags attached—a backstage visit from Paul Newman, a portrait on the wall of Sardi's, a *New York Times* caricature by Hirschfeld (of which I received a grand total of eight). By contrast, the blandishments of success in film and TV seem crass and garish. The money is so lavish, the celebrity is so outsized, the competition is so keen and so public that a rigid hierarchy inevitably asserts itself. I love to work in film and television. I can't imagine my career without them. But after a few too many soundstages and shooting locations, a few too many makeup chairs and craft service tables, a few too many early calls and queasy naps in overheated trailers while waiting for the next camera setup, it's only a matter of time before I come running back into the arms of my old friends in the New York theater.

I've had hundreds of those friends. Let me tell you about four of them.

Comedians is a corrosively serious play. It throbs with anger and political heat. Its author, the English playwright Trevor Griffiths, is a near-revolutionary zealot, wielding theater as a club to smash down what he sees as Britain's smug, complacent class system. Yet *Comedians* is about comedy, too. It crackles with edgy laughter. It is a compelling, unsettling blend of fizzy gags and harsh drama. I acted in it for four months in 1976.

The setting of *Comedians* is a dank grade school classroom in Manchester, in the north of England. On a rainy evening, a group of six working-class men straggle in. They are attending an adult education class in stand-up comedy led by an old-time music hall comic with the gravitas of a stern university professor. He takes the class through a series of warm-up drills in preparation for a comedy competition the men will attend later that evening. Act II is the competition itself, where each of these men presents his carefully crafted stand-up routine at a nightclub. In a canny piece of stagecraft, the theater audience becomes the audience for the competition. In front of the crowd, some of the would-be comedians kill. Some of them die, glazed with flop sweat. Act III is the aftermath of the competition, back in the classroom later that night. The centerpiece of this final act is a long, polemical argument in the empty room between the old comic and his prize pupil. The pupil is a dark, angry, genius comedian named Gethin Price. In our production, Gethin was brilliantly played by Jonathan Pryce, the young actor who had created the role in England the year before.

True, *Comedians* has its hidden political agenda. But it is dangerously funny and it buzzes with ideas about performance, ambition, social resentment, and rage. In an instance of life imitating art, our director was himself a master of comedy. Our rehearsal period with him was an ongoing master class in the art and craft of making people laugh. Years before, this man's own work as a comedian, together with the likes of Lenny Bruce, Mort Sahl, and Shelley Berman, had helped to revolutionize the genre. Since then he had evolved into one of our finest directors, for both stage and film, winning a trunkload of Oscars and Tonys. He was also hilarious fun to work with. With improvisational glee, he took the all-male cast through his own set of comedy drills, striving to put us all in touch with the comic's urge to amuse. These exercises went on for days, long before he began to actually stage the play. He held group sessions in which we would all take turns telling our favorite jokes. He conducted improvs, giving all of us the intense experience of both succeeding and failing at being funny. He told vivid, self-mocking stories of his own history as a performer. He played recordings of great comic monologists (for the first time I heard the voice of the amazing Ruth Draper). And he brilliantly dissected the nature of comedy itself—its components of hurt, need, and anger—and impressed on us his own deeply held belief that comedy is a serious matter.

Comedians had a respectable run, but it wasn't a hit. Its startling mix of comedy and rage was a bitter pill for Broadway audiences, and a lot of theatergoers must have expected something very different from a director who had won four Tony Awards for staging the plays of Neil Simon. As for the director himself, we could all see by the time we opened that *Comedians* had been a disappointment to him. The production hadn't lived up to his hopes and he blamed himself for its short-comings. But for me, working with him was inspiring, revelatory, and ecstatic fun. He is high on the list of the best directors I have ever worked with, or ever will. He was Mike Nichols.

I left *Comedians* early to begin work on a major Broadway revival of Eugene O'Neill's *Anna Christie*. The Norwegian star Liv Ullmann was to play the title role. Our director was José Quintero. José could not possibly have been more different from Mike Nichols, but his status in American theater was equally lofty. Where Mike was dry, ironic, and devilish, José was an active volcano of passion. He was a trans-planted Panamanian who, years before, had embraced Eugene O'Neill as a kind of spiritual savior. He directed O'Neill's plays with a Holy Roller's messianic zeal (and he directed them nineteen times). He even claimed to converse with the dead playwright's ghost.

I was cast opposite Liv as a seagoing Irish coal stoker named Mat Burke. In the play, Anna Christie has come home to her father's barge, moored at a New York dockside, to leave behind her wretched life of prostitu-tion. Out at sea, in Act II, father and daughter rescue

Mat from a shipwreck and take care of him onboard the barge. As the story unfolds, Mat falls hard for Anna and asks her to marry him, never knowing of her shameful past. When he learns of it in the last act, the devout Catholic stoker is consumed with anger and humiliation. It doesn't help when he discovers that Anna was brought up Lutheran. Anna desperately tries to persuade Mat that his love has cleansed her and that she is worthy of him. In a scene of near-Wagnerian passion, Mat kneels with her and asks her to affirm the truth of her protestations by swearing on his dead mother's crucifix. The crucifix hangs on a chain around his neck where he had promised he would always wear it.

To stir us to an emotional pitch for such scenes, José periodically resorted to a kind of Pentecostal style of directorial invocation. In one rehearsal, five actors were running through the opening minutes of the play in which the bedraggled Anna staggers into a tavern. I was not in the scene, but I sat to the side, watching the action. On her entrance Anna croaks her famous first line:

"Gimme a whiskey, ginger ale on the side. And don't be stingy, baby."

Halfway through the scene, José stopped the action. We all sensed that one of his arias was about to begin. With a hypnotic glare, he focused his attention on Liv. Starting slowly, he began to create for her a detailed portrait of the debased life of a dockside prostitute. As he continued, his eyes widened. His face contorted. Spittle collected on each side of his broad mouth. His rich, accented voice rose, trembled, and broke with sobs. Steadily gathering steam, he spoke for at least fifteen minutes. He invoked scenes of his youth in Panama City, when great naval ships would dock there. He painted extraordinary verbal pictures of the streets of the city, "WHITE with SAILORZ!" He described hundreds of them lining up outside the bordellos.

"And they would go EEN! And they would come OUT!" José cried. "And each had their NEEEDZ and their PERVERSIONZZ!"

All of us sat there transfixed. Reaching a climax, he grabbed a ten-dollar bill from his pocket and thrust it into Liv's hand.

"THERE!" he roared. "You are MINE. I have BOUGHT you!"

He proceeded to push and tug her around the room. Finally he thrust her in a corner where she cowered near tears.

"NOW," he ordered at last, looming over her. "Start the scene AGAIN!"

When José directed the moment with Mat's dead mother's crucifix, he unleashed another of his inspirational perorations on me. At its height he tore a chain from around his neck. On it hung a crucifix. With tears in his eyes he told me that it was *his* mother's crucifix, which she'd given *him* before *she* died. Just like Mat's mother, she had begged José to always wear it. He snatched my prop crucifix from me and strung his mother's around my neck. He told me to repeat the scene, armed with this sacred talisman. Maybe the crucifix worked a little magic. Maybe the scene played a little better the next time through. But José's mischievous partner, Nick, told me later in confidence that José's mother was still alive, happy, and well. She was living in the comfortable house José had bought for her back in Panama City.

"And, by the way," Nick added, "that crucifix doesn't belong to him."

Anna Christie was hardly my finest hour. Nor Liv's. Nor José's, for that matter. And it is curiously absent from most of our résumés. The play is ungainly and long, and our leaden production didn't do much to help it out. Liv was a little too stately for her part, and no one would ever mistake me for a coal stoker (*Times* critic Walter Kerr was right when he claimed that I played Mat Burke as though I'd "been spun from a children's merry-go-round"). The performances were exhausting, yet they rarely earned us more than a tepid response from the crowds. Indeed, the most memorable moment of our run was on one sultry July night when the massive 1977 East Coast blackout struck in the middle of one of my interminable Act III speeches. I suspect that a lot of people in the audience that evening were hugely relieved that the show came down an hour early. But if the show was far less than triumphant, there was one major compensation. The experience of working with José Quintero, that big-hearted, larger-than-life, pounding steam engine of human emotion, did not completely make up for those six months of depletion and disappointment. But it helped.

There is a number missing from my 1970s Broadway scorecard. That number is zero. Zero musicals. I performed in not a single production of a Broadway musical in that entire decade. In fact, I learned early on that the worlds of "legit" and "musical" theater on Broadway are virtually two separate professions. The people from those two different worlds rarely even know each other. I had done lots of light opera in my college days, and a few musicals in summer stock. But my singing and dancing skills had little to recommend them besides their slap-happy enthusiasm. I couldn't possibly measure up to the hundreds of amazingly talented song-and-dance performers who fiercely competed every day for the minuscule number of musical-theater jobs in and out of town.

But, to my amazement, the undisputed king of Broadway director-choreographers took an interest in me. Bob Fosse always loved to get his thoroughbred singer-dancers to act. In my case, he seemed intent on getting an actor to sing and dance. When he was casting the new Kander and Ebb musical *Chicago*, he called me in to audition. He had me in mind for the role of Amos, the hapless cuckold best remembered for his melancholy song "Mr. Cellophane." Through my agent I was told to learn Bert Williams' classic ballad "Nobody" and to come in and sing it for Bob Fosse. I worked my head off with a coach, came to my audition, and sang my heart out for Bobby.

Bob Fosse was a small man. He was pale, wiry, and balding, with the fidgety fixity of a mongoose. He wore a signature uniform of black jeans, black dance shoes, and a black shirt with the sleeves rolled up above his elbows. He appeared to have a half-smoked cigarette permanently affixed to the corner of his mouth. Curiously, for an ex-dancer his posture was not great. Although he was always grimly focused on the job at hand, his gray eyes twinkled with mischief and he loved everything about show business. My audition seemed to charge him with excitement. After my song, he had me read a speech written for the lead role of Billy Flynn, the razzle-dazzle trial lawyer. He brought me back two more times in the coming weeks, shifting me back and forth between Billy and Amos, two vastly different characters. I was not really right for either role, but Bob seemed restless and frustrated that he couldn't squeeze me into either one. Soon afterwards, Jerry Orbach was aptly cast as Billy Flynn and Barney Martin as Amos. I was neither surprised nor disappointed. I'd gotten a lot further than I'd expected. I'd had two callbacks for a big Broadway musical. I'd had my Bob Fosse moment. That was enough for me.

But as it turned out, all those auditions ended up landing me a Bob Fosse job after all. Four years later, Bob was halfway through the murderously difficult shooting period for his autobiographical movie *All That Jazz*. The film was loosely based on the creation of *Chicago* all those years before. In the movie, Roy Scheider plays a character that unmistakably represents Bob himself. During the rehearsals for *Chicago* Bob had suffered a massive heart attack that stopped production for a period of months. An identical episode is the central crisis of *All That Jazz*. In the script of the film, when production is suspended the producers go to a rival director to take over the show. For this role Bob had cast an actual director, filmmaker Sidney Lumet.

When the film's shooting schedule ran over, Lumet was forced to pull out for another project. Bob had to find a replacement fast. He thought of me. He called up and asked me to play the part, as if he were politely asking me for a favor. I couldn't say yes fast enough.

And so it was that in 1978 I finally crossed the line that separated legit and musical theater in New York. Ironically enough, I did it in a movie. My role was actually featured in only two dialogue scenes, tart but brief. As the rival director in the script, I was clearly the embodiment of all of Bob's Broadway nemeses—Hal Prince, Michael Bennett, Gower Champion, *et al.* He directed the scenes with relaxed, sardonic humor, and with the offhand precision of a choreographic taskmaster. My cynical little role was acid fun, but the real joy of doing *All That Jazz* lay elsewhere. I appeared in a huge production number that came at the very end of the film. I was nothing more than a glorified extra in the sequence—one of a dozen minor characters from the film who sit in the audience of a hallucinatory rock concert. The concert features Roy Scheider and Ben Vereen belting out "Bye Bye Life" to herald the death of Scheider's character. For nine days of shooting, I saw Bob Fosse indefatigably at work. I saw Ben Vereen, Ann Reinking, and Kathy Dobie hurl themselves into his athletic choreography, duplicating every move and gesture, through at least fifty angles and at least three hundred takes. I never saw a trace of nerves, fatigue, or bad humor from any of them. There was just strength, concentration, commitment, and talent. In those nine days, the musical gang put the legit gang to shame.

Twenty years later, in 2002, I did my first Broadway musical. Three years after that, I did my second. Taken together, I played about six hundred performances. I never missed a single show. I was nominated for two Tony Awards for Best Actor in a Musical. I even won one of them. But I had watched Bob Fosse direct his thoroughbreds through nine days of shooting on *All That Jazz*. In six hundred shows I never quite got over the nagging feeling that, as a song-and-dance man in the Broadway musical theater, I was a total fraud.

In the mid-1970s, a friend from my Harvard days wrote a play. The Manhattan Theatre Club organized a first reading of the play in its old theater on the Upper East Side. As a favor to my friend, I showed up to read one of the parts. The play's milieu was trailer-trash Appalachia. I dimly recall that the plot involved an episode of hostage-taking and the siege of a rural shack. Beyond that, I remember almost nothing about the reading. I might have forgotten it altogether if it weren't for a young actress in the cast that day. She was a pale, wispy girl with long, straight, cornsilk hair. She appeared to be in her late teens. She was so shy, withdrawn, and self-effacing that I couldn't decide whether she was pretty or plain. The only time I heard her voice was when she spoke her lines. She had a high, thin voice and a twangy hillbilly accent. She was so lacking in theatrical airs that I surmised that perhaps she wasn't an actress at all. Maybe she was the real thing. Maybe the play was even based on her own story. Maybe the playwright had brought her in for the occasion, from Kentucky or West Virginia. Certainly her performance in the reading provided the only authentic moments of the entire afternoon.

The young woman had a strange name. How could she possibly be an actress, I wondered, with a name like that?

Imagine my amazement a few months later when this same young woman showed up for the first day of rehearsal for *Trelawny of the "Wells"* at Lincoln Center's Vivian Beaumont Theater. Joe Papp had hired us both to join the play's cast of eighteen. That pale waif with the lank yellow hair had landed her first job in New York theater, just weeks after getting her degree from the Yale School of Drama. Since I'd first laid eyes on her, she had utterly transformed herself. Mingling with a cast of strangers, she was vibrant, animated, and

radiantly beautiful. You would never know from looking at her that this was her first professional gig. I was
floored. I'd been watching actors act my whole life. I
wasn't easily taken in. But when I'd mistaken her for
a hayseed hillbilly at that play reading a few months
before, either I had been a myopic fool or this young
woman was a brilliant actress.

In the coming weeks, she was a joy to work with.
Joy, in fact, defined the entire experience of *Trelawny
of the "Wells."* The play is a late-nineteenth-century
romance by Arthur Wing Pinero about a theater
troupe based at the fictional Wells Theatre in London.
The Lincoln Center production was my second time
around with the play, having done it at Long Wharf a
few years before in a different role. It is arguably the
best play ever written about the intoxicating allure of
the stage. The passionate thespians in *Trelawny* are
breathless with the high seriousness, reckless folly, and
occasional heartbreak of the acting profession. Because
they are enacting their own stories, actors always love
performing the play (possibly more than audiences
love watching it). The shared affection of the onstage
troupe always spills over into their offstage lives. This
was certainly true of our Lincoln Center production. It
was delirious fun. The magic of theater floated down
on us like fairy dust. We all fell in love with each other.

The superb cast assembled by director A. J. Antoon included Walter Abel, Aline McMahon, Mary Beth Hurt, Michael Tucker, and, in another professional debut, the very young Mandy Patinkin. In the midst of all this luminous talent, that fresh-faced Yale grad with the funny name more than held her own. In the fairly thankless role of Imogen Parrott, the Wells' hard-boiled leading lady, she lit up the stage. Everyone in the show sensed that she was destined to do great things.

Later that year, I was hired to direct a comedy revival for the Phoenix Theatre, yet another nonprofit rep theater based in Manhattan. It was to be one of four American offerings in a season intended to celebrate the American bicentennial. Of the three other shows being produced, one was an evening of two one-acts that included Tennessee Williams' *27 Wagons Full of Cotton*. This was the three-character play from 1955 that eventually evolved into the notorious film *Baby Doll*. The one-act was to be directed by my old Long Wharf boss Arvin Brown. He needed to find a sensational young actress to play the bravura role of the voluptuous, dim-witted Baby Doll. Word had gotten around about the terrific young Yale Drama School girl who had fared so well in *Trelawny of the "Wells"* at Lincoln Center. She was called in to read for the part. Since I was one of the four Phoenix directors that season, I was there for her audition. When she walked in, I greeted her warmly, introduced her to the other three directors, then sat down beside them behind a table and witnessed a little piece of theater history.

For her audition she wore a nondescript skirt, blouse, and slip-on shoes. She carried a second pair of shoes and a box of Kleenex. As she made small talk with Arvin about the play and the character, she unpinned her hair, she changed her shoes, she pulled out the shirttails of her blouse, and she began casually stuffing Kleenex into her brassiere, doubling the size of her bust. Reading with an assistant stage manager, she began a scene from *27 Wagons Full of Cotton*. You could barely detect the moment when she slipped out of her own character and into the character of Baby Doll, but the transformation was complete and breathtaking. She was funny, sexy, teasing, brainless, vulnerable, and sad, with all the colors shifting like mercury before our eyes. From the first second there was no question that she would be offered the part, so the four of us just sat there and enjoyed her performance. She was hired. She played Baby Doll. She was the talk of the town. She was nominated for a Tony Award for best featured actress in a play. This was the first of at least thirty major award nominations she would eventually receive. Nobody would argue with

the statement that she is the greatest American actress of the last fifty years.

A moment of history? Of course. It was the last time Meryl Streep had to audition for anything.

Nichols, Quintero, Fosse, and Streep may stand out, but they are only four out of scores of extraordinary figures that dropped in and out of my life during the 1970s. New York was a stricken city in that decade. It was destitute, filthy, and dangerous. Actors, hookers, and muggers peopled the theater district in equal numbers. Dark theaters outnumbered the ones with running shows. Most of my theater friends spent far more time unemployed than employed. Life was not easy for any of us. And yet we all belonged to an intensely active, optimistic, and interdependent community. My tight-knit gang gathered for potluck supper parties, diligently trooped off to see each others' shows, sang Irish ballads in crowded taverns, and biked furiously through Manhattan traffic as if we owned the town. We shared a sense that we belonged to New York theater and it belonged to us, that in spite of setbacks and struggles we were doing what we'd chosen in our lives, that good things were happening for us, and that we'd all make it in the long run. In that vital community, I had more reason than anyone for optimism and hope. Leaping from one show to the next, season after season, I felt like the luckiest actor in town.

But in this bright picture there were dark shades. For one thing, my parents had entered a period of impermanence and anxiety. My ascendance in the theater profession precisely coincided with my father's precipitous decline. After his ignominious dismissal from McCarter Theatre he and my mother had spent a forlorn year on that farm outside of Princeton, departing only after my little sister was safely ensconced in college. In the next years, they moved a half dozen times, an itinerary that resembled the wanderings of Odysseus. Duplicating the precarious lifestyle of his younger days, my father pursued one pipe dream after another. He never lost his sunny positivism or his buoyant humor, but with every move his exploits became a little more quixotic. And through it all, with a poignant air of forced cheeriness, my mother remained his most ardent booster.

They first moved to Vermont, where Dad attempted to start a performing arts center in Brattleboro. When that failed, he tried selling Norwegian prefab kit homes to out-of-state buyers. When nothing came of that, Mom persuaded her brother, my wealthy Uncle Bronson, to buy an old Vermont farmhouse and hire Dad to restore it for resale. Next was Tampa, where Dad took a job as an artist-in-residence at the University of South Florida, with my mother on hand as an active faculty spouse. After that, the pair bounced back and forth between my brother's and my sister's hometowns of Amherst and Ithaca. During this stretch, Dad undertook his most fanciful project yet. Purely on spec, he created a long epic poem set during the Trojan War, written in the style of Homer's *Iliad*. At all of his whistle-stops he landed temp teaching jobs, at schools like Cornell, U Mass, and Ithaca College, or directed student shows for their undergraduate theater groups. In each of these settings he was a popular and inspiring mentor, beloved by faculties and students alike. But he never stuck around for long.

My folks had reached their seventies by now. Their best days were drifting farther and farther into the past. They began to lose more and more of their old gang, those hard-drinking, hard-smoking bohemians from their younger years. My mother had fewer and fewer friends, and fewer and fewer people were around who remembered my father's best work. With the burden of old age and nagging insecurity, Dad was growing increasingly fretful and prone to fatigue. But he and my mother kept moving on, moving on. Wanderlust never quite released them from its grip.

Meantime I was acting away on Broadway. I was loving my work, expanding my horizons, and making a bigger and bigger name for myself. But despite the pleasure and pride I took in my fat Broadway résumé, my concern and guilt at my parents' increasing sense of dislocation weighed me down. Nor was this the only burden I carried during those frenetic years. Onstage I was a confident, respected actor, constantly employed and consistently in demand. But in my offstage existence, things couldn't have been more different. By the time I reached the end of the 1970s, my personal life had come apart at the seams. All the verities of my first thirty years had utterly failed me. Every time I walked out a stage door I left the warm embrace of the theater and came up against the real world. In that world I was hanging on by a thread.

27.
Adolescence

We all have to go through adolescence. If you're lucky you go through it when you're actually an adolescent. With me, it kicked in at thirty, about fifteen years late. For a compulsively good boy—a dutiful son, a committed husband, a doting father—my late adolescence was like a hair-raising ride on a runaway train. I clung for dear life to my seat on that train. There seemed to be no way to control its speed or direction. At a certain point I knew I was going to crash. I swung crazily between exhilaration, confusion, emotional exhaustion, and guilt. I was in an altered state of consciousness. I had no perspective. It would be years before I realized that the whole mess had been inevitable. The crash was long overdue, but it had to happen.

In distant hindsight, my life up to the age of thirty resembles a stately edifice, constructed over many years, only to be reduced to rubble in an instant. Emerging from a wildly unpredictable childhood, I had followed an orderly path. By its very nature, a theater career is *disorderly*, but I had pursued mine with as much rationality and discipline as I could muster: a Harvard education, British academy training, rigorous work in rep theater, and success on Broadway. I had married at an absurdly young age, but my wife was resourceful and supportive, and our son didn't arrive until we'd been married for a sensible six years. To all appearances we were a model family. So what was missing from this picture of happy domesticity?

Simply this: my adolescence.

In the theater, love and sex are occupational hazards. We actors are no more lovesick and libidinous than anybody else, but our working life is a chemistry lab of emotions and urges. It renders us uniquely susceptible. Let's say two people are hired to portray two characters who fall in love. The two have never met. They are attached to other partners. At their first rehearsal, they don't even appeal to each other all that much. But they set about to learn their lines and rehearse their scenes, always striving toward the closest possible imitation of the truth. In an atmosphere of erotic intimacy, the play begins to come to life in the rehearsal studio. A director with the intensity of Svengali does his damnedest to stir a mutual attraction between the two. They gradually discover seductive qualities in each other. They turn each other on. They start to hang out together after rehearsals in restaurants and bars. They think they are hiding their titillating secret from the rest of the cast, but in fact everyone else is on to them. On a night of giddy excitement, they open their play. The two act out their love relationship in front of hundreds of people. They touch the audience deeply. They are elated by their success. Somewhere around this time, they finally sleep together. Onstage, night after night, they go through the motions of their pretend passion. Offstage, their passion is genuine. They are madly in love. Their lives become a kind of ecstatic chaos. Eventually the magic begins to dissipate. Life's complications begin to wear them down. The play itself begins to bore them. They break up. Long after the show closes, they both look back and wonder what in the world they had been thinking.

Is it any wonder there are so many affairs among actors? The miracle is that there are not many more.

I know whereof I speak. I acted in some twenty plays in and out of New York in the 1970s. In eight of them I had an affair with an actress in the cast. I staged a one-man sexual revolution, a dozen years after the actual sexual revolution had liberated my own generation. My backstage infidelities were dignified only slightly by the fact that they were, in a manner of speaking, serially monogamous: each time I would fall into an agony of love, replete with tears, longing, and late-night phone calls. Each time, my marriage would lose a little more tensile strength. Repeatedly I would feel on the brink of ending it and starting anew. Yet in each of these affairs, I had involved myself with a woman who was so enmeshed in her own relationship with someone else that there was no realistic possibility of my committing to her. Although I did not admit it to myself, this was probably a relief. It may even have been an unconscious choice. It allowed me to crawl back to my marriage, wallowing in a mire of confessional self-flagellation. It was Hickey's dynamic, from *The Iceman Cometh*, but without the booze and the whores. Lacking the courage of my own concupiscence, I brought as much misery to my wife and my lover-of-the-moment as I had brought upon myself.

With the reckless passion, comical clumsiness, and destructive power of a rampaging elephant, I had finally reached my adolescence. But adolescence, too, comes to an end eventually. That runaway train goes too fast. It races out of control. Along comes one curve it can't quite navigate. It crashes spectacularly. You survive the cataclysm, you crawl out of the wreckage, you wipe the blood from your face and check your limbs for broken bones. Then you stagger away from the crash site and get on with the rest of your life. For me, this was the story of the last few years of the 1970s.

In 1977, Liv Ullmann was the most beautiful and celebrated film actress in the world. From her modest beginnings in the Norwegian town of Trondheim, she had risen to the status of an incandescent international star. She had played leading roles in several films of Ingmar Bergman, the great Swedish *auteur.* The naked intimacy of her performances in those films perfectly matched Bergman's bleak vision of human emotion, spirituality, and sexuality. She was spoken of

as Bergman's muse. Their offscreen romantic attachment had ended a few years before, but it was still inextricably linked to the power of their collaborative work. She had most recently appeared in Bergman's harrowing *Scenes from a Marriage*. In that film, it was impossible to imagine any other actress in the role Bergman had created for her. In her memoir *Changing*, published that same year, Liv fearlessly described the tortured passion between the two of them during their long affair. These passages read like scenes from a Bergman film. I was destined to reenact a few of those scenes myself.

One day in late spring 1977, I got a phone call from Alexander Cohen. Alex was one of the last great one-man Broadway producers, a throwback to a bygone era. A call from him was always good news. In his baritone growl, Alex said he wanted me to play Mat Burke opposite Liv Ullmann in *Anna Christie* on Broadway for the upcoming season. I knew next to nothing about either the role or the play, but I was elated at the offer. I dashed out to a bookstore, bought the play, and read it that very afternoon. My heart raced and my fingers trembled as I turned the pages. I was going to perform these scenes with Liv Ullmann!

My excitement was boundless, but underneath it another emotion began to stir. At the time, I had just extricated myself from my most recent ill-fated love affair. Jean and I had regained a measure of equilibrium and had once again resolved to make our marriage work. It was a cycle we had repeated two or three times in the preceding couple of years. As I read *Anna Christie*, my giddy anticipation was tempered by a sense of foreboding. This could be trouble. The cycle could start all over again. How could I prevent it? In the case of Liv Ullmann, I was already in love.

I met Liv at our first rehearsal. Sure enough, she cast a spell. In person she had a kind of heartbreaking beauty. No man in the room could take his eyes off her, nor any woman. She was a mix of playful and serious, vulnerable and tough, shy and daring. She disarmed us all with her earthiness and her willingness to be one of the gang. She was clearly accustomed to being treated like a queen, and yet she charmingly deflected everyone's adulation. Her broad smile and ready laugh lit up the room. In the ensuing days, the work did not come easy for her. She had a regal bearing and a sensuous bloom of health that made her oddly ill-suited to the role of the downtrodden Anna, and with her heavy Nordic accent she struggled to master O'Neill's yeasty slang. But she loved the high drama of José Quintero's direction and she poured herself into the work. Watching her day by day, the whole cast became smitten with her. None more than I.

Prior to Broadway, we took the show out of town. Our first stop was Toronto. The production's major players were put up at the Sutton Place Hotel. The company plunged into a week of tedious tech rehearsals at the Royal Alexandra Theatre. Outside of the gravitational pull of New York, Liv and I became closer and closer. We began spending all our time together, inside the playhouse and out. After our first Toronto performance, she invited the cast to celebrate with champagne in her dressing room. After twenty minutes, everyone began to peel off and say goodnight. Finally only Liv and I were left. The two of us sat alone in the room for another hour, laughing and talking in a thickening haze of drunkenness. Two or three times the stage-door man tapped on the door and asked us when we were going to leave and let him lock up. With too much champagne in us, we finally left the theater and climbed into the back of Liv's car. Her impassive driver took us back to the Sutton Place Hotel. That night, the night we first performed *Anna Christie*, was the beginning of a year-long affair. Ever since that night, the Sutton Place Hotel has loomed in my mind as a grim landmark. It memorializes a moment shot through with a dizzying mix of joy, pain, and guilt, the first night of a year that changed everything.

By prior arrangement, Jean came up to Toronto a week later to join me for a short visit. She brought along five-year-old Ian. I had not told her about what had transpired between Liv and me. In a state of numb paralysis, I had done nothing to forestall her trip. The visit was horrific. On the very first night Jean was there, I blurted out to her the news of my latest infidelity. Her first response was incredulous laughter ("You're kidding!"). This was quickly followed by bewilderment, then rage, and ultimately a kind of deranged despair. I was so choked with my own tears and guilt that I was blind to my unintended cruelty toward her. In retrospect it appalls me. There was plenty wrong with our marriage, but I'd had neither the honesty nor the courage to flatly state that I wanted it to end. Instead I blamed our troubles on some inexorable outside force that had me in its grip. How can we go on, I wailed, when I keep doing this to you? How can you endure it? I'm such a bastard! Why don't you throw me out? The scene could have been scripted by Eugene O'Neill.

In essence that evening was the beginning of the end of our ten-year marriage. Jean flew home early with Ian, leaving me to grapple with a turbulent new reality of my own devising. The pre-Broadway tour continued for two more months. After Toronto we played Washington and Baltimore. The out-of-town run constituted a de facto separation from Jean and a de facto live-in relationship with Liv. Between Liv and me, passions ran so high that it was almost impossible to sort them out. We loved each other's company, but from the very outset our relationship was beset with insecurity and strife. Following the age-old pattern of stage romances, the play had released a torrent of need in both of us. She longed for a simple love relationship, a safe haven from the unwanted glare of celebrity and star worship. In me she was looking for a strong and defiant protector. I was completely incapable of assuming that role. I was a tangled mass of conflict, woefully lacking in self-knowledge. On the one hand I was a horny teenager in a thirty-year-old body, grasping insatiably for all the sex I had never allowed myself. On the other, I was an escapee from an unhappy marriage and a defecting father, tortured with guilt and doubt. With such baggage, the affair was unlikely to be good for either of us, but this prevented neither of us from hurling ourselves into it. In the coming months, things only grew more troubled and intense. But by some miracle, despite all the tempestuous offstage drama of our relationship, the two of us managed to put on our costumes every night, walk out onstage, and *act*.

As the weeks passed, more complications weighed on us. The backstage world of *Anna Christie* grew claustrophobic. It became the least fun show I'd ever been in. A subtle hierarchy took hold in the company, with Liv at the top. My friendships with three-fourths of the cast evaporated. Although Liv never invoked the privileges of stardom, an entourage gradually formed itself around her, answering to her every whim. It was comprised of our director, our company manager, Liv's dresser, an older character actress in the cast, and their various traveling companions. Of this inner circle of fawning courtiers, I was the only heterosexual. I wrestled disconsolately with the role of royal consort. After every show the group would merrily carouse in a restaurant, striving mightily to flatter and entertain their queen bee. At the end of such evenings I would squire Liv back to her hotel room and leave the others behind. Everyone tacitly understood my courtly function. My male ego, fragile at the best of times, swung crazily between swaggering pride and cringing humiliation.

In those days, everywhere Liv went she was treated like visiting royalty. In every city, she was invited to glittering A-list events to which I would dutifully escort her. Rudolf Nureyev greeted us in his Toronto dressing room after a performance with Canada's Royal Ballet. Ethel Kennedy hosted us at a lawn party at Hickory Hill, her rambling family seat. We sat on either side of Henry Kissinger at Sweden's embassy in Washington.

We had chummy lunches with the likes of Bibi Andersson and Ingrid Bergman. With fellow partygoers Katharine Graham and Teddy Kennedy, we witnessed a gleeful frat-boy food fight between George Stevens, Jr., and Bob Woodward at Stevens' Georgetown home. Our show's press agent engineered an after-theater soiree in honor of Liv and Elizabeth Taylor. On another night we shared an intimate dinner with Richard Burton, Robert Preston, and their wives. Burton began that evening gracious, charming, and sober. Liv and I watched in fascination and horror, exchanging eye-rolling glances, as too much drink gradually turned that splendid man into a boorish, self-loathing sot.

At such moments I could hardly believe that I was in the presence of such powerful, notorious figures, or that I was witnessing such larger-than-life behavior. It was both exciting and unsettling. On the one hand, I was thrilled to be so close to the white-hot center of the celebrity firmament. On the other, I knew very well where I stood. All eyes were on Liv. I was strangely invisible. I was an awkward, ungainly presence, regarded by all as tolerable, perhaps necessary, but vaguely embarrassing—if, that is, they noticed me at all.

In retrospect, my comparative anonymity strikes me as a blessing. Back then, show business was not yet subject to the frantic 24/7 scandalmongering of our present era. Our affair had all the elements of a sensationally lurid tabloid serial, tracking the undoing of four lives. But in our case, the press was merciful. It turned a respectful blind eye to all of us. This was partly the result of a greater degree of circumspection among entertainment reporters in those days, and partly it was because of their worshipful regard for Liv. Whatever the reasons, only a single brief mention of our relationship ever appeared in the national press. In a Q&A feature for her Sunday gossip column, Liz Smith was asked about Liv Ullmann's love life. Smith succinctly noted a "heavy affair" with her costar in *Anna Christie*. The subtext of the sentence was unmistakable: "Let's leave these people alone."

The torrid weeks passed by, and we continued to perform our ponderous production of *Anna Christie*. My role was a monster. I'd never worked so hard onstage, and rarely to such little effect. It slowly dawned on me that, for most of the audience, the show's main attraction was neither the play nor the production but Liv. As I bellowed my way through my speeches on one side of the stage, I would occasionally glimpse the audience gazing at the other side, where Liv was simply standing and listening, staring straight out into the lights. People were transfixed. Who could blame them? She was beautiful, the show was turgidly un-dramatic, and I was a lousy Mat Burke. But that adoring, misdirected gaze did little to shore up my faltering self-esteem.

The most torturous period of our affair was during the first months of the Broadway run. When the tour ended, the heady swirl of life on the road smashed up against the reality of home. Back in the city, I was sur-rounded by all the touchstones of my everyday New York life—my apartment, my friends, and, most of all, my son, who had been pining for my return. I was ut-terly unprepared to leave any of this behind. Reach-ing out desperately for some semblance of normality, I moved back in with Jean. Liv was aghast. My feck-less decision left her feeling abandoned, humiliated, and deeply injured. For weeks I shuttled between her and Jean, bicycling inanely between my apartment and Liv's hotel suite on Central Park South, in the mad at-tempt to meet the needs of two very different women. I was frantically shoveling to fill two bottomless pits, yawning on either side of me. It was *Scenes from a Marriage*, but with two separate leading ladies. And through it all, the curtain went up eight times a week on *Anna Christie* at the Imperial Theatre on Forty-fifth Street, like the relentless tolling of a dooms-day bell.

I cut a strange figure during that time. I looked like a character from a Dostoyevsky novel. I had lost a lot of weight. I was pale, drawn, and perpetually seized with fatigue. I'd had my hair permed into tight Irish curls for the role of Mat Burke, altering my appearance so completely that friends did double takes when they ran into me on the street. One of them, actor (now director) Don Scardino, hadn't seen me for months. As I shot by on my bicycle one day, he hailed me from the sidewalk. I pulled over and dismounted. He sized me up and greeted me, with a trace of concern in his voice: "How's it goin'?" To Donnie's astonishment, I instantly burst into tears.

I was falling apart. I needed help. Thankfully, I had a place to go. It was a stuffy room in a musty apartment at Eighty-sixth and Broadway. The apartment belonged to a woman I'll call Miriam. Miriam was my therapist. The room was her office. Six months before, I had sought her out in an attempt to put my emotional life in some kind of order. At the time I had been involved in an earlier extramarital entanglement. That one had been stormy as well, but compared to the cyclone that was battering me now, it had been barely a drizzle.

Miriam was a blocky, wizened little Jewish woman with the demeanor of a chain-smoking tortoise. When

I first met with her, the grave rituals of therapy were brand-new to me. I seized on them hungrily. Until that moment, my entire life had been characterized by a fretful eagerness to please. The fear of anyone's *displea-sure* had dominated my every thought. Small wonder I had ended up an actor: God forbid that anyone should have known the *real* me. Such fears had taken their toll. They had turned me into a rusty strongbox of dark secrets, waiting to be pried open. When my sessions with Miriam cracked open that box, the relief was overwhelming. The simple act of saying things out loud that I had kept shamefully to myself since childhood sent an electric jolt through my entire system. Exposed to the air, my demons took flight. The sources of my guilt, fear, and shame turned out to be compelling evidence that I was—surprise!—merely human. In those early sessions with Miriam, a great weight was lifted from my shoulders. I practically hyperventilated with optimism and hope. I had no inkling of the turmoil up ahead.

Months later, when I arrived in New York after the pre-Broadway tour of *Anna Christie*, I was in the midst of the biggest emotional meltdown of my life. I went straight to Miriam to pick up where we had left off. My sessions immediately took on a combustible new intensity. A couple of times a week I would stagger into her office, flop into an overstuffed chair, and tearfully recycle the psychic garbage of the past three decades and the past few days. The process was murky and messy. In fits and starts I lurched toward some measure of self-possession. There were no eureka moments and no clear, definable results. I couldn't even tell whether Miriam was a good or bad therapist. Some sessions were breathlessly illuminating and some were a pointless waste of time. But looking back, it is impossible for me to imagine surviving that chapter of my life without them.

A few months after I went back to Miriam, things got a little weird. My therapy began to echo the antic confusion of the rest of my life. In the misguided belief that she could solve everyone's problems, Miriam allowed herself to get drawn into the fiery dramatics of my situation. She herself joined the cast of characters of the frenzied passion play that Jean, Liv, and I had been acting out.

Of the three parties in my romantic triangle, I was clearly not the only one in emotional crisis. My hand-wringing indecisiveness had unstrung Jean and Liv as well. Our days and nights, in the apartment, the hotel, and the theater, were filled with drunken rages, frenzied suicide threats, and tumblers of vodka hurled through the air at crowded parties. Such scenes had all the earmarks of lunatic farce, but they were deadly serious and searingly painful. Both women were in just as much agony as I was. In desperation, first Jean, then Liv, made the same crazy decision. They went to Miriam. Miriam was just as crazy as they were: she took them on as patients. That made three of us, all tramping up to Eighty-sixth and Broadway for separate sessions with the same little old Jewish lady. She had taken on the untenable role of Mommy to three squabbling children. Her revolving-door treatment of the three of us was reckless, inexpert, and verging on the unethical. It was further compromised by her starstruck infatuation with Liv and by her transparent hope that my marriage to Jean would survive (when we finally split up, Miriam wept like a jilted teenager). In hindsight, my estimation of her therapeutic skills has slipped considerably. But at the time, we were all crazy enough to try anything.

Somehow, whether through Miriam's intervention or in spite of it, the three of us all survived. The year left us a lot sadder, but a good deal wiser. *Anna Christie* mercifully closed. Jean and I separated for good. I moved out of the apartment I'd shared with her and into a tiny one-bedroom flat on West End Avenue, living alone for the first time in my life. Ian's days were divided between the homes of his two parents, fifteen blocks apart. My relationship with Liv sputtered along sporadically, depending on where in the world her work took her. A couple of times I traveled with her to Scandinavia, and she returned periodically to visit me in New York. The affair grew less stressful but it was hardly stress-free. Instead of Jean, Liv's new rival was my solitude. Crouched in my little apartment like an ascetic hermit, I began to savor my solitude like precious oxygen. In solitude I felt as if I was finally learning who I was. I was drunk with it. And it finally won out. Six months after the close of our show, Liv and I finally broke up. Predictably, the breakup was fraught with pain, anger, and tears. But it was a blessed relief for me and the best possible thing for her. It had been an important time for both of us. For me it had been essential. But it was time for us both to move on.

The preceding year had revealed to me some unpleasant truths about myself—my neediness, my fragility, my cowardice, and my fear. These failings had driven me to scenes of wild, irrational behavior that until then I hadn't thought myself capable of. My ego had crumbled calamitously under all of the pressure, but in time I began the long process of rebuilding it. I struggled to overcome my weaknesses and find new sources of strength. I had learned a basic truth of human nature, that the stress and strain of relationships can change us beyond recognition, blurring the lines be-tween kindness and cruelty, loyalty and betrayal, love and hate. The great goal in life is to understand and forgive each other and ourselves. These simple insights eased me out of my emotional paralysis and nudged me toward self-awareness. And who knows? It might pos-sibly have added a new dimension to my acting as well. I was in the drama business, after all. Who knew that nothing on any stage or screen could touch the high drama of real life?

A few years later I ran into Liv in the wings of Radio City Music Hall. It was the first time we had seen each other since our breakup. Along with a hundred other celebrities, we were participating in a big benefit event for the Actors' Fund of America. The moment was dreamlike and surreal. We stood alone in a ghostly half-light filtering into the wings from the vast Radio City stage. A pop orchestra played in the distance. Dozens of stars milled around nearby in the cavernous backstage. Thousands of people rustled in the audito-rium just yards away from us. In our own little bubble, Liv and I hugged each other with genuine affection. She told me how happy I looked and I truthfully told her the same thing. To all appearances our lives had righted themselves. I felt a sudden, surprising rush of gratitude. In a flash of rueful irony, I realized that a desperately unhappy year had cleared the way for a much happier life.

Life, of course, is not quite so tidy. No story of a family's dissolution leaves everyone unscarred. The events of that year had taken their heaviest toll on the one person least equipped to deal with them. My son Ian turned six that year. At such a young age, he couldn't begin to understand the forces that had split up his parents. Jean and I did our best to explain things to him in terms that he could understand, but this was a tall order. She was consumed with bitterness, I with guilt, and we barely understood the situation ourselves. Despite our best efforts, Ian was completely bewildered by our separation. He had been living the life of a happy Upper West Side kid, beating a path between home, school, play dates, and the wilds of Central Park. Suddenly things were not so simple. His days were now encumbered by frequent treks between his parents' two apartments, by the terse, angry exchanges between the two of them, by the blunt questions of his schoolmates, and by the earnest looks of concern on the faces of his best friends' mothers. Jean and I struggled to compensate for all these new burdens he carried. We worked harder than ever to make his life active and fun. All things considered, he

managed his difficulties extremely well, soldiering on
with a good-natured fortitude and courage that belied
his young years. But even his best times were tinged
with melancholy. He clearly longed for Jean and me to
get back together, to restore the Eden of his younger
days. But he was too young to understand that this
was never going to happen.

A marriage had come to an end. The change left
the three of us reeling. For each of us, every day was
a battle to dispel the gloom. But in the midst of all the
pain, I sensed that my life had changed for the better.
The same could not be said for Jean or Ian. The separation had been a bitter blow to both of them. In time
we would all walk away from the train wreck of my
late adolescence, but their injuries would take longer to
heal. They continued to grieve for a past that was gone
forever. Their grief saddened me as well. But despite
it, and despite the grim loneliness of my solitary life, I
was not looking backwards. I was looking ahead. In my
homely little flat, I slowly taught myself the rudiments
of self-sufficiency and self-knowledge. I put my adolescence behind me and wearily embraced adulthood
at last. I was patiently waiting for my next chapter to
begin.

28.
My Biggest Mistake

C hoices can drive an actor nuts. Having to choose between two job offers is a high-class problem, to be sure. Most actors spend their days pining for even one. But if a choice is a luxury, it can also be a torment. We actors are always looking for the main chance, the big break, the next rung on the illusory ladder of success. When a choice presents itself, a broad range of considerations comes into play—the roles, the material, the venues, the visibility, the other talent, the artistic fulfillment, the dough. The most compelling factor is the mysterious signal that comes from your gut: What do you really want to *do*? But sometimes the answer to that question is maddeningly difficult to formulate. Choosing between two jobs (not to mention three or four) necessarily means turning something down. Faced with a major choice, every actor is haunted by the dire scenario of declining a role that then brings undreamt-of glory to some other actor. I myself must hold the record for the most Tony Awards won by actors in roles that I've turned down. Inherent in every choice is the potential for making a terrible mistake. In the course of his career, an actor tiptoes through a minefield of such mistakes. In the fall of 1979, in choosing my last acting job of the decade, I made a whopper.

In the spring of that year, I participated in a reading of a new play at Joe Papp's downtown Public Theater. It was an interesting play with an arresting title: *Salt Lake City Skyline*. The play was a loosely historical re-enactment of the trial leading up to the 1915 execution of Joe Hill, the radical union organizer. It was written by one of Papp's in-house playwrights, a contemporary of mine named Thomas Babe. Tom had been a friend at Harvard, although I had never worked with him there. Along with my old rival Timothy Mayer, he had been codirector of that long-ago Harvard summer theater that I had spurned in favor of my doomed Great Road Players in Princeton. At the time of the play reading, Joe Papp was in his glory years. If he summoned you to read a play, you showed up. But I was also eager to do a favor for Tom Babe, a man I liked and admired, in an effort to bury an old hatchet.

The reading was unexpectedly powerful. Ten good actors had been assembled for the occasion. I read the lead role of the immigrant Joe Hill, in a Swedish accent that owed a good deal to my recent friendship with a certain Norwegian film star. The other major role in the play was the sentencing judge from the Joe Hill trial. It was played by the dour, ironic, and very imposing Fred Gwynne, the only actor I had ever shared a stage with who was taller than I was. Typical of such occasions, the cast read through the script once in a Public Theater rehearsal studio. Then about thirty of the Public's friends and staff members filed in and we performed the play full-out, standing before our little audience at a row of black music stands. At the play's climax, the judge dolefully sings the anthemic union ballad "I Dreamed I Saw Joe Hill Last Night," then BANG! Joe Hill is shot by a firing squad. Blackout. As the reading drew to an end, we could hear sniffles and muffled sobs. When it was over the crowd applauded strenuously and tearfully. I had asked my big brother, David, to come to the reading that day. He still remembers it as one of the most moving moments of theater he has ever seen. Unrehearsed play readings can sometimes have that effect.

A few months after we did that downtown reading, I went back to work on Broadway. I joined the cast of Peter Hall's production of *Bedroom Farce* at the Brooks Atkinson on Forty-seventh Street. That show's producer was Robert Whitehead, one of the great gentlemen of the New York theater. In his day, Bob had produced such historic Broadway fare as *The Member of the Wedding, A Man for All Seasons,* and the premieres of four major plays by Arthur Miller. With his impeccable suits, his urbane mustache, and his mane of white hair, Bob radiated class. Late in the run of *Bedroom Farce,* he came to my dressing room. He was giddy with good news. He was all set to produce the American premiere of Harold Pinter's *Betrayal* for Broadway. Peter Hall himself was slated to direct it, having just staged it in London to loud acclaim. Roy Scheider and Blythe Danner were already cast in it. Bob breathlessly announced that Hall wanted me to play Jerry, rounding out the three characters. This was wonderful news, of course, but Bob took more pleasure in delivering it than I took in receiving it. Joe Papp, you see, wanted to mount *Salt Lake City Skyline* at the Public Theater at the very same time. Even as Bob spoke, I could feel the burden of *choice* descending on my shoulders.

Joe Papp was the very opposite of Robert Whitehead. If Bob was a Broadway aristocrat, Joe was a Lower East Side street tough. Since the late 1950s, he had built the New York Shakespeare Festival from a downtown church basement workshop into an indispensable American institution. Having introduced free Shakespeare in Central Park in 1962, he had since grabbed hold of the enormous Astor Library on Lafayette Street and turned it into the Public, a sprawling, splendidly renovated five-theater incubator of new American plays and musicals. A list of productions begotten at the Public reads like a history of New York theater in the last thirty years of the twentieth century. Such Tony-winning creations as *That Championship Season*, *A Chorus Line*, and *Hair* only scratch the surface of his prodigious output.

This miraculous body of work was the result of a unique good cop/bad cop management partnership at the top of Joe's organization. The good cop was his producing partner, a genial and warmly persuasive man named Bernard Gersten. The bad cop was Joe himself, a charismatic, irascible, fearless, mercurial, and frequently impossible man to deal with. He had a kind of genius for throwing people off guard and bending them to his will. To that end, he cultivated a complex love-hate relationship with everyone who worked with him, including even Bernie Gersten himself. The first time I met Joe had been years before, at a Shakespeare audition in a rehearsal room at the Public. In front of six or eight staffers, he greeted me that day with a booming voice, cigar in hand:

"John Lithgow! The son who has outstripped his father, as every son must!"

Zap! By some sixth sense, he had found my emotional sore spot and plunged a needle straight into it. I was stunned and confused. On the one hand, he was complimenting my nascent success. On the other, he was airily dismissing my father's entire life's work, without knowing a thing about my relationship with him. I was frozen in place, caught somewhere between flattery and outrage. Just like that, Joe Papp had me right where he wanted me. A man like that is incredibly hard to say no to.

And there I was, years later, caught between Bob Whitehead and Joe Papp, between Broadway and downtown, between Harold Pinter and Thomas Babe, between *Betrayal* and *Salt Lake City Skyline*. I twisted myself into knots trying to decide between the two jobs. I spoke on the phone with Bob Whitehead, who was incredulous that I would even consider turning down *Betrayal*. Then I spoke to Joe, who did a classic Joe Papp number on me:

"Whaddya wanna do another English play for? That's all y'been doing! You're an American! You should be playing an American! Everybody thinks you're a limey!"—(this, notwithstanding the fact that Joe Hill was a Swede). "That Harold Pinter thing's already been done! That's all the Broadway crowd wants! Something that's already a big deal in *London*!" (pronouncing the word as if it were week-old fish). "That's safe stuff! It's soft! Come on down here and show everybody you've got some *balls*!"

Never the most decisive actor in town, I was a reed in the wind, blowing this way and that. The deciding vote was cast by my agent at William Morris. This was a young man to whom I'd recently been relegated after my longtime rep, Rick Nicita, had decamped for an upstart agency in Los Angeles called CAA. My new agent took the Joe Papp line. Let's go with the bold choice, he proclaimed. Let's be daring. Let's take *Salt Lake City Skyline*! So I did. I called Bob Whitehead and told him my decision. To Bob it sounded as if I had chosen dirt over gold dust, but without a trace of ill will he wished me well.

Anyone might have guessed the outcome. With a full production in the Public's churchlike Anspacher Theater, *Salt Lake City Skyline* wilted into an inert and preachy bore. The reviews said as much. My brother barely recognized it from that exhilarating play reading six months before. We played for three weeks to half-empty houses. Joe Papp had sat through half of a dress rehearsal and had never been heard from again. At a desultory party on our opening night I learned the reason that my new agent at William Morris had so strenuously urged me to choose the Babe play: he also represented its director.

And *Betrayal*? It opened halfway through our brief run, with Raúl Juliá in the role of Jerry. The show was an unqualified success, hailed as one of Pinter's greatest works. It was the talk of the town, destined to play to sell-out crowds well into the following season. In every bio of Robert Whitehead, it is listed first among his many great successes. Since that hit Broadway premiere, there have been hundreds of revivals of it all over the world. Gallingly, I've been asked to play Jerry in it, three or four more times. By contrast, *Salt Lake City Skyline* was never performed again. In the next thirty years, the two plays would come to symbolize the biggest professional mistake I ever made.

A few nights before we closed, Bob Whitehead and his wife, Zoe Caldwell, came downtown to see our show. Afterward, they made their way to my makeup table through a crowd of half-dressed actors in our cluttered common dressing room. Bob was aglow with his recent Broadway triumph. In possibly his most gracious moment, he complimented me warmly on my performance. He said that, while he'd been baffled by my decision to pass on *Betrayal*, having seen me in the role of Joe Hill he could understand why I'd chosen it. Fred Gwynne slouched nearby, listening to the exchange. After the Whiteheads left, he put a hand on my shoulder, shook his head, and looked at me with a world-weary smile on his long, mournful face. He didn't have to say a word.

But that is not the end of this cautionary tale. There is another chapter.

While the cast of *Betrayal* merrily continued their sold-out run on Broadway, I ate my heart out with self-recrimination and regret. But because *Salt Lake City Skyline* had closed so abruptly, I was available for other work. Before long, another job did indeed materialize. I was hired to play a small supporting role in a live network TV production of *The Oldest Living Graduate*, a recent play by the Texas writer Preston Jones. Headlining the show would be Henry Fonda, Cloris Leachman, and George Grizzard. The play would be broadcast from the campus theater of SMU in Dallas, but the cast was scheduled to rehearse for three weeks in Los Angeles prior to the live performance. This modest job was a far cry from a leading role in a hit Broadway show, but I was happy to put a few thousand miles between me and the thrumming New York success of *Betrayal*. In the month of March 1980, I flew west to begin rehearsals. It was a trip that was destined to completely change my life.

Soon after my arrival in Los Angeles, I called up Walter Teller. Walter and I had been good friends for a dozen years. I had met him on the night that Nixon defeated Hubert Humphrey, in November of 1968. That was the month when I'd sneaked home from England to direct *As You Like It* for my father in Princeton. Walter's parents and mine were part of a crowd of Princeton friends who had gathered for an election-night party at the house of a gung-ho Democratic couple. Walter and I had tagged along with our parents, the only members of our generation in attendance. He was smart, cynical, and funny. Like so many of my college friends of that era, he was highly educated and totally directionless. I took to him immediately. We spent the evening skulking in the basement of the house, playing pool, drinking beer, bemoaning the ascendancy of Richard Nixon, and hatching a lifelong friendship.

In the years between that election night and my West Coast trip, Walt had gone to law school at Berkeley, had turned to entertainment law, had moved to Los Angeles, and had joined a booming law practice there. This career path had put a continent between us. We hadn't connected for ages. When I reached him in his L.A. office, he was delighted to hear from me. We arranged to have supper the following night at El Coyote, a clamorous Mexican restaurant on Beverly Boulevard in Hollywood. That evening, over enchiladas, beans, and beer, I spent an hour bringing Walter up to date on the events of my last couple of years. It was a pretty gloomy narrative, but it was leavened by Walt's usual drollery and wry perspective. At a certain point, I paused for a breath and a swig of Dos Equis. Walter chose that moment for a twinkly pronouncement.

"Well, I have something for you," he said.

"What's that?" I asked.

"Mary Yeager."

Walter proceeded to tell me all about a friend he'd made since arriving in town. It was a story that grew more intriguing with every sentence. Mary Yeager was a professor of economic history at UCLA. Considering the tweedy mustiness of academia, she was a stunning anomaly—blond, blue-eyed, and attractive, with a passing resemblance to the young Julie Christie. She had grown up a farm girl on the plains of northern Montana, but from childhood she had methodically plotted an escape from her preordained life as a farmer's wife. Her planned escape route was an East Coast college. Her farmer father had only allowed her to apply to two schools, refusing to pay for more than two application fees. She'd selected Smith and Middlebury. Sadly, she was turned down by both.

After receiving her rejection letters, she wept for two days. Then she wrote a letter to the admissions officers at Middlebury and told them she was coming anyway. Taken aback by her fierce tenacity, they agreed to make room for her after all.

The following September, as if grabbing the last stagecoach out of town, Mary Yeager left Montana behind her. She spent four grueling years at Middlebury, struggling to fill the holes in her small-town Montana public school education. After Middlebury, she earned a Ph.D. in history at Johns Hopkins University in Baltimore. Then she won an appointment as the first-ever female tenure-track history professor at Brown. Finally she had ended up on the faculty of UCLA, two years before my supper with Walter Teller at El Coyote. By now she was thirty-five years old, just like me. She had married young, but, like me, her marriage had ended three years before. Walter had been going with a longtime girlfriend during the entire time he had known Mary, but as he recounted her story it was clear that he adored her. And something told him that she and I were exactly right for each other.

Walter fixed us up. With lawyerly craft, he hatched a benign two-faced plot. He told Mary that we would swing by on a Saturday and take her out to lunch. Telling me nothing of the plan, he proposed that he and I play tennis that same morning on a public court near her home. That Saturday, after two sweltering hours of tennis, he blithely suggested to me that we drop by Mary Yeager's apartment and see if she wanted to join us for a bite to eat. I liked the idea. As we pulled up to her Santa Monica address, I noted that her apartment was in a building situated at the corner of Montana Avenue and Harvard Street. Montana and Harvard? The coincidence sent a tiny shiver of destiny right through me. Walter rang the doorbell and Mary opened the door, betraying not a trace of impatience at the fact that we had arrived an hour later than he had told her to expect us.

She was even prettier than Walter had described. Decked out for an elegant Santa Monica lunch date, she wore beige pants, strappy sandals, and a white cotton sweater dotted with little embroidered flowers. I, on the other hand, sported mismatched tennis gear that featured dirty gray sneakers, navy socks, and an old red polo shirt soaked with sweat. Flushed with athletic exertion, my face matched the color of my shirt. My dripping hair stuck out porcupine-style. I was a clueless embarrassment to chivalrous manhood. When Walter introduced me to Mary, I cheerily greeted her and wetly shook her hand, without the slightest notion that there was anything wrong with this picture.

Mary knew next to nothing about my world. Her closest brush with show business was at the age of eleven when her father erected the first drive-in movie theater in the state of Montana, in a wheat field outside the town of Brady. When Walter had mentioned me to Mary, she had never heard of me. I was the first actor she had ever met. I later learned that Walter had hyped me to her as "the best theater actor in New York." This had led her to picture me as a handsome matinee idol, someone along the lines of the dark, dashing Kevin Kline (a stab in my envious heart!). So for her, my appearance on the doorstep that day was a deeply underwhelming disappointment. Her mistaken first impression of me was twofold: I was Australian, and I was gay.

Fortunately, she was too polite to slam the door in our faces. Off we went for a notably *in*elegant nosh at the long-gone Westside Delicatessen on San Vicente Boulevard. The three of us had a fantastic time. We laughed ourselves breathless for ninety minutes. When Walter and I dropped Mary off afterwards, I kissed her cheek at the curb in front of her home. We arranged to get together the next day to see a Sunday-afternoon showing of the film *Norma Rae*. We spent that entire Sunday talking and laughing on her living room couch. We never got to *Norma Rae*. I went to UCLA on Monday morning and watched her give the first lecture of her survey course on American Economic History. From her lips I heard the name "Joseph Schumpeter" for the first time. Who would have dreamed that the name "Joseph Schumpeter" could ever sound so sexy?

By Tuesday, Mary had left for an academic conference in Washington, D.C. She was gone for three days. The days were punctuated by a dozen phone calls between us. She returned just in time to go with me to a weekend barbecue for the cast of *The Oldest Living Graduate*. It was her introduction into the exotic backstage world of show business. She hobnobbed at poolside with leathery Harry Dean Stanton and callow Timothy Hutton. She chatted with Henry Fonda, the first screen legend she'd ever met in the flesh. After the barbecue, a manic Cloris Leachman insisted on giving us a Cook's tour of her vast home, perched atop Coldwater Canyon. More bemused than starstruck, Mary navigated the events of that afternoon like a research scholar stumbling onto a captivating new field of study.

The following week, my flying visit to Los Angeles came to an end. I had spent every possible hour with Mary. I left for Dallas to perform *The Oldest Living Graduate* on television. By that time, the die was cast. Walter had been right. Mary and I were made for each other. We've been together ever since. It was the best deal Walter Teller ever struck.

God probably never intended for actors and professors to marry. When an actor weds a professor, they are both asking for trouble. By nature, a professor's life is orderly and predictable. Years in advance, she knows what courses she'll teach, what conferences she'll attend, and what faculty committees she will serve on. She carefully doles out months and years of time to conduct research and write books. If she is to amass a substantial body of work and build a distinguished academic career, nothing must distract her from her clearly defined scholarly mission.

By comparison, an actor's life is scatterbrained chaos. He never knows where his next job is coming from, or when. A stray phone call from his agent can send him to another continent for a three-month gig on three days' notice. With every new offer, his career is totally rejiggered. Given a choice between jobs, he can bore the bark off a tree with his agonizing equivocations. Worse still, months can go by with no jobs at all. When this happens, an actor's gloom and self-doubt can make him an insufferable conjugal partner. But the opposite can also apply: a professor with a book deadline or a pending promotional review is no walk in the park, either. The twin disciplines of academia and show business require two completely different emotional skill sets and temperaments. On the face of it, a marriage between an actor and a professor can never work.

Ours does. It has for thirty years. Who knows why? Perhaps our differences have somehow bound us together. Mary is earthbound and practical, I am airheaded and artistic. She is restless and mercurial, I'm phlegmatic and plodding. She is pessimistic and contrary, I'm optimistic and accommodating. She is fearless and combative, I'm fretful and politic. She is openhearted and generous, I'm self-absorbed and tight-fisted. She shuns the spotlight, I am drawn to it like a heliotropic flower. Shakespeare is Greek to her, economics is Greek to me. Spectator sports? She is frostily indifferent, I am rabidly passionate. And yet from the first day we met, we have never bored each other for a second. For both of us there is no one else in the world whose company we would prefer. She has brought a tough-mindedness and reassuring order to my life, and I have brought a measure of disruptive fun and happy disorder to hers. By now, it is impossible for either of us to imagine life without the other.

After my lunch with Mary at the Westside Deli, the next four years passed with lightning speed. They were jam-packed with momentous changes for both of us. For a while we played a transcontinental tug-'o-war, struggling to choose between my life in New York and hers in Los Angeles. Mary took a sabbatical from UCLA to test the waters in Manhattan. She weighed job offers on the East Coast. We snooped around for a bigger Upper West Side apartment. One day my agent called. He'd made an appointment for me to read for a film based on John Irving's bestselling novel *The World According to Garp*. At my audition, I read for the role of the transsexual Roberta Muldoon. Director George Roy Hill cast me as Roberta and I shot the film in and around New York. Halfway through the shoot, Mary was granted tenure at UCLA. This news abruptly ended our geographical tug-'o-war. She won. I was heading west. But before leaving town, Mary and I got married at City Hall, with nine-year-old Ian as my best man. Arriving in Los Angeles, I joined Mary in the apartment at the corner of Montana and Harvard. Ian became a frequent visitor. Mary gave birth to our daughter, Phoebe. Soon after, *Garp* was released. The next year, our son Nathan came along. We bought a house, minutes from UCLA (where we have lived ever since). Rick Nicita was my agent again and Walter Teller was now my attorney. Awards began to pile up for my performance as Roberta Muldoon. When I won the New York Film Critics' Award, my old friend David Ansen gleefully called me with the news. Hollywood embraced me with open arms. After *Garp*, I played a back-to-back string of wildly different roles in major Hollywood films: *Twilight Zone, Footloose, Terms of Endearment,* and *The Adventures of Buckaroo Banzai.* Celebrity struck like an avalanche. I escorted Mary to the Academy Awards for two successive Oscar nominations. We barely knew what hit us. Our lives had been hurled into a completely new level of reality. If we hadn't had each other we might not have survived our dizzying flight into the ozone. But we did. We had each other. And we've had each other ever since.

A cautionary tale? Indeed. But it is a cautionary tale with a difference. This cautionary tale has a happy ending, right out of O. Henry. It is an ending shot through with one blazing, life-affirming irony:

None of these things would have ever happened if I hadn't made the biggest mistake of my career.

Let us examine for a moment what my wife's professorial colleagues might call "a counterfactual." I choose *Betrayal* and I celebrate a gratifying success on Broadway. But look what I miss out on? I never meet Mary Yeager. I completely forgo my life with her. Phoebe and Nathan are never born. A thousand happy events in our lives never take place—birthday parties, school plays, graduation ceremonies, camping trips, foreign countries, Christmas mornings, Halloween nights, swimming lessons, bicycle lessons, weddings, baby steps, pets. My professional life is impacted as well. I never achieve that unique dual citizenship as a Broadway and Hollywood actor that has been my calling card ever since. Everything of substance that has defined the second half of my life simply never happens. Such an alternate universe is completely inconceivable to me. Each of these things I hold near and dear. They will live in me forever, long after everyone else has lost all memory of a hit Broadway play in 1979.

And what is the moral of this story? It is a truth at the heart of my whole life:

Acting is pretty great. But it isn't everything.

Coda

Years after my father died, my thoughts continued to dwell on memories of him. The most vivid of those memories was that evening in 2002 when I first read him a bedtime story. As I relived that evening again and again, an idea gradually began to form in my mind. On that long-ago night, my mother, my father, and I made our deepest connection with each other. But that's not all that happened. By chance, I also stumbled across a nugget of pure gold. The nugget was called "Uncle Fred Flits By." That Wodehouse short story was a work of comedy genius, a fine-tuned machine for manufacturing riotous laughter. Best of all, it was a story that almost no one west of the Atlantic Ocean had ever heard of. I began to imagine a theatrical performance consisting of nothing more than "Uncle Fred

Flits By" enacted by a single actor on an empty stage. It would be a kind of storytelling magic act. With nothing more than the actor's sleight of hand, four settings, ten characters, and a parrot would all come to life in front of an audience. I would be the actor. And the story, for all its loopy hilarity, would be suffused with my own poignant history with it.

With no clear notion of what I would do next, I began to commit the story to memory. I printed it out on twenty sheets of paper. Each morning and evening I would take the family dog on long, leisurely walks, carrying the pages and running my lines. Passersby would see me staring into space, working my features spasmodically, and muttering to myself. They steered clear of me without a word. I assigned myself a single paragraph for each dog walk and wouldn't return home until it was safely stowed in my brain. After a month, the dog was exhausted, but I could recite the entire story to myself from beginning to end.

I enlisted the help of Jack O'Brien, a good friend and a splendid stage director, to help me spin "Uncle Fred" into a piece of theater. Jack was uncannily suited to the task. He and I shared a distinct strand of theatrical DNA. As a young man, he had worked with several alumni of my father's old Ohio Shakespeare festivals, so he felt an ineffable connection to my father's legacy. Together we approached André Bishop, artistic director of New York's Lincoln Center Theater Company. We asked him for a rehearsal room to try the piece out. André readily obliged. The three of us assembled a group of twenty friends and well-wishers. They arrived in the subterranean Ballet Room of the Vivian Beaumont Theater on a late morning in January 2008. They had no idea what I was up to.

I spent five minutes telling the little crowd my brief history with "Uncle Fred Flits By." I told them about my father, my mother, and my siblings. I told them about *Tellers of Tales*. I had brought along our old copy of the book, and I showed it to them. I told them about the Amherst condo and the night I read to my parents. Then, with no set other than a table and chair and with no prop other than the old book, I sat down and began to read the story out loud to them. After a few paragraphs, I looked up, took off my glasses, placed the open book on the little table, and proceeded to perform the rest of the story by heart.

The little performance was a revelation. Our friends loved it. They thought the story was hilarious. They experienced the same sense of discovery that I had felt six years before when I had read it to my folks. But most of all they were captivated by my five minutes of introductory storytelling. They wanted to hear much more of it.

After they disbanded, Jack, André, and I discussed how to expand the piece into a longer evening, something more suitable to a ticket-buying crowd. Judging from the response of our little audience, stories of my own family were clearly going to be my richest source materials.

At the end of our conversation, André took a cheery leap of faith. He invited me to perform the show for several weeks that very spring, on dark nights at the little Mitzi Newhouse Theater. Jack signed on to help me mount it. Within a month I had added enough new material to forge a ninety-minute solo show. In April and May I performed it on Sundays and Mondays, fourteen times in all. It was warmly received in the press. With so few performances in such a small theater, tickets were impossible to come by. It was the biggest little hit in town. I called it *Stories by Heart.*

For the next couple of years, the show continued to evolve. I toured it to cities all over the country. I appeared in theaters, opera houses, and concert halls, in front of audiences large and small.

Galveston. Lexington. Scottsdale. Reno. I even performed it at London's National Theatre. In every city, old friends from every chapter of my life showed up and reconnected with me. Most stirringly, I presented the show at the McCarter Theatre in Princeton, at the Great Lakes Theatre Festival in Cleveland, at Harvard's

Loeb Drama Center, and at the Colonial Theatre in Pittsfield, Massachusetts, just north of Stockbridge. On those nights, ghosts hovered over the crowd and smiled warmly at me from the wings. Wherever I went, I secretly invoked the spirit of my father. I imagined him watching every performance. I picked out his booming laugh in the audience. I heard his voice in my speech and felt his movements in my limbs. I especially loved paying tribute to him from the stage and bringing him back to life, both for friends who had loved him and for people who had never heard of him. I wish he could have seen it. I think he would have liked it.

Old age is a hardship for a man of the theater. Live long enough and you outlast all the people who remember the events that shaped your life. In 2002, toward the end of my month in Amherst, I was chatting idly with my father in the condo living room. As I recall, my mother was busying herself in the kitchen nearby. In a few days I would leave the two of them and return to Los Angeles. Anticipating my departure, all of us were feeling a little morose. For some reason, my father and I took up the subject of theater critics. I had recently suffered through the critical failure of a big Broadway musical in which I'd played the leading role. The *New York Times* notice had been hard on the show and dismissive of me. The review had tormented my father. It was only the latest of many moments when my bad press had driven him crazy. As he had often done before, he'd even written an unsent letter of vehement protest to the *Times* reviewer. In our conversation, the two of us were trying to figure out why he took these things so hard.

"Why does it bug you so much, Dad?" I asked. "I've had lots of good reviews in my time and lots of bad ones. Pans really don't bother me that much anymore. I think they upset you more than they upset me."

"I don't know," he answered, perplexed. "I guess I must have some vicarious investment in what you do. I experience it all through you. After all, I didn't have a career of great achievement . . ."

"Whoa!" I shouted. "Dad! Stop right there! You take that back! I'm not going to let you get away with that! You've had a *magnificent* career! Look what you created.

Look how many lives you changed. You gave so many people their first jobs. You inspired them. You introduced thousands of people to theater. To Shakespeare! Strangers come up and tell me that all the time. You're my hero. I would never have done any of this if it weren't for you. I owe you everything. And I'm one of hundreds. *Thousands!* I'm not going to let you *say* that!"

Dad blinked and wrinkled his brow as I worked myself into a righteous passion. I ended my diatribe. After a moment's silence, he turned toward the kitchen and called out in a tremulous voice: "Did you hear that, Sarah?"

It was deeply important for him to hear my rant, for me to deliver it, and for my mother to overhear the exchange and bear witness. It was one last gift the three of us were able to give each other. For me, it was a reaffirmation of the love and respect I felt for my father. For my mother it was a validation of her long life of unstinting support for him. And for him it was one last round of applause, one last rave review, one last ovation. Nine years later, at the beginning of 2011, I completed this book. I have come to see it as their story as much as mine. If you have reached this sentence, you yourself have finally finished it. This particular drama has come to an end. It is time for me to take a bow, wave to the crowd, and leave the stage.

Acknowledgments

I've written books before, but they've been picture books for children. These were all in rhyming verse and none was over thirty pages long. *Drama* is something else altogether. I could not have undertaken it without the encouragement and support of several people. Robert Miller, Julia Cheiffetz, Jonathan Galassi, and Jean Strouse helped me get started. My publisher, Jonathan Burnham, and my editor, Tim Duggan, added fuel to the fire. Tim in particular helped me shape and focus the book and reminded me often, at crucial moments, to "show, don't tell." Steve Martin read the very first completed draft of the book, and his acute editorial advice provided ample evidence that he has completely missed his calling.

I am a hopeless self-archivist, so the process of gathering photos from the past sixty-five years was fitful and arduous. I was helped by Matt Weinberg, who haunted the Harvard Theatre Collection; Frank Vlastnik, who camped out at the Lincoln Center Library of the Performing Arts; and Zoe Chapin, who tended to the business of photo credits, permissions, and fees.

As described in the preceding pages, the book was inspired by an autobiographical one-man show which I first performed in early 2008. This was the first time I had written material for myself based on events from my own life. Here, too, I required a lot of encouragement. Therefore thanks are also due to Jack O'Brien, who egged me on to write the show, and André Bishop of Lincoln Center, who gave me a setting to present it in. The warm reception for the piece helped prod me to expand it into a book. An actor thrives on applause, so I thank my New York audiences as well.

As the book neared completion, Mr. Duggan's assistant, Emily Cunningham, took it in hand and marshaled the talents of her HarperCollins colleagues to steer me through the last stages of the publication process. Everyone I met in the offices of Harper persuaded me that my book was in expert hands.

Thanks finally to each person who appeared in this drama. Major and minor players alike, from every chapter of my life, gave me all the material I needed for my first long-form piece of writing. Chief among these people are the main characters of my early years: my sisters, my brother, my mother, and especially my late father, Arthur Lithgow. As in every other thing that I have attempted, my wife, Mary, was forbearing and supportive. This time, I was venturing into her area of expertise. She is no stranger to the challenge of writing a book over the long haul. I could have never sustained the effort without the benefit of her experience, wisdom, and love.

Image Credits

All images are courtesy of the author unless noted below:

p. 11: Photograph by Axel Bahnsen. Courtesy Arthur Lithgow papers, Kent State University Libraries, Special Collections and Archives.

p. 13: Photograph by Axel Bahnsen.

p. 17: Courtesy *Yellow Springs News.*

p. 26: Photograph by Gerald Hornbein.

p. 29: Photograph by Axel Bahnsen.

p. 62: Courtesy Stan Hywet Hall & Gardens.

p. 97: Photograph by Gerald Hornbein.

p. 102: Photograph by Bootsy Holler.

p. 109: Photograph by Gerald Hornbein.

p. 156: Courtesy Harvard Theatre Collection, Houghton Library, Harvard University.

p. 159: MS Thr 546 (71), Harvard Theatre Collection, Houghton Library, Harvard University.

p. 170: MS Thr 546 (147), Harvard Theatre Collection, Houghton Library, Harvard University.

p. 186: MS Thr 546 (155), Harvard Theatre Collection, Houghton Library, Harvard University.

p. 205: © Zoe Dominic. Courtesy National Theatre of Britain.

p. 221: Malcolm Davies Collection © Shakespeare Birthplace Trust.

p. 245: Photograph by Jim McDonald. Courtesy Billy Rose Theatre Division, The New York Public Library for the Performing Arts.

p. 269: Photograph by Van Williams. Courtesy Billy Rose Theatre Division, The New York Public Library for the Performing Arts, Astor.

p. 312: Photograph by William L. Smith. Courtesy Long Wharf Theatre.

p. 330: Photograph by Martha Swope. Courtesy Billy Rose Theatre Division, The New York Public Library for the Performing Arts.

HARPER LUXE

THE NEW LUXURY IN READING

We hope you enjoyed reading
our new, comfortable print size and found it
an experience you would like to repeat.

Well – you're in luck!

HarperLuxe offers the finest in fiction and
nonfiction books in this same larger print size and
paperback format. Light and easy to read, HarperLuxe
paperbacks are for book lovers who want to see
what they are reading without the strain.

For a full listing of titles and
new releases to come, please visit our website:

www.HarperLuxe.com